"From the moment Jane Hampton Cook first toured the White House as an employee there, she herself was lit by a fire to tell the untold story of the woman who could be called our Founding Mother, Dolley Madison. Jane possesses both the scholarship and storyteller's passion for bringing new generations into the intimate, immediately daring intrigues of our nation's history. In short, she brings *The Burning of the White House* story alive in a way that emboldens us now to be better citizens, and to count our blessings for our forebears' acts of great courage and prescience to imagine a better world for future Americans who will find themselves surprisingly inspired by the tales of those who built our democracy."

—BOBETTE BUSTER, story guru, former adjunct professor, University of Southern California School of Cinematic Arts, writer/producer, and author of *Do Story: How to Tell Your Story So the World Listens*

"Jane Hampton Cook once again brings to vivid life stories of the White House and its occupants and the times in which they lived. In her latest book, we learn about the figures around James and Dolley Madison—both historical and ordinary—who were witnesses to the divisive time in our nation's history when we came dangerously close to losing the capital city and perhaps the Union itself."

—ANITA MCBRIDE, assistant to President George W. Bush and chief of staff to First Lady Laura Bush, and executive in residence at the Center for Congressional and Presidential Studies, School of Public Affairs at American University

"Author Jane Hampton Cook has done it again! She has written a well-researched new book entitled *The Burning of the White House—James and Dolley Madison and the War of 1812*. It is filled with historic facts, figures, and insightful stories about the buildup to the war, the lives of the fourth President of the United States and the First Lady, and the Executive Mansion. It is a wonderfully documented study of one of our nation's early historical events."

—NANCY THEIS, presidential writer for President Ronald Reagan, George H.W. Bush, and George W. Bush

"Jane Hampton Cook has emerged as one of America's leading and important historians, especially on the country's early days. In her new book, *The Burning of the White House*, Cook reveals new facts about that awful event which were previously unknown. Her writing is lively and engaging, honest and fresh. Cook asks the reader to simply enjoy her book and no doubt many will. I did!"

—CRAIG SHIRLEY, Reagan biographer and presidential historian

"Jane Hampton Cook's latest book proves to the reader to look to our past for the strength to guide us in our country's future. In *The Burning of the White House*, the Madisons, through their commitment, bravery, and love of country, provide us an excellent lesson in hope and a determination to save our beloved nation. This book is more than an excellent tribute to people of substance; it is a reminder of what we nearly lost and must preserve."

—DR. LINDA SUNDQUIST-NASSIE, retired American history teacher and author of *The Poetess of Song*: *The Life of Mary Shindler*

"*The Burning of the White House* is a lively, engaging read. It's told through some characters we don't often meet, such as Senator Rufus King—Federalist and bitter opponent of President Madison—and offers a unique, fresh twist on a familiar story."

—MATTHEW GILMORE, editor, H-DC, Washington, D.C. History Network

THE BURNING OF THE WHITE HOUSE

THE BURNING OF THE WHITE HOUSE

JAMES AND DOLLEY MADISON AND THE WAR OF 1812

JANE HAMPTON COOK

REGNERY
HISTORY

Regnery History™ is a trademark of Salem Communications Holding Corporation; Regnery® is a registered trademark of Salem Communications Holding Corporation

Cover image: 2013 White House Historical Association

Cataloging-in-Publication Data on file with the Library of Congress

ISBN 978-1-62157-478-1

Published in the United States by
Regnery History
An imprint of Regnery Publishing
A Division of Salem Media Group
300 New Jersey Ave NW
Washington, DC 20001
www.RegneryHistory.com

Manufactured in the United States of America

10 9 8 7 6 5 4 3 2 1

Books are available in quantity for promotional or premium use. For information on discounts and terms, please visit our website: www.Regnery.com.

Distributed to the trade by
Perseus Distribution
250 West 57th Street
New York, NY 10107

CONTENTS

PART THREE

Author's Note

This book began when I toured the White House in February 2001 as a new staff member. I'm not sure who told me, maybe it was my new boss Nancy Theis or one of the Secret Service agents who guarded the rooms during public tours and answered questions. Regardless, a tidbit of sentimentality stood out and stuck with me in the years to come.

When you tour the White House, you enter on the east side and walk through the ground floor corridor, past the windows overlooking the Jacqueline Kennedy Garden, and the library. Then you walk up a set of stairs, which gives you the sense of stepping up to power, as the design intended, to enter the State Floor through the grand East Room. The chandeliers glisten overhead as your eye beholds the full-length portrait of Martha Washington across the room. As you walk through the East Room, you pass the intersection of the red-carpeted Cross Hall in the center, which creates a stately image on television for presidential news conferences.

You also see the full-length portrait of George Washington by Gilbert Stuart. Taking a right turn, you walk through adjoining doors that run parallel to the Cross Hall. Subsequent adjoining doors allow you to enter the beautiful Green Room, Blue Oval Room, Red Room, and State Dining Room before exiting through the Cross Hall and north entrance.

An arrangement in the Red Room is where I first caught the sentimentality about James Madison's wife, Dolley, and the War of 1812. Above an adjoining doorway between the Red Room and State Dining Room hangs Gilbert Stuart's portrait of Dolley Madison. Though it was not called the Red Room at the time, Dolley had decorated this parlor in sunny yellow and placed her pianoforte and guitar here to make it her beloved music room.

Fittingly, Dolley's portrait faces the East Room with a view of the George Washington portrait that she saved in 1814. In this way, when all of the adjoining doors are open, as they are for public tours, Dolley continues to keep her eye on Washington. Though the arrangement is a fun tidbit, it made an impression on me and ignited a desire to learn more.

Several months later, I was part of the White House staff who evacuated the White House and adjacent Eisenhower Executive Office Building during the terrorist attacks on September 11, 2001. I never posted the page about the president's education policies on the White House website that we had planned that day in my role as "web gal," as President George W. Bush called me.

The terrorist attacks of 9/11 changed everything, including restricting public tours of the White House for a time. We tried to compensate by creating 360-degree tours of the State Rooms online. But in the days that followed those attacks, I sometimes thought about the Madisons and the War of 1812, when British Admiral George Cockburn wanted to be a guest at the White House so he could take his bow and terrorize its occupants. At some point, too, I saw Cockburn's handiwork—the scorch marks—in the lower level of the White House, which isn't part of modern public tours.

I wondered what it was like in 1814 to live in the grand White House and sleep at night with the possibility of being attacked, similar to the aftermath of 9/11. Were James and Dolley Madison afraid? Did they take precautions? Why did Cockburn want to attack Washington, D.C.?

Two years later, in 2003, my writing journey began in earnest. I left my position at the White House and received an educational research fellowship from the White House Historical Association and the Organization of American Historians to research the White House and its occupants. I'm forever grateful for this opportunity because it helped me to launch a book-writing career while also allowing me time to work through some medical challenges that were keeping my husband and me from having children.

The research fellowship led me to write a thirty-page version of this book as part of a collection of unpublished short stories about the White House. Though I wrote other published books over the years, I kept coming back to this story and expanding my research. I read Dolley's letters and studied Admiral Cockburn's correspondence, Madison's writings, Senator Rufus King's correspondence, and others from this time period.

In 2012 I took a weekend intensive class on story structure with Bobette Buster, a film guru. Bobette combines the best of both worlds of scholarship and entertainment. The daughter of a former history professor, she is an adjunct professor at the University of Southern California and also on the guest faculty for Pixar, Disney Animation, Disney Channel, Sony Animation, Twentieth Century Fox, the University of Milan, and others.

Bobette challenged me to think about how the attacks of 1814 changed Dolley and James. Was there an authentic, *nonfiction* arc of change? I reread more writings and discovered that they both underwent natural, organic 180 degrees of change that was real, not fiction.

Bobette also encouraged me to include the stories of average Americans, people to whom readers could relate in some way. Let's face it, very few people have become a president of the United States or been married to one. Her advice led me to create what I call an "average Joe" and "average Jane" point of view in this book. I've included several ordinary Americans who played an extraordinary role in moving the big-picture story forward. People such as attorney Francis Scott Key, newspaper editor Joseph Gales, architect Benjamin Latrobe, and U.S. Navy commander Joshua Barney made choices and expressed emotions that we all experience and can relate to, such as rejection, injustice, anger, love, and hope.

Likewise, the polarization of party politics today can help us better understand the contributions of the Madisons, who tried to change the culture, fought for what they believed in, overcame great loss, discovered a purpose in life beyond their own family circle, and sacrificed self for the well-being of others.

My own humanity played a small role in writing this book. Pregnant with my third child, I was just about ready to write the chapter on how the British "toured" the White House when I went into labor a few days early. Two nights later, while my infant son was snuggly asleep in the hospital nursery, I suddenly was ready to write that chapter. I pulled out my laptop at 11 p.m. and the words just flew out of my fingers.

While I can't give you a literal tour of the White House today, I hope you will make new discoveries as you *tour* this book. The facts come from reliable summaries of history, biographies, and records. Anything in quotations is something that somebody wrote in a letter, diary, or newspaper. We all know that communication methods change over the years. Technology transforms time. Fashions of the day soon become the costumes of the past. But the human heart doesn't change. The need for love, purpose, a second chance, renewal, faith, and hope are as real today as they were two hundred years ago.

While Dolley still keeps her eye on Washington in the White House, may we keep an eye on her and the others in this book to discover what history can show us today.

Enjoy,

Jane Hampton Cook

PART I

1813: A Fiery Prelude

If our first struggle was a war of our infancy, this last was that of our youth.
—James Madison, fourth president of the United States

This 1810 drawing by architect Benjamin Latrobe shows the north view of the President's House. *Courtesy Library of Congress*

CHAPTER ONE

The Pirate

"One thousand dollars reward will be given," began the bold announcement in Philadelphia's *Democratic Press* on August 16, 1813.

As usual, this newspaper published many advertisements that day. These classifieds were mostly mundane ads for two-story brick houses, feather beds, and looking glasses, among other fineries. Unfortunately, because slavery was still common, the offer to sell the services of a thirteen-year-old African boy was also included. But thanks to religious Quakers who morally opposed slavery, the practice was gradually being abolished in Pennsylvania.

What stood out as highly unusual that August day was this advertisement from Mr. James O. Boyle, a naturalized Irishman from Pugh Town, the northernmost point in Virginia. Why would someone living more than 179 miles away pay for an advertisement in a Philadelphia newspaper? The answer was simple: American zeal. This man was a patriot, and his homeland was under attack.

One thousand dollars was a mighty sum. Tickets to President James Madison's inaugural ball—the first for a president—had cost only four dollars each four years earlier, in 1809. The going rate for room and board for congressmen in the nation's capital, Washington City, was around twelve to sixteen dollars a week. Mrs. Madison's beloved pianoforte in the charming yellow music room of the newly renovated President's House had totaled a mere $458. Not even Gilbert Stuart's superb painting of George Washington, which hung in the State Dining Room, had cost as much as $1,000. Congress had paid only $800 for this national art treasure as a gift for the opening of the President's House in 1800. Yet, the reason for Boyle's award was far more tantalizing than its high dollar value.

"For the head of the notorious, incendiary, and infamous scoundrel, the violator of all laws, human and divine, the British Admiral George Cockburn," the ad continued. If Cockburn's head wasn't possible, other facial parts would suffice: "Or five hundred dollars for each of his ears on delivery to James O. Boyle."

The time had come to slay the British Goliath, whether with a musket, bayonet, or slingshot. Any weapon would do. Boyle wasn't alone in his David-like quest. Many Americans, especially those living along the Chesapeake Bay in Maryland and Virginia, wanted to see Admiral Cockburn's head on a plate.

In the spring and summer of 1813, America's second war with England—the War of 1812—had expanded from traditional fighting between armies and navies into the terrorizing of private citizens by pillaging redcoats. Cockburn may have been a British admiral, but he was acting with a pirate's swagger.

━━━━━

Not long after 4:00 a.m. on May 3, 1813, British Rear Admiral Sir George Cockburn gleefully watched his fifteen small boats launch his squadron's latest attack. Before him was the fishing nook of Havre de Grace, Maryland, a stage stop on the road between Baltimore and

Philadelphia. Cockburn's target was a small battery of cannon on shore. His order was firm and succinct: Fire!

As the admiral later reported to his superior officer, "A warm fire was opened on the place at daylight from our launches and rocket boat, which was smartly returned from the battery for a short time."

His excitement accelerated. The British launch boats didn't let up. "Their fire rather increasing than decreasing" while the American fire "out from the battery soon began to slacken."

Cockburn, a forty-one-year-old Scot who had started living aboard Royal Navy ships at age nine, smiled with a buccaneer's glee as his men fired yet another round at the battery. Named Congreve after the English colonel who invented them, these rockets left a red glare as they soared toward the battery. William Congreve was a British engineer who had created these weapons based on ones fighters in India had hurled at British forces in a recent war. In Congreve's version, the warhead was a cone-shaped cylinder attached to four-foot wooden poles. By changing the elevation of their A-shaped launching frames, Royal Marines could adjust the distance of the Congreve rockets, which could soar as far as two miles.

As Cockburn attacked Havre de Grace that morning, one rocket soon did something that none of the others had done so far. The weapon struck and killed a local militiaman, who was returning fire from shore. Scared by their friend's death, the rest of militia fled to the woods. Only the brave Irish American John O'Neil stood his ground and stayed with the battery.

Cockburn next ordered fifteen launch boats carrying 150 marines to land on shore to burn the entire town. Why commit such an atrocity? The residents weren't employed by the federal government. Nor were they housing a U.S. warship. Their crime, in Cockburn's view, was taking precautions to defend themselves and signal that his marines were coming. After learning that Cockburn had burned some boats in nearby Frenchtown, they had placed cannons—two six-pounders and one nine-pounder—on Havre de Grace's banks.

Their efforts had backfired. Instead of repelling the British, their warning shots had attracted them. As Cockburn reported: "I observed guns fired and American colors hoisted at a battery lately erected at Havre de Grace at the entrance of the Susquehanna River."

The sight of these new defensive weapons had given the rear admiral the justification he'd been looking for to invade and burn the town. "This of course immediately gave to the place an importance, which I had not before attached to it, and I therefore determined on attacking it."

After all, the more cannon, gunpowder, tobacco, flour, and livestock Cockburn could capture, the better he could bolster and feed his forces. He also had his eye on the bigger picture. With any luck, he could dampen the resolve of average Americans to fight him in the future.

———

Cockburn didn't know it, but Havre de Grace was one of the most patriotic places in America. Incorporated as a city in 1785, this Maryland locale sat at the top of the Chesapeake Bay and intersected with the Susquehanna River. Proud of the American Revolution and its heroes, the town's founders gave their streets patriotic names, such as Congress and Union Avenues along with Washington, Adams, and Franklin Streets.

Though its boulevards were distinctly American, the city's name was decidedly and purposefully French. When the Marquis de Lafayette, a Revolutionary War hero and French general, sailed down the river and saw this genteel spot, he called out exuberantly: "*C'est Le Havre*," or "This is the Havre." The spot reminded him of the beloved French port city Le Havre de Grace, which means "harbor of grace." Flattered by the marquis's compliment, the townspeople named a street for Lafayette and their fishing town for their French twin.

By 1789 this herring hamlet was so well regarded, patriotic, and genteel that congressmen from Pennsylvania and Maryland initially thought it would be an ideal location for the nation's new capital. More than twenty cities and locales vied for the honor, which, of course, was ultimately given to the hundred-square-mile district that became Washington City.

Despite failing to become the nation's capital city, Havre de Grace grew in population. By the time Cockburn launched his rockets against it in 1813, this fishing hamlet was part of Harford County, whose population had topped two thousand in the 1810 U.S. Census.

━━━━━━

Cockburn had arrived for his American mission less than three months earlier. With Britain's war against the French emperor Napoleon Bonaparte winding down in Europe, the Admiralty in London had ordered him to relinquish his command in Spain and travel to British-controlled Bermuda. From there he had sailed to Lynnhaven Bay, the mouth of the Chesapeake Bay, to await the arrival of his commanding officer, Admiral Sir John B. Warren, and receive instructions. While there he had accomplished his first raid: pillaging the pantry of the Cape Henry lighthouse, not far from where the Jamestown settlers had first landed in America in 1607. Warren soon joined Cockburn and shared a top secret letter from Henry the third Earl Bathurst, the British secretary of state for war and the colonies.

"It having been judged expedient to effect a diversion on the coast of the United States of America," Bathurst had written, noting the plans of the U.S. military to "wrest from His Majesty" Upper and Lower Canada in the 1813 military campaign. British naval forces were to attack towns and frighten vulnerable residents along the Chesapeake Bay.

Raiding should be easy, the British top brass had reasoned. With such a weak militia system and thousands of regular U.S. troops deployed to Canada, the U.S. government could not possibly protect every nook and cranny on its jagged eastern shore. If successful, these raids would convince American politicians to withdraw U.S. troops from Canada and defend their homeland instead.

Warren had ordered Cockburn to enforce a British blockade of the Chesapeake. By the end of April 1813, Cockburn had swept up the bay and burned five schooners in Frenchtown. After one of his men deserted, he rightfully feared that the deserter would tell the people of Havre de Grace of his plans.

Cockburn had long despised deserters. He believed in a practice called impressment, in which British ship captains possessed the right to search U.S. merchant ships and seize anyone they suspected of being a deserter, proof or not, U.S. citizenship papers or not.

Desertion and mutiny frequently threatened the size of Cockburn's and other British commanders' forces—and thus their ability to sail— and the British response to it had given Congress a moral reason to declare war against England on June 18, 1812. More than any other qualm with Britain, American government leaders had long despised their use of impressment. The U.S. State Department later estimated that 5,000 men—both deserters and bona fide U.S. citizens—had been impressed.

Some Americans, such as John Quincy Adams, the top U.S. diplomat to Russia at the time, had concluded that the number was higher. On his voyage to Russia in 1809, Adams had witnessed a British captain attempt to impress a legitimate American sailor. He believed impressment was as immoral and unjust as the slave trade. Realizing that hundreds of cases had been unreported, he'd calculated the number of impressments to be much higher, at 9,000. To many Americans, the British government had used desertion as an excuse to take or impress legitimate U.S. citizens and force them to fight for England and against their own nation. No matter that Parliament needed every man it could find to fight France's Napoleon, England was denying a man's right to his citizenship or to change it, which was an insult to U.S. sovereignty and independence.

This conflict between desertions and impressment had affected the timing of Cockburn's decision to attack Havre de Grace. Knowing that one of his men had escaped near the town, Cockburn had smartly delayed his invasion plans in case the deserter had warned the town. The evidence from his spyglass suggested that the rascal had indeed betrayed him.

For two days he watched from a distance as 250 Maryland militia vigilantly patrolled the shore. They had kept their arms ready night and day. Then by May 2 they had fled, perhaps feeling exhausted or deceived by the deserter. They went home to quietly rest that night. Taking advantage of their absence, Cockburn ordered his men to fire upon their battery before dawn on May 3. Now it was time to invade.

Admiral Cockburn delighted as his marines landed on shore and marched through town with as much confidence and ease as if they were local residents. Cockburn's captain, Lieutenant Westphal, "very judiciously directed the landing of the marines on the left, which movement added to the hot fire they were under, induced the Americans to commence withdrawing from the battery to take shelter in the town."

As this pirate-like admiral observed, some Americans hid behind trees or inside houses and aimed their muskets at his invading marines. "They commenced a teasing and irritating fire from behind their houses, walls, trees etcetera, from which I am sorry to say my gallant first lieutenant received a shot through his hand whilst leading the pursuing party," Cockburn wrote.

Despite his injury, Lieutenant Westphal continued the pursuit "with which he soon succeeded in dislodging the whole of the enemy from their lurking places and driving them for shelter to the neighboring woods."

Cockburn hated this type of dastardly guerilla warfare. He complained that the Americans took "every opportunity of firing with their rifles from behind trees or haystacks, or from the windows of their houses upon our boats…or whenever they can get a mischievous shot at any of our people without being seen or exposed to personal risk in return."

His lieutenant "had the satisfaction to overtake and with his remaining hand to make prisoner and bring in a captain [John O'Neil] of their militia. We also took an ensign and some other individuals."

Cockburn's marines then divided into groups of thirty to forty and went from house to house, prompting more Havre de Grace residents to flee to the woods. From his ship the admiral couldn't see what happened when his men entered the houses, but he could see the results after they left: smoke and flames.

As he watched the increasing inferno, Cockburn may have sneered: *Wonder what little Jemmy thinks of his war now?* He had frequently mocked James Madison, who was a mere five feet, four inches tall. Yet, he really didn't understand the genius of America's fourth president. Though Madison was short in stature, he possessed a giant intellect. He had one of the brightest minds in the United States.

Unknown to Cockburn that day, President James Madison was about to make a choice that he hoped would change the trajectory of the war and send Cockburn home—permanently.

CHAPTER TWO

Mighty Little Madison

P resident James Madison had no idea that Havre de Grace was in flames that day. The nation's capital city was sixty-eight miles from the inferno. In those days before the telegraph and telephone, news traveled slowly.

Hence, while Cockburn took pleasure in attacking American civilians after dawn, the president sat in the President's House in Washington City and prepared to send the U.S. Senate a request—perhaps the best opportunity for peace since the war began. On Madison's mind that May morning was a hopeful mediation proposal to end America's war with England.

"The high character of the Emperor Alexander," began the president's letter to the U.S. Senate. Alexander was the youthful, dashing emperor of Russia, the czar who competed only with Napoleon, France's emperor, for power in Europe.

The chief architect of the U.S. Constitution, Madison was the key political power player in America. He'd recently been contemplating an opportunity for triangulation in his foreign policy.

Emperor Alexander had proposed to mediate a peace treaty between Great Britain and the United States. Russia would act as a neutral party, a friend to both countries, in an effort to end the war. Would the honorable President Madison accept?

More than anything, Madison wanted to say yes. How he longed for a true solution to America's problems with England. With the war going poorly along the Canadian border—including the embarrassing surrender of Fort Detroit in the Michigan Territory in August 1812—the more quickly he could achieve peace with fair trade and respect for the citizenship of U.S. sailors, the better.

But past diplomatic failures had led to the current war in the first place.

———

Each direct negotiation with the British before the War of 1812 had failed. First, in 1809, not long after assuming office, President Madison had tried to negotiate with David Erskine, the top British envoy to the United States. They soon came to an agreement for resuming trade, making reparations for an attack on a U.S. ship in 1807, and repealing Britain's Orders in Council, which were policies by the British government that oppressed U.S. trade to gain the advantage in England's war against France.

The Orders in Council required U.S. ship merchants to receive British licenses to trade with other European countries and dock in British ports before selling their cargo throughout Europe. These orders, along with the practice of impressment, were the greatest sources of strife between the United States and Great Britain. Complicating these disagreements were Napoleon's reciprocal orders that required neutral ships, including American vessels, to first obtain French licenses and visit French ports before selling their goods in Europe.

Unable to be in two places at once, U.S. merchant ships couldn't first visit both France and England. To make matters worse, many British sea captains raised U.S. flags and forged paperwork to sneak their cargo into French-controlled ports. At the same time, both French and English sea captains confiscated American ships, sailors, and their cargo. So, while impressment was the moral impetus for the war, England's and France's anti-American trade policies served as the economic and political catalysts.

How happy Madison had been to seal that agreement with English envoy Erskine in 1809. The president had been so confident of success that he had sanctioned U.S. trade with Britain once again. Hundreds of American sailors and dozens of ships had sailed exuberantly for Europe that summer with high hopes of earning money for their cotton, sugar, indigo, coffee, and other goods without British interference.

The problem, however, was Erskine's bosses. Saying he had exceeded his instructions, the British government disavowed Erskine's agreement shortly after the paperwork arrived in England. This put all of the American ships that had just set sail at increased risk for capture and confiscation by British sea captains. With no other viable options, Madison reinstated trade restrictions against England.

The failure of the Erskine agreement infuriated the pro-British Federalist Party in America, especially in New England. A Southern Republican—whose party later became the Democratic Party—Madison was aware of their opposition.

"We regard Erskine's arrangement as little, if any, better than an act of swindling," Robert Troup, a Federalist in New York, complained in a letter to a U.S. senator.

Troup was a Revolutionary War veteran who represented an Englishman's real estate interests in New York. His Federalist sentiments were typical. Some New England foes accused Madison of insulting the prince regent of England—the future King George IV—who ruled instead of his living but insane father, King George III.

"Hence the adjustment with Erskine was accompanied with expressions so offensive towards the king as would ensure its rejection," complained Timothy Pickering, a former secretary of state, Federalist, and U.S. senator from Massachusetts.

The British government then sent Francis Jackson, Erskine's successor, to Washington City. Jackson soon proved as haughty as he was hostile. Negotiations with him and another British envoy failed, as did U.S. diplomats negotiating in London. The United States and England were deadlocked.

With Madison's support, a majority of Congress declared war against England on June 18, 1812.

Because Madison was informally considered to be the father of the Constitution and the man who most influenced its three-branch blueprint, who would dare question the constitutionality of his decisions as he led America's second war with England? Yet, despite his high character and past contributions, his enemies were growing stronger with each passing political tide.

═══════

Madison likely sat in his office on the second floor of the President's House to write his May 3, 1813, letter to the U.S. Senate. Thomas Jefferson, Madison's immediate predecessor and the nation's third president, had used this space, which came to be known as the Green Room, as a dining room to entertain. But because the floor could hold only fourteen seated guests, Madison converted it into his office.

In May 1813, Madison's secretary, Edward Coles, was ill and recovering in Philadelphia. Without a secretary, Madison wrote and made copies in his own hand. Emperor Alexander's offer gave him hope. Maybe the tensions with England were too great and the U.S. government needed an arbitrator. Perhaps a fresh approach, such as mediation by a third party, would work.

"The high character of the Emperor Alexander being a satisfactory pledge for the sincerity and impartiality of his offer, it was immediately accepted," Madison wrote of his decision.

Though he'd learned of the Russian offer in late February 1813, politics had prevented him from officially notifying the Twelfth Congress at the time. The Senate and House had adjourned a few days later, right before Madison's second inauguration on March 4, 1813. He also didn't have time to write the emperor a letter of acceptance and receive a reply before the new Thirteenth Congress began a special summer session at the end of May to resolve war issues.

A letter could only travel as quickly as the ship delivering it. As Madison had learned, correspondence with his diplomat John Quincy Adams in Russia took an average of eight weeks in one direction between May and September. Depending on the severity of the frozen water imprisoning Russia's capital in winter, ship travel took six to eight months the rest of the year. Passage also depended on whether U.S. ships could make a journey without being captured or detained by English or French ships or their allies.

Madison decided to use the timing of Congress's adjournment between March and May to his advantage. Why wait to send a letter of acceptance to Emperor Alexander when he could send members of a delegation instead? What better way to prove his sincerity for achieving peace? Hence, Madison took a political risk to negotiate peace.

He explained his decision this way to Congress: "Three of our eminent citizens were accordingly commissioned, with the requisite powers to conclude a Treaty of Peace with persons clothed with like powers on the part of Great Britain."

He had chosen Albert Gallatin, his Treasury secretary, and U.S. Senator James Bayard of Delaware, to join Adams in Russia. Adams's peace delegate nomination was obvious. Since 1809, he had developed relationships with Russian government officials and secured promises from them to trade with U.S. merchants. His success was a key factor in Alexander's decision to favor the United States by offering to mediate the peace treaty.

In choosing Bayard, Madison flattered the Senate by trusting one of their own for this important task. Bayard's selection also gave Madison a chance to prove that his intentions were bipartisan. Bayard was a

Federalist, albeit a moderate one, who opposed declaring the war but supported funding it.

Then there was Gallatin. Oh, Albert Gallatin. How Madison respected and treasured his friend and cabinet member. A naturalized U.S. citizen who came from Switzerland, Gallatin understood Europeans better than most members of the U.S. government. He'd also been very loyal to both Presidents Jefferson and Madison as leader of the Treasury. The past few years had tried and tested the nation's finances in ways that neither Gallatin nor Madison could have imagined. The need to fund the war had led Gallatin to pressure Congress to raise taxes, authorize millions in loans, and enact other unpopular measures. Senators and U.S. representatives who opposed the war had prevented Congress from adequately funding the war. Gallatin's popularity with them was especially low.

Madison believed that Gallatin deserved this gallant opportunity. Sending his Treasury secretary abroad would send a strong signal that America was serious about peace. Hence, Gallatin, Bayard, a few members of their families, and other assistants, including Madison's stepson, left in April 1813 to ensure a summer arrival in St. Petersburg.

"[A]s further proof of the disposition on the part of the United States to meet their adversary in honorable experiments for terminating the war, it was determined to avoid intermediate delays," the president explained of their departure before receiving confirmation by Congress. They needed to make the eighty-day journey before the sailing season in Russia ended.

Now he needed the U.S. Senate to trust his reasoning and motives for selecting these peace negotiators and sending them overseas without first receiving Senate consent. As the man who defended the Constitution clause by clause in debates at the convention that created that document in 1787, Madison knew better than anyone the power of the president to nominate diplomats and the duty of the Senate to vote to confirm them. The Senate wanted an end to the war, and Madison knew it.

"The issue of this friendly interposition of the Russian Emperor, and this pacific manifestation on the part of the United States, time only can decide," he concluded his letter.

Thus, the president did what he often did. He relied on the roles of government as defined by the law while also appealing to common sense. Politics, however, often defies even the most practical decisions.

———

That day, while Madison wrote Congress in hopes for peace, Jared Sparks became an eyewitness to the destruction of Havre de Grace. An ordinary citizen, Sparks held extraordinary observation skills. He later reported that the Royal Marines entered a house and plundered "it of such articles as could be of any service to them." They used their hatchets to open locked drawers and then slipped the booty into their knapsacks. When their looting was complete, they torched the home.

"This was not a work of much time, and as soon as it was accomplished, they set fire to the house, and entered another for the same purposes." The marines repeated their ritual. Again. And again.

———

Knowing his men were carrying out his orders, Cockburn decided to join them. He landed on Havre de Grace's shore easily, as if he owned the town. In that moment, he did. As he'd written to Admiral Warren three days before the attack, "*Should resistance be* made, I shall consider [what I take] to be prizes of war."

Resistance or not, at some point he saw his prize: a fine carriage. What a beauty it was. Should he take it? This vehicle belonged to a local ferry owner. Word was that another ferry owner along the river had sunk some of his boats to make the water too shallow for British ships to navigate. The decision had made the low water even more difficult to traverse. Realizing that his seventy-four-gun ships were too large, Cockburn was forced to transfer some of his men to smaller vessels to reach Havre de Grace. He "found that the shallowness of the water would only admit of its being approached by [smaller] boats."

Cockburn liked the carriage, which newspapers reported cost $1,000. He gave the order to seize it. His men complied, taking the carriage to a launch boat and transporting it to his flagship. By doing so he sent a retaliation message to ferryboat owners throughout the Chesapeake.

Not long after he landed, the admiral encountered "two or three ladies who had courageously remained in their houses, during the whole commotion," as Sparks chronicled. They implored him to save their houses. These women "endeavored by all the powers of female eloquence to dissuade him from his rash purposes."

The admiral was not immune to the sweetness of females. He was married to his cousin Mary and was the father of two children, including a daughter. Yet, he was unrelenting. Orders were orders. Why should he change them?

The ladies were concerned about an elderly woman's home, which was already damaged. Would he really stoop to such an atrocity by burning it completely? Though they didn't dare tell him, the older woman was the mother of John Rodgers, who commanded the USS *President*. Under Rodgers' leadership, the forty-four-gun *President* had captured nine British vessels in 1812. Fortunately Cockburn was unaware that Rodgers's mother's house was the source of their pleading.

"But when they [the ladies] represented to him the misery he was causing, and pointed to the smoking ruins under which was buried all that could keep their proprietors from want and wretchedness, he relented and countermanded his original orders," Sparks noted.

Though the Rodgers house was partially damaged, it wasn't completely destroyed. Cockburn then ordered all of the burning to stop. By this time forty of the sixty houses in Havre de Grace were ablaze. Those not on fire were "perforated with balls or defaced by the explosion of shells." Debris, such as mattress feathers and broken glassware, filled the streets. Following the example of Cockburn's capture of the carriage, officers sent fine tables and other quality items back to their cabins as mementos.

The Royal Marines weren't entirely malicious that day. After pleading by John O'Neil's daughter, Matilda, they released the spirited militia captain who'd stayed at the battery when others fled early that morning. Cockburn was also so impressed with Matilda's courage that he gave her a small turtle shell box to remember him. She didn't need a token to remember someone as unforgettable as Cockburn.

The British also spared the structure of St. John's Episcopal Church—how seemingly kind of them. The inside was another matter. They destroyed every window and pew, including the pulpit.

Cockburn felt justified in burning and destroying Havre de Grace. He wanted "to cause the proprietors to understand and feel what they were liable to bring upon themselves by building batteries and acting towards us with so much useless rancor."

Such illogical justifications were the pirate-like norm for this rear admiral. Most men of honor respected those who acted in self-defense; Cockburn punished people for it.

He likely ended the burning and released O'Neil not as a result of the pleas of women but because better treasure awaited him nearby. Someone gave him news of an even more enticing prize: an ironworks foundry.

Hence, after four hours, Cockburn and his men left Havre de Grace. "I embarked in the boats," he wrote. They traveled eight miles to Principio Creek in Cecil County. The Principio Foundry was one of only three in the United States that used the advanced technology of machines to bore cannon from solid metal castings. The foundry, one of the nation's largest, was worth $20,000.

"The most valuable works of the kind in America, the destruction of it therefore at this moment will I trust prove of much national importance," Cockburn bragged.

Personally leading this expedition, he spent the rest of the day there. His men destroyed fifty-one large-caliber guns and 130 small arms. Delighted at his success, Cockburn further boasted about accomplishing so much with so little: "After being 22 hours and constant exertion without nourishment of any kind."

For the British, the cost was very low: "I have much pleasure in being able to add that excepting Lt. Westphal's [hand] wound we have not suffered any casualty whatever."

In contrast, the people of Havre de Grace had suffered great losses of life, dignity, and property.

"But the most distressing part of the scene, was at the close of the day, when those, who had fled in the morning, returned to witness the desolation of their homes, and the ruin of all their possessions," Jared Sparks reflected.

Those whose houses were burned now owned only the clothes on their backs. "They returned wretched and disconsolate, and seemed overwhelmed with the thoughts of the misery and want which awaited them," Sparks continued. Neighbors who had something left offered clothes and other necessities to those who now had nothing at all.

The people of Havre de Grace didn't understand why the war had come to their shore. Sparks described their sense of injustice: "No reasons of a public nature could have induced it. No public property was deposited there, nor were any of its inhabitants engaged in aiding the prosecution of the war." He couldn't "assign any cause other than the caprice of its projector, for this violent attack on a defenseless and unoffending village."

Though drunk with power and feasting on adrenaline, Cockburn was not satisfied when he returned to the thirty-six-gun HMS *Maidstone* after his near-twenty-four-hour rampage. He never was. Only one thing could quench his war-thirsty spirit: defeating the Americans. More than anything, he seemed to want revenge, glory, and promotions. He sought revenge for British deserters who had abandoned his ship in New York a decade before and also for his insane king's embarrassing loss of the American colonies and their commerce a generation earlier.

Cockburn wanted glory for England and the crown. Perhaps he also had his eye on a promotion. Admiral of the fleet was a nice proposition. What better way to accomplish all of these things than to follow orders and invade other towns along the Chesapeake? If successful, he just might get a crack at the best prize of all: the destruction of Washington City. Now that would put him on glory's fast track with the admiralty in England.

To do this Cockburn needed something that he didn't have—a superabundant force. His hundreds of marines were hardly the thousands he needed to seize Norfolk, the town harboring a valuable U.S. military ship, much less this degenerate nation's capital city set in an unprotected wilderness.

Though the admiral had his eye on Washington and the president, he was also intrigued by the president's sociable, buxom wife: Dolley Madison. So was everyone else.

CHAPTER THREE

Hello, Dolley

To Dolley Madison, Cockburn was more than just a pirate. He was also a savage.

"We cannot be surprised at a breach of promise in our enemies, when we think of their savage style of warfare at Havre de Grace and other places," Dolley wrote in a letter on May 6, 1813, three days after the burning.

The news had come by stagecoach to the Madison-leaning Washington City newspaper the *National Intelligencer*. Bombarding a U.S. military ship in war was expected, but burning a sleepy town? That was barbaric. Inflicting suffering on innocents, especially women and children? Why, that was nothing less than terrorism.

As she'd done many times before, Mrs. Madison wrote that day to Phoebe Morris, the twenty-two-year-old daughter of her dear childhood friend Anthony Morris. Dolley had first met Anthony in Philadelphia, where her family, the Paynes, had moved in 1783, when she was fifteen.

Dolley was the oldest of eight Payne children—four boys and four girls. Though Dolley carried an Irish lineage on her mother's side, Anthony reflected that "her complexion seemed from Scotland, and her soft blue eyes from Saxony." With a "stately step and the sweet engaging smile," teen Dolley had brought an air of freshness to Anthony and his friends: "She came upon our comparatively cold hearts in Philadelphia, suddenly and unexpectedly with all the delightful influences of a summer sun...with all the warm feelings, and glowing fancies of her native state."

Dolley had spent most of her childhood in Hanover County, Virginia, on a plantation north of Richmond. Her parents were Quakers, Christians known as the Society of Friends. Because they believed that everyone held the potential to carry God's grace in their hearts, the Friends opposed war and dividing people by class or race. With such an egalitarian view, Quakers were generally hospitable people, known for opening their homes to anyone who called. These tenets of equality eventually led many Quakers, including Dolley's parents, to oppose slavery.

But Virginia law prohibited the freeing or manumission of slaves. When lawmakers changed this statute in 1782, the Paynes and other Quakers did just that: they freed their slaves in Virginia, abandoned a rural life, and moved to an urban locale to start over. As the nation's second-largest city and the home to many Quakers, Philadelphia was a logical choice.

When it came to marriage, however, many in the Society of Friends shunned outsiders, even Christians who were not Quakers. Soon after Dolley married Congressman James Madison in 1794, her Philadelphia Friends excommunicated her. Not only was he not a Quaker, but he was also seventeen years older than she. Worse, he was a plantation slave owner.

Many Quakers were also upset that she'd not waited a full year to marry after the death of her first husband, John Todd, a Quaker who died along with 10 percent of Philadelphians in the 1793 yellow fever epidemic. What they didn't realize was that Dolley's first marriage was more out of duty to her father than deep love for Todd. The increasingly impoverished Mr. Payne had insisted that she marry Mr. Todd to ease his pocketbook so he could feed her younger siblings. Agreeing dutifully, Dolley married Todd and had two children with him. Their youngest, an infant, also died in the yellow fever epidemic. By that time, her father also had died, likely of alcoholism. The death of her husband and father left Dolley vulnerable.

As a young widow with a two-year-old son, named Payne, she needed the financial security that marrying Congressman Madison would give her. But she also knew he was highly attracted to her. Theirs wouldn't be a match of duty from his point of view.

"He thinks so much of you in the day that he has lost his tongue, at night he dreams of you and starts in his sleep a calling on you to relieve his flame for he burns to such an excess that he shortly will be consumed," Dolley's aunt had conveyed to her of Madison's affection.

Madison was so taken with her that he worried another man would steal her away. "He hopes that your heart will be callous to every other swain but himself," Dolley's aunt continued. His worry was understandable. As Anthony had observed, "She could raise the mercury in the thermometers of hearts to fever heat."

Madison needn't have fretted. While she may not have been madly in love with him at the time, she clearly respected and held some affection for him. "I give my hand to the man who of all others I most admire," Dolley wrote to a girlfriend on her wedding day to Madison. "In this union I have everything that is soothing and grateful in prospect and my little Payne will have a generous and tender protector."

Yet, she also closed that letter with her old name, Dolley Payne Todd, followed by a mysterious postscript. Perhaps showing her wedding-day jitters, she added, "Dolley Madison, Alas! Alas!"

Though many Quakers abandoned the new Mrs. Madison, Anthony Morris continued to be her Quaker friend. Their ties were strengthened years later after Anthony's wife died. Taking his teenage daughter Phoebe under her eagle-like wings, Dolley had embraced her with the affection of a mother tending her nest. In the winter of 1811, Phoebe lived in the President's House, where Dolley taught her etiquette and introduced her to society. An extrovert who felt energized around people and at parties, Mrs. Madison helped many girls transition from gullible teens into polished young women.

By May 6, 1813, much weighed on Dolley's mind. Besides Havre de Grace, she pored her heart out to Phoebe about the great change in her life. She had a personal stake in her husband's acceptance of Emperor Alexander's mediation offer. Her now-grown son Payne had gone to Russia as a secretary for Mr. Gallatin. The decision made her anxious. "I have been sad at the departure of my child," she confessed.

She was also deeply sad for Phoebe and Anthony, who had been seeking a diplomatic appointment to Bermuda. British Admiral Warren had refused to grant permission for Anthony to cross the English blockade and enter Bermuda. By doing so Warren had defied the usage of nations for accepting passages for diplomatic voyages.

Because Bermuda was fast becoming a staging post for the Royal Navy, Warren didn't want Anthony or other Americans to discover key intelligence, such as the number of British marines and soldiers who were flocking there after fighting Napoleon in Europe.

As she often did, in her sugary way, Dolley steered Phoebe to hope for an alternative appointment for Anthony in her letter on May 6, 1813. "I trust in Heaven that all or both has happened for the best and that you will be consoled by a voyage somewhere else," she added. "My husband was never more provoked, and was never more anxious to promote the good, and gratify the wishes of a friend than he is now to serve your dear father."

Though Dolley didn't know it at the time, Anthony had traveled through Havre de Grace shortly after Cockburn's attack. No one yet knew that the fallout was just beginning.

Cockburn also wrote a letter on May 6. Addressed to Admiral Warren, it highlighted his latest conquests: George Town and Fredericstown. Not to be confused with Georgetown outside of Washington City along the Potomac River, these hamlets "situated up the Sassafras River were places of some trade and importance." From Cockburn's viewpoint, they were the "only river or place of shelter for vessels at this upper extremity of the Chesapeake which I had not examined and cleared." Before invading them, he ordered his launch and rocket boats to monitor the water two miles below. They intercepted a small boat navigated by local residents.

Then he "sent forward the two Americans in their boat to warn their countrymen against acting in the same rash manner the people of Havre de Grace had done."

With a goal to weaken their spirit as well as capture muskets and ammunition, Cockburn set about "assuring them if they did, that their towns would inevitably meet with a similar fate, but on the contrary, if they did not attempt resistance, no injuries should be done to them or their towns."

He justified his actions by promising "that vessels and public property only would be seized, that the strictest discipline would be maintained, and that whatever provisions or other property of individuals I might require for the use of the squadron should be instantly paid for in its fullest value."

Thus, Cockburn invoked his signature strategy. Though he would loot the houses of those who didn't fight back or shoot at his marines, he wouldn't burn those houses. Americans who defended themselves, in contrast, would find themselves homeless. Cockburn waited for an answer from his latest target. When none came, he made his choice. His boats advanced.

"I am sorry to say I soon found that the more unwise alternative was adopted, for on our reaching within about a mile of the town between two projected elevated points of the river, a most heavy fire musketry was opened on us from about 400 men divided and entrenched on the two opposite banks."

Similar to Havre de Grace, many residents fled to the woods after firing from their houses. "The towns, which [excepting the houses of those who continued peaceably in them and had taken no part in the attack made on us] were forthwith destroyed, as were for vessels laying in the river, and some stores of sugar, of lumber, of leather, and other merchandise."

After defeating George Town and Fredericstown of the Sassafras, Cockburn directed his force to another town located off a branch down the river. This place gave him what he most wanted to see: no will to fight.

"Here I had the satisfaction to find that what had passed at Havre, George Town, [and] Fredericstown had its effects, and led these people to understand that they have more to hope for from our generosity than from erecting batteries and opposing us by the means within their power."

He was "well pleased with the wisdom of their determination on their mode of receiving us." Then he received a messenger from another nearby town, Charlestown, on the Northeast River. Like a criminal pleading for his life to a judge, the messenger explained to him that his townspeople were at the admiral's mercy.

"I am assured that all the places in the upper part of the Chesapeake have adopted similar resolutions." Indeed. Many townspeople along the Chesapeake were now so frightened of pirate Cockburn that they would willingly dismantle their batteries and other defenses in exchange for a promise that he wouldn't burn their buildings. Such was the demise of the American spirit nearly forty years after the start of the American Revolution.

Confident that he would rid the region of vessels and other warlike stores by force and fear, this pillaging British admiral left the upper Chesapeake and traveled two hundred miles to Lynnhaven Bay, the Chesapeake's southern mouth. No matter that he had concluded that Baltimore and Annapolis were too well fortified to attack with just a few hundred men; he still couldn't help but smile. To this uniformed buccaneer, hadn't his mission of terror been a success so far? Yes, it had. Overwhelmingly so.

Yet it wasn't enough. Cockburn had bigger plans. Up next? A target of national consequence.

"I have little doubt of this city faring exactly as did Havre de Grace," architect and engineer Benjamin Latrobe wrote from Washington City to his father-in-law in Philadelphia on May 8, 1813.

That same day, Latrobe also conveyed alarming news to his new business partner, Robert Fulton, the steamboat builder and inventor, in New York.

"An express arrived this morning stating that the British were preparing to burn Annapolis.... The post boy who is since come in, says that no bombardment however has taken place," Latrobe wrote, noting that Madison had said that Washington City was not in danger.

Born in England in 1764, Latrobe was the son of a French Huguenot father and an American mother originally from Pennsylvania. With an obvious talent, he trained as an architect and engineer in Europe. The death of his first wife motivated Latrobe to move to the United States in 1796 to seek a new life in his mother's native country. He then married Mary Hazlehurst, a Philadelphia friend of Dolley's, and built the impressive Bank of Pennsylvania, the first Greek Revival style building in the United States. President Jefferson, an architectural enthusiast, was impressed with Latrobe's professional expertise and training and named him as surveyor of public buildings in Washington in 1803. Charged with completing the Capitol started by Dr. William Thornton, Latrobe finished the south wing housing the U.S. House of Representatives in 1811 and fulfilled requests from President Madison for the President's House.

After learning about Havre de Grace in May 1813, Latrobe was also worried about another *Washington*, the steamboat he had ordered from Fulton for the Potomac Steamboat Company. Though the vessel was complete, the British occupation of the Chesapeake and the blockade of the East Coast had prevented it from being delivered to Washington City. The attack on Havre de Grace solidified in Latrobe's mind that the danger "which surrounds us will assuredly prevent the steamboat being brought around," as he wrote to Fulton. He was correct.

Rejection was also on Latrobe's mind that day. The War of 1812 had negatively affected him in several ways. Because it needed to fund the war, Congress had suspended all construction on the U.S. Capitol, the primary focus of Latrobe's job as surveyor of public buildings. Congress also still owed him $600 for furnishings he had bought for the President's House and the marine hospital.

More than the lack of work, the war had emphasized a painful reality, one he had known for years but had hoped his architectural accomplishments would override. Worried about the lack of defenses for Washington City, Latrobe had offered his engineering services to a general. The officer had told him that engineers weren't needed in the army, because anyone could dig a trench.

Latrobe had also offered to sell a ship to the navy secretary, who told him the law wouldn't allow it. He had made suggestions on fortifying Alexandria and Fort Washington, but no one listened. He'd also offered his engineering services to the military directly to President Madison, who revealed the truth behind these multiple rejections.

"Our honest, patriotic, firm—but influenced president tells me plainly that he dare not employ me because I am unpopular," he'd written to a friend.

How had Latrobe become so unpopular? Hadn't he received critical acclaim for working hand in hand with the Madisons to renovate the interior of the President's House as a splendid backdrop for their republican ideals? Hadn't he improved the shoddy construction of the U.S. Capitol and elevated the interior to a state of magnificence? Hadn't he created the Navy Yard and its attractive arch? Yes, he had.

Though a brilliant architect, Latrobe had failed to charm members of Congress by showing them his plans and flattering them by letting them make suggestions. More than that, the original Capitol architect, Dr. William Thornton, had been a thorn in Latrobe's side from the start.

On the first day Latrobe visited the Capitol in 1803, a brick had fallen from a scaffold and hit him in the head. The blow was so hard that it took a week for Latrobe to recover. Though seemingly accidental, the brick incident raised speculation about Thornton's involvement in hurting Latrobe. Thornton's venom against Latrobe soon came out so strongly in letters to Congress that Latrobe eventually sued him for libel. Latrobe had raised legitimate concerns. The wood Thornton had used in the then-three-year-old U.S. Capitol was already rotting, the ceiling leaked, and the Senate chamber needed better heating. Though he'd won his case, Latrobe lost his popularity nonetheless.

Now that President Madison had plainly told him he was too unpopular to assist the war as an engineer, Latrobe decided to move to Pittsburgh and become a blacksmith.

"This war has among many other changes, totally changed my plan. It is my intention to resign my public situation and go and live at Pittsburg in Pennsylvania," Latrobe explained in a letter to his brother in London. He planned to move his family in the summer of 1813 and build steamboats for Fulton in Pennsylvania.

To his brother, Latrobe also confided his biggest fears. "But this unfortunate war accounts for everything that is abominable. I expect it will end either in a few months or last for many years, in which case your Congreve rockets may be tried on our towns and our torpedoes under the bottoms of your ships."

As he prepared to move to Pittsburgh, Latrobe had one more hope for doing something to save Washington City. As soon as he could, he would provide Fulton with an update on his role as a secret agent.

By mid-May, Dolley received a reply from Phoebe, who had swiftly answered her May 6 correspondence. "Before you receive this letter my dear Mrs. Madison, you will no doubt have seen Papa," Phoebe began. Indeed. Anthony had recently arrived in Washington City after traveling on the stagecoach between Philadelphia and Baltimore: "But tell him if you please that we were rejoiced to learn that he was safe at Havre de Grace."

Phoebe also expressed what many average Americans were feeling about the terrorizing British military. Though she didn't call for

Cockburn's head on a plate, as others did, she fumed over the injustice of the redcoats' tactics.

"Every person condemns the pitiful conduct of the enemy in destroying our unfortified towns and pilfering their poor inhabitants." Phoebe had another reason to write Dolley. A friend had asked her to write an introduction for him to Mrs. Madison.

"I have shown him your picture, that he might have some idea of Mrs. Madison; besides those descriptions of her which he must often hear; but I have told him that hers is that face which neither pen nor pencil can faithfully portray." Phoebe thought the picture was the "dignified representative of our sex in every female virtue adorned with all her sex's beauty, grace and loveliness."

The drawing was a gift that Dolley had given Phoebe four years earlier as a "resemblance of your 'parent's friend.'" She likely gave it to her because she sensed that in her new role as wife of the president, she would no longer have the ability to be as close to her old friends as she once was. Mrs. Madison couldn't have been more correct.

As the summer of 1813 progressed, Dolley would soon realize that she wouldn't have time for anyone but her husband. Pressure greater than anything he had yet experienced would weigh on him. The war would threaten their doorstep. He would soon need her sole, undivided attention. His presidency—his life, in fact—would depend on it.

CHAPTER FOUR

Dueling Strategies

"**A**nd now, if I could, I would describe to you the fears and alarms, that circulate around me," Dolley wrote on May 13, 1813, to her cousin and husband's secretary, Edward Coles.

Ten days after the British burned Havre de Grace, the people of Washington and adjacent Georgetown panicked over rumors that the redcoats were on their way to destroy the nation's capital city. An American general had acquired intelligence of a British plan to invade Washington under darkness.

"It is to land as many chosen rogues as they can about fourteen miles below Alexandria in the night, who may arrive before day and set fire to the offices and President's House when, if opposed, they are to surrender themselves as prisoners," Dolley explained.

A frigate had recently stopped at the mouth of the Potomac River. The ship's commander had sent a rowboat to another ship that anchored nearby. Too scared of being captured to wait around to discover the

33

frigate's intent, the American who watched this exchange shared the news, stirring fears of a British invasion.

"For the last week all the [Washington] City and Georgetown [except the Cabinet] have expected a visit from the enemy, and were not lacking in their expressions of terror and reproach," Dolley wrote about the contrast between the panic of the people and the call for calm coming from her husband's cabinet. Chief among them was the secretary of war, General John Armstrong, who was a little too cool for comfort.

———

"Madison and General Armstrong [the war secretary] declare that there is not any danger. A town meeting, however,...has appointed a committee of vigilance, and will, I hope, rouse the sleeping administration a little," Latrobe explained to Fulton about the cabinet's attempt to keep calm in the capital city.

Two days before Cockburn attacked Havre de Grace, Armstrong had proudly issued a new manual for the regular military, not to be confused with the ragtag militia, which he disdained. Called the "Rules and Regulations of the Army of the United States," the document outlined strict guidelines for promotions, ranks, and war staff responsibilities.

Though Cockburn's eye was clearly on causing trouble on the Chesapeake Bay, Armstrong looked much farther away: to Canada, particularly to Kingston. His strategy was so focused on the northern campaign that he seemed oblivious to the movements of the British along the Chesapeake.

Earlier in April 1813 a rider from Baltimore had rushed to Washington City with a stunning report. He had notified both Armstrong and the navy secretary, William Jones, that Baltimore was in imminent danger of attack.

How did each respond? While Jones darted to Baltimore, Armstrong was cool and dismissive. Indeed, Armstrong continually dismissed concerns about the Chesapeake as if swatting pesky flies. In his view the true plague facing America wasn't the nearby coast, but the cost of failing to capture key cities in Canada. If U.S. forces could conquer Canadian border towns, then the British would have no choice but to end the war and raise the northern boundary by ceding Canadian cities to America in a final peace treaty. So he, and many others, reasoned.

———

How did Dolley, a former Quaker, react to the rumors of an attack on Washington in mid-May 1813? Did pacifism reign in her heart or did self-defense kick in? Her tenacity dictated her response.

"We are making considerable efforts for defense. The fort is repairing, and 500 militia, with perhaps as many regulars are; and to be, stationed on the green near the windmill, or rather, near Major Tayloe's. The 20 tents, already look well," she wrote Edward, assuring him that the military was responding swiftly.

Major Tayloe, a known Federalist, owned a red-bricked mansion called the Octagon House. He had earlier rejected a design by Latrobe and instead employed Federalist Dr. Thornton to build this eight-sided mansion a few blocks west of the President's House. The Octagon was the finest privately owned mansion in town.

Unlike Dolley, some ladies were so frightened by the rumor that they packed their wardrobes and prepared for flight.

"I do not tremble at this, but feel affronted that the admiral [of Havre de Grace memory] should send me notice that he would make his bow at my drawing room soon."

To her surprise, Dolley's drawing rooms—a Republican term for levees or open house parties that she held at the President's House—had attracted the notice of America's top enemy.

———

Though Dolley and the president's cabinet sought to appear strong in the wake of rumors that Cockburn would attack Washington in May

1813, some people—including Latrobe—had concluded that Madison was a weak leader.

Though his wife Mary had privately painted an unflattering image of Mr. Madison, she still held fondness for Dolley. Like Anthony Morris, Mary was a longtime Quaker friend of Dolley's from Pennsylvania. Knowing her friend's personal taste, Mary had occasionally shopped for Dolley in Philadelphia. "Tomorrow you will receive your box containing the hat and turban," Mary had informed her in April 1809.

At the time, Benjamin Latrobe was working with the Madisons to renovate the President's House. Congress had authorized $5,000 for the project.

Focusing primarily on the state or main floor, James and Dolley had split the state floor into two parts: one for entertaining and one for conducting official business. The East Room served as the Cabinet Room. With Latrobe's help they converted the room next to it, the Green Room, into Madison's office. They chose the next three rooms overlooking the South Lawn as a suite for entertaining: the oval room in the center, the adjacent west parlor, and the large corner room on the west. These rooms featured interior doors that connected each other as a suite while each also opened to a hallway. Visitors could enter the state floor from the north door.

Latrobe had scoured the shops of Philadelphia and Baltimore for curtains, china, and cutlery. When he couldn't find enough lightweight damask fabric for the formal center oval room, he'd settled on Dolley's preference for the boldest possible color in the heaviest fabric: red velvet.

"The curtains! Oh the terrible velvet curtains! Their effect will ruin me entirely, so brilliant will they be," he'd confessed to her. The oval room's red curtains stood out from the cream wallpapered walls, white wood work, and a large French plate mirror over the mantel on the east wall. The style was Grecian and featured forty pieces of furniture, including two sofas and dozens of chairs, which were painted in white and gold or mahogany lacquer and depicted the U.S. coat of arms.

In contrast, Dolley had chosen lighter-weight satin and damask for the curtains and décor of the smaller room in between the oval room and State Dining Room. Set in a sunny yellow motif, this room became her music room, complete with a pianoforte and guitar for entertaining. Given her sunny personality and the attention she gave to decorating the room, this was likely her favorite of the three entertaining rooms, which is where a miniature painting or engraving of her hung.

On May 13, 1813, Dolley was also worried about another matter regarding Edward, who was the president's only paid executive staff member. He prepared and copied letters for the president and delivered messages to Congress. Coles's secretarial skills were as valuable to Dolley as they were to her husband. She relied on him to help her orchestrate and implement her weekly Wednesday evening open house parties and other social occasions.

A bachelor, Coles had become a favorite among the single society belles attending Dolley's events. Though a southerner who came from a family who owned a plantation not far from Thomas Jefferson's homestead, Monticello, Edward's Quakerism emerged more strongly than his culture.

In March 1813 Edward had traveled to Philadelphia for medical treatment for hemorrhoids from Dr. Physick, who'd treated Dolley years earlier for a knee wound. Discouraged by his lack of improvement, Edward had written the president and asked to be relieved of his duties as his secretary. Dolley's May 13 letter was a response on behalf of her husband. Employing Dolley for the task kept the matter private and unofficial.

"Your letter caused me great affliction my dear cousin. The continuation of your illness and Payne's reluctance at leaving America, left me not fortitude to write you until now," she wrote, explaining that she'd received a letter from Payne from aboard his ship "in which he expresses satisfaction at all around him."

Relieved that Payne was well, Dolley desperately wanted to convince Edward to return to James's service. "We indulge this pleasing hope, in addition to that of your remaining with us, to the last—not that I would, for the world, retard any plan for your prosperity," she wrote, noting that she longed for his happiness.

Though she knew how much Edward wanted to travel west and establish a colony for freed slaves, she wanted him to serve her husband a little longer. Thus, she used the sweetness of family ties as a strategy to bring him back.

"And that of your connections—Among them there are none, who feel a more affectionate interest for you than Mr. Madison and myself. I hope you will believe, that such is our regard and esteem for you, that we should consider your leaving us, a misfortune."

She enlisted another strategy, answering his worry that his absence was burdening the president. Dolley assured him, "Mr. M. can do very well without a secretary until your heath is re-established."

In reality, with the Russian mediation offer and other pressing business in the upcoming special summer session, her husband really needed Edward's assistance. She also needed help planning parties during the summer to give James informal opportunities to speak with members of Congress.

Dolley reminded Edward of another rational truth about the West: "The winter is not a season for emigration—so that next spring or summer you will be better able to make your election—to go, or not to go."

She also invoked their shared faith. Edward was a devout Quaker. Though the Society of Friends had abandoned her, she had not fully abandoned their beliefs. She understood the pacifism of Quakers but she also believed in self-defense, as did many of them. She wanted Edward to know that she was not afraid of Cockburn or the threats against Washington City.

"In my eyes as I have always been an advocate for fighting when assailed, though a Quaker—I therefore keep the old Tunisian saber within my reach," she told Edward.

The Tunisian saber was likely a diplomatic gift that James had received while serving as Jefferson's secretary of state years earlier. A diplomat from Tunis and Algeria in Northern Africa visited Washington during that time. Folklore from that culture suggested that a woman who could dance with a sword on her head without the weapon falling carried her husband's honor. Whether or not Dolley was aware of this symbolism, she tapped its meaning nonetheless.

In the darkest hour of the nation's capital, Dolley would soon carry her husband's honor unlike any wife of the president who preceded her.

———

While Armstrong dismissed rumors about British attacks on Washington City and Baltimore, the nation's third-largest city, Elijah Mix did just the opposite. He was so concerned that he took major steps to prevent an assault.

Mix had written President Madison a letter in April 1813 requesting financing to experiment with warfare technology. Madison agreed. Following up on the president's decision, Navy Secretary Jones had written a letter to the commanding Naval officer in Baltimore to authorize Mix's secret mission.

"A Mr. Elijah Mix will call upon you by my order to furnish him with such aid in carrying into effect his plans for the destruction of the enemy's ships," Jones had explained, fearing the British were in close proximity to Baltimore and the upper Chesapeake Bay. His instruction was as clear as it was concise. "You will furnish him with 500 pounds of powder, a boat or boats and six men."

He continued, "His plan is that of Fulton's torpedo." Robert Fulton, the builder of the steamship, had taken the name torpedo from an Atlantic Ocean fish that releases an electric discharge to incapacitate its enemies. The experiments focused on an explosive charge attached to the end of a long pole, which exploded when it touched the hull of a ship.

Jones had confidence in Mix, who had been a prisoner aboard the *Emolus*, a British Navy cruiser supposedly lost early in the war. Instead, Mix had run the vessel ashore and seized its dispatches. A commissioned sailing master, Mix had recently served on Lake Ontario from the winter of 1812 through the spring of 1813.

"He is an intrepid zealous man and means to perform the service in person...the greatest privacy ought to be observed," Jones had written.

Latrobe had served as the secret agent and financer behind the mission for Jones. Earlier on March 21, 1813, he had written to Fulton that "if I were unmarried, and under 25, I would borrow a few pairs of torpedoes, and if am not much mistaken, they should succeed in some stormy night at Norfolk, with the aid of two canoes.... The more dreadful the wind is, the darker, the better."

Knowing that the U.S. envoy to France, Joel Barlow, had sent several torpedoes from France, Latrobe had searched the Navy Yard. He'd found them buried in a heap and a barrel. Because the U.S. Navy didn't have financing authorized for the project, Latrobe had put up his own money to pack and mail them to Mix under the label "mathematical instruments."

While all of Washington worried about the rumors of an invasion by Cockburn in mid-May, Latrobe focused on saving Washington through a covert operation. He wrote Fulton that their secret mission was under way. "Mix should be at Old Point Comfort (the lighthouse in Hampton, Virginia). The English Fleet is collected in Lynnhaven Bay."

Without Edward's secretarial help, Madison continued to rely on his own hand to write letters. His indignation against British tactics came out through his pen.

Twenty days after the burning of Havre de Grace, he sent a message to Congress. Deriding "the spirit and manner in which the war continues to be waged by the enemy," he called their tactics a "savage fury."

Cockburn's recent jaunt up the Chesapeake was nothing less than "a system of plunder and conflagration." Both were "equally forbidden by respect for national character and by the established rules of civilized warfare."

Then Madison focused Congress's attention on good news: the success of the *Hornet*. "In continuation of the brilliant achievements of our infant Navy," he wrote, "a signal triumph has been gained by Captain Lawrence and his companions in the *Hornet*."

The *Hornet* was an American sloop of war that had destroyed a British sloop of war, the HMS *Peacock*. The speed and skill of the *Hornet*'s crew were unparalleled. Madison believed the conquerors deserved the "highest praise" and full compensation from Congress. The House of Representatives agreed. The up-and-coming James Lawrence received a promotion to captain.

Madison's eye, however, like his war secretary's, was far less on fortifying the Chesapeake and much more on continuing to bolster the Navy and Army in the North. The military's top focus remained squarely and supremely on the Great Lakes and Canada. A victory there could change the direction of the war and force Britain to end its abusive practices against U.S. trade and sailors.

"On the lakes our superiority is near at hand, where it is not already established," Madison wrote hopefully.

On military matters, this scholarly president deferred to plans created by the War Department and its generals. As a young man fresh out of college, Madison had served for a brief time in his local militia in Orange, Virginia. Once the Revolutionary War began in earnest, his sickly nature and small physique made this rich man a poor soldier. He exchanged a musket for books and pens, drawing upon them to serve at the convention to abolish Virginia's royal charter and set up Virginia's new government, and later, in the Continental Congress during the last years of the Revolution.

Over the years Madison filled his mind with books on political science, such as Joseph Priestley's *An Essay on the First Principles of Government*. Military science was better left to captains and major generals. Now as president, he had to rely on them for military decisions and success above his own instincts. Surely this was the best strategy he could employ?

━━━━━━

John Armstrong was one reason that Albert Gallatin had been eager to leave Washington and go to Europe as a peace commissioner. Gallatin had opposed Armstrong's appointment as secretary of war in February

1813 and distrusted his loyalty to the administration, and for good reason. Though Armstrong had served as the top diplomat for the United States to France under Presidents Jefferson and Madison, many doubted his loyalties to them.

The questions had started in 1810 after Armstrong had forwarded President Madison a letter from Napoleon's foreign secretary. In vague terms the letter indicated that Napoleon would revoke France's trade restrictions against America.

Missing was Armstrong's assessment or analysis of the letter and the foreign secretary's true intentions. Madison had taken Napoleon at his word and issued a proclamation to reinstate trade restrictions against England if Parliament didn't do the same and revoke its policies against America. Armstrong soon left his post and returned to America with fanfare, as if he were the hero of the decade. For awhile, he was.

New York's governor honored him with a dinner, and audiences applauded him when they learned of his presence in theaters. In Philadelphia, he received an even warmer welcome at a sumptuous dinner of prominent citizens. Then came more flattering offers. One friend suggested that he run for governor of Pennsylvania. Another went much further. No, he shouldn't run for governor. He should become president of the United States!

"I am a great favorite with both parties," Armstrong confessed to a friend, though doubting the attention would last. As a military man and diplomat, he'd long enjoyed the nonpartisan status that came with those positions. "This cannot from its own nature, be of much duration."

The reason? Armstrong wasn't a naturally charismatic fellow. He could be sharp, intense, and taciturn. He preferred winning battles to winning friends. The French government had often complained that he didn't socialize enough and hid behind testy notes.

Armstrong's triumphant return to America had included a visit to Washington City on December 20, 1810. The president and his cabinet received him warmly.

General James Wilkinson, who was in Washington at the time of Armstrong's return, confessed to a friend that "Armstrong may take the White House this time two years if things are well managed."

Things were not. Armstrong didn't run for governor of Pennsylvania, the state of his birth to Scottish American parents.

"Our future destiny is not, as you know, in our keeping," Armstrong had written to his brother-in-law. "What mine may be is very doubtful."

Realizing that he'd rather manage an estate than engage in presidential engineering for himself, he bought a sheep farm in New York off the Hudson River and settled there in 1811.

But a stronger reason emerged. The promising letter of free trade with France that Armstrong had forwarded to Madison had proved to be deceptive. Napoleon had merely suggested through his foreign secretary that he *might* lift his policies—called the Berlin and Milan Decrees—not that he had actually done so. He had not and did not.

The fallout for American ships that believed Napoleon had lifted his policies against them was disastrous. As one Federalist observed, "To the astonishment of their owners they find that the Berlin and Milan Decrees are not repealed; the officers of the [French] government seize and detain them."

Because Madison had trusted Armstrong about Napoleon's intentions, American ships were in increased danger of having their cargoes plundered. This added to the perception that Madison favored France over England. Although Madison believed that France deserved war from the United States, he also understood that America couldn't handle two wars with two European powers. To him, England was the greater threat. To his political adversaries, France was the worst menace. This division over foreign allies and foes divided the two parties.

Albert Gallatin and other members of Madison's cabinet had blamed Armstrong because he'd forwarded the letter without giving an assessment on the French government's sincerity. As a result, he'd embarrassed the president.

But Armstrong's popularity made him a threat to Madison's administration. When War Secretary William Eustis resigned after several military failures in 1812, Madison considered his options for replacing him. Two men turned him down. Talk of Armstrong's political prospects as governor or president may have planted an idea in Madison's mind of tapping his services in some other way to keep him from securing a place on the next presidential ballot. Hence, the president offered the post to the petulant Armstrong as a way to keep him loyal.

━━━━━━

Were the threats real to Washington in 1813? Or was this propaganda? The small size of Cockburn's force made it doubtful that he could pull off an attack on Washington. His timing, however, would be ripe. In the weeks following the attacks on Havre de Grace, members of Congress were flocking to the nation's capital for the special summer session. The surprise one legislator would bring would lead Madison to question his choices and strategies.

CHAPTER FIVE

Knickerbockers

Elijah Mix had heard the truth about Cockburn's maneuvers. He had abandoned the Upper Chesapeake. No invasion of Washington City was imminent as May 1813 came to a close.

Cockburn and his ships now docked in the mouth of the Chesapeake Bay in Virginia. Admiral Warren had departed for Bermuda in a convoy of forty vessels loaded with American treasure from the towns they had attacked in the Upper Chesapeake.

Could Mix attack them before they traveled elsewhere, such as back up the Potomac River to Washington City? Mix and his men took their powder machines and experiments with them to Gosport Naval Yard in Norfolk, Virginia. There they developed a secret strategy to row a boat near an anchored enemy ship and then drop a torpedo into the water. He expected that the torpedo would drift toward the ship and explode.

After Mix arrived off Norfolk's coast and quietly set about to launch his weapon of surprise, another torpedo, a political one, shot from

America's largest city into Washington City. What a force this Knicker-bocker would prove to be.

———

After a ten-year absence from national elected office, Rufus King of New York returned to the U.S. Senate determined to take a firm stand. This time Madison had gone too far. King knew immediately what he should do on June 2, 1813, during the special session of the Thirteenth Congress.

King was the most experienced politician in Washington, second only to the president. Their lives had followed similar paths. Like Madison, he had started his public service career as a legislator after the American Revolution. Madison had served in the Virginia House of Delegates and on the Governor's Council, and King had taken his place in the House of Representatives of the Massachusetts General Court. King had subsequently served in Congress under the Articles of Confederation, which met in New York City. There he had met the wealthy Miss Mary Alsop.

Still representing Massachusetts, King went on to participate in the Constitutional Convention, where Madison proposed the Virginia Plan, which created a foundation for the new Constitution. Both supported ratification of the U.S. Constitution and strategized together on how to convince Americans to support it. After marrying Mary, King moved from Massachusetts to New York.

When George Washington became president, the New York State Assembly chose the logical, authoritative King as its first U.S. Senator under the Constitution. A few years later, during John Adams's presidency, King served as the top U.S. diplomat to England. He felt comfortable in London, in part because New England's manufacturing and mercantile economy was similar to England's. As a result, he made many English friends and became increasingly pro-British, while Madison, a Republican Party leader, leaned more and more toward France, whose agricultural economy was similar to that of his beloved Virginia.

When Jefferson became president, King remained in his diplomatic role in London while Madison, now Jefferson's secretary of state and head of all diplomats, became his boss. King realized that his Federalist leanings would become increasingly at odds with President Jefferson's Republican policies. Hence, King returned to New York in 1803 and retired to private life.

His retirement lasted only five years. Soon America discovered just how different King's and Madison's politics were from each other when they ran against one another in the 1808 presidential election. King became Federalist Charles Pinckney's running mate. Madison beat them handily in the Electoral College to become president. King spent the next four years observing Madison's politics while living a private life in New York. Things suddenly changed in 1813.

"You will have observed in the public paper the notice of my appointment to the Senate," he had written to his friend, Christopher Gore of Massachusetts, on February 14, 1813. The New York State Assembly had chosen King, its most veteran politician, to serve in the Thirteenth Congress in the U.S. Senate. Upon his return to public life, King wrote: "Of one thing you may be assured that this appointment has been made without solicitation, nay, without the expression, or existence, of a wish for it on my part."

Despite pretentiously denouncing ambition for power, he knew that his return to the Senate in 1813 as a senior statesman was historic because of his stature. "I shall probably pass the next winter at Washington; the changes of men, as well as measures are so complete, that there will not be a single member of the Senate except myself, who belonged to that body during the time of General Washington."

When King arrived in Washington City in late May 1813, he had only a few things in common with Madison. Both bore a bald spot on tops of their heads with their hair framing the sides. What remained of King's reddish brown semicircle was graying and curly. What was left of Madison's hair was white, wavy, and loose. Hair loss, age, and intellect were about all they seemed to share in the summer of 1813.

King made his move on June 2. As a moderate Federalist attorney, he tapped logic more than passion as he addressed his fellow senators. He argued that the president had exceeded his authority by not seeking the advice and consent of the U.S. Senate before sending peace envoys to Europe, particularly Treasury secretary Albert Gallatin.

King submitted three resolutions. Up first was a request that Madison send the Senate copies of the "communication from the Emperor of Russia, offering his mediation to bring about a peace between the United States and Great Britain, together with copies of the answers to such communications." King wanted specifics. He didn't just want to read the letters. He wanted to know the "dates at which" the correspondence was "respectively received and answered." He rightfully suspected that Madison had delayed revealing the offer until after the conclusion of the Twelfth Congress and his inauguration.

King's second resolution called for the president to send copies of the commissions given to Gallatin, Adams, and Bayard. These first two requests seemed harmless enough, an act of transparency. The third resolution was much sharper and more pointed: "That the President of the United States be requested to inform the Senate whether Albert Gallatin...retains the office of secretary of the department of the treasury."

That wasn't all. If Madison had kept Gallatin as Treasury secretary while also appointing him as a peace envoy, King wanted the president "to inform the Senate under what authority, and by whom, the powers and duties of the head of the treasury department are discharged during the absence of Albert Gallatin from the United States."

On June 3, 1813, the Senate considered King's resolutions. By close margins, it voted against the first two requests. But the third request intrigued the senators because it raised an important question. Could Gallatin legally serve as both Treasury secretary and a peace commissioner? Many wondered if Madison, the father of the Constitution, had just exceeded the power of the executive branch by stealing authority from the legislative. To King, this was a golden opportunity to undermine the president.

What he didn't realize was that by doing so, King might just thwart the remaining political goal that he shared with Madison. Though they may not have realized it, both men wanted the same thing for their country: peace. They simply had different opinions on how to achieve it.

———

Meanwhile another New Yorker contemplated his next move. His name was Washington Irving, and he had visited Washington City two years earlier, in 1811, with an eye for writing a satire about the place.

"I arrived at the inn about dusk; and, understanding that Mrs. Madison was to have her levee or drawing-room that very evening, I swore by all my gods I would be there," Irving had written in January 1811 of his visit to the President's House.

Because he was born in New York on April 3, 1783, during the same week that New Yorkers learned of the peace treaty ending the Revolutionary War, Irving's mother named him after George Washington. When New York City was the nation's capital, six-year-old Irving met President Washington. Little Washington was so impressed with the giant Washington that he painted a watercolor of him.

By 1811, twenty-eight-year-old Irving wasn't a typical American Joe or even a George. Many readers, especially New Yorkers, knew him by other names, including Jonathan Oldstyle, a pseudonym for his Federalist-leaning literary achievement called *Morning Chronicle* and, later, *Letters of Jonathan Oldstyle.*

To most he was Diedrich Knickerbocker, whose satirical 1809 book poked fun at the self-importance of New Yorkers and coined the name knickerbockers. The work was so successful that he'd received acclaim from Sir Walter Scott, Scotland's foremost historical novelist and poet. Scott had recently written a letter to a friend of Irving's claiming that "our sides have been absolutely sore with laughing" after reading Knickerbocker's *History of New York.* "There are passages which indicate that the author possesses powers of a different kind...let me know when Mr.

Irving takes pen in hand again, for assuredly I shall expect a very great treat."

Writing another work was on Irving's mind when he arrived in Washington in 1811. Just as he was drawn to meeting the first U.S. president, so he was attracted to meeting the fourth member of the president's club and, more especially, his charismatic wife.

Irving headed to the President's House, where "in a few minutes I emerged from dirt and darkness into the blazing splendor of Mrs. Madison's drawing-room. Here I was most graciously received; found a crowded collection of great and little men, of ugly old women and beautiful young ones, and in ten minutes was hand and glove with half the people in the assemblage."

Oh, how the vivacious Dolley impressed him. "Mrs. Madison is a fine, portly, buxom dame, who has a smile and a pleasant word for everybody."

With such great source material for his next comedic work, he continued his observations with humor. "Her sisters, Mrs. Cutts and Mrs. Washington, are like the two merry wives of Windsor. But as to Jemmy Madison—ah poor Jemmy!—he is but a withered little apple-john."

Ever the life of the party, Irving charmed Dolley with his comedic and satirical talents as much as she charmed him. He boasted that "Mrs. Madison is a sworn friend of mine, and indeed all the ladies of the household and myself great cronies."

Like many who came to Washington, Irving had been searching for something. Though tasked by his brothers to report on how politics might affect their family business in New York and London, which funded Irving's travels, part of him had dabbled with the idea of an appointment. Secretary Monroe suggested that Irving become the secretary for the top U.S. diplomat to France at the time, Joel Barlow.

"The President, on its being mentioned to him, said some very handsome things of me, and I make no doubt will express a wish in my favor on the subject," he reported to his brother, noting that he hadn't made a direct application for the position. "I shall let the thing take its chance." But in his heart, he knew he was an independent mind, unsuited for serving the American public through politics or a government position. "I should only look upon it as an advantageous opportunity of acquiring information and materials for literary purposes, as I do not feel much ambition or talents for political life."

He was determined to write more satire, especially when the diplomatic secretarial appointment did not materialize. "Should I not be placed in the situation alluded to, I shall pursue a plan I had some time since contemplated," he wrote, wondering if he should reveal his real motivation "of studying for a while, and then travelling about the country for the purpose of observing the manners and characters of the various parts of it, with a view to writing a work."

He was confident in his best gift without being cocky. "Which, if I have any acquaintance with my own talents, will be far more profitable and reputable than any thing I have yet written."

Then he warned his brother. "Of this, however, you will not speak to others."

Indeed, great secrecy and a hoax had surrounded his satire on the history of New York. He had invented newspaper accounts of the disappearance of Diedrich Knickerbocker to build interest in publishing Knickerbocker's *History of New York* as a way to pay the presumed deceased Knickerbocker's bills. The ruse worked and his satire was a bestseller. Irving had hoped the President's House and his travels would give him another success.

No matter what, however, "I am determined on one thing—to dismiss from my mind all party prejudice and feeling as much as possible, and to endeavor to contemplate every subject with a candid and good-natured eye."

His next opportunity to receive compensation for writing had not left him good-natured. Returning to Washington in December 1812 for his family's business, he had felt "tied by the leg to the footstool of Congress."

Worse, he had also accepted a job to review books for a magazine. He didn't like it, saying he was "wickedly made the editor of a vile farrago, a congregation of heterogeneous articles that have no possible affinity to one another." Writing reviews made him "stagger under the trash."

Then something exciting happened. He, along with 400 guests, attended a Washington City dinner saluting America's newest naval hero, Stephen Decatur. "It was the most splendid entertainment of the kind I ever witnessed. The city assembly room was decorated in a very tasteful manner with the colors and flags of the Macedonian."

Decatur had commanded the USS *United States* in October 1812. In a battle off the coast of Azores, a group of nine islands 1,000 miles west of Portugal, a wounded Decatur defeated the HMS *Macedonian*. Decatur's victory over this British vessel was a source of American pride. According to Irving, "The room was decorated with transparencies representing the battles…and the whole entertainment went off with a soul and spirit which I never before witnessed."

Now, in June 1813, with the war a year old, Irving needed new material for the *Analectic Magazine* in Philadelphia. While Senator King took jabs at Madison from the Senate floor, Irving sought something fresh to write about for his magazine. Should he write about the withered apple James Madison and his delectable wife? Recalling the splendid dinner for Decatur, he longed to write something more nautical, more heroic. What would that be? In the midst of war, the patriotic Irving decided to put aside being a satirist and take up the pen of a journalist.

———

John Armstrong's politics were also a complicated mixture of opinions and contradictions. As a transplanted Knickerbocker, sometimes his loyalty was to the North, particularly to New York, where he lived, and Pennsylvania, where he had grown up. Because he disdained the power of the South, he met with New York Federalists in advance of selecting nominees for the presidential election in 1812. What he disliked about Madison and Jefferson was their southern backgrounds. How he longed for a man of the North to take the presidency! He had secretly concluded that southern domination must end with Madison's presidency.

As much as he loved the North, Armstrong loved the military more. When tensions with Great Britain escalated and diplomacy continue to fail, he had complained that the government and nation lacked the spirit needed for war.

"We are a nation of Quakers [pacifists], without either their morals or their motives," he quipped.

Congress's declaration of war had affected Armstrong's politics and decisions in 1812. As a dedicated military man who had fought for his country during the revolution, he couldn't fully embrace the Federalists who opposed the war, especially those who supported New England's secession from America. "They [Federalists] behave like idiots when they oppose or obstruct it. A war will give them another chance of ascendancy and I know not anything else-that will do so."

As a diplomat, he had seen firsthand how unwilling France was to cooperate and embrace U.S. trade. He also understood the bully that England had become to America.

Armstrong felt war was the only remaining option. Presidential candidate DeWitt Clinton's opposition to the war had worried Armstrong. Backing from both Federalists and anti-war Republicans had boosted Clinton's chances of winning. Though Clinton was from New York, Armstrong had concluded that Clinton's ambition would backfire and give the South more power. As he had written to his New York friend Justice Spencer: "The effect will be to perpetuate, not put down, the policy of the South."

Armstrong's sense of duty, the military, and patriotism had led him to support Madison for president in 1812. After the war started, he had become a brigadier general in the regular army, which assigned to him the prestigious job of defending New York harbor.

Now as a member of Madison's cabinet in 1813, Armstrong watched Senator King's maneuvers with great interest. Should he approach his fellow knickerbocker with an opportunity? When the time was right, of course.

━━━━━━━

King offered his resolutions from the floor of the U.S. Senate, which was located in the two-winged U.S. Capitol building on Pennsylvania

Avenue. Years earlier, in 1791, Pierre Charles L'Enfant, a French veteran of the American Revolution and military engineer, had meticulously planned a grand grid for the future city of Washington. He had designed many streets to crisscross at traditional right angles while others cut through diagonally. L'Enfant had hoped that spouting fountains, cooling ponds, lush green spaces, botanical gardens, and grand edifices would one day transform this muddy marsh into a western Paris. Wanting Washington's classical buildings to rival old Athens, he envisioned the Potomac River as a seaport for trade exceeding Alexandria—the one that anchored Egypt's Nile River.

With great enthusiasm and wonder, L'Enfant had ridden out with George Washington in 1792 to show him a hill cascading to the Potomac River. Here was an amazing spot to build the U.S. Capitol. This was the best place to showcase a grand imposing powerhouse fit for the halls of a Congress that represented the people. Adding a national mall would increase the location's grandeur. Giddy with excitement, he described the hill as a "pedestal waiting for a monument." Washington agreed.

The final plans, however, did not come from L'Enfant but from Dr. William Thornton. For all of his vision, artistic eye, and skilled architectural hand, L'Enfant was unable to get along with other people. He was fired for his inability to work effectively with city commissioners. Saving the day, Thornton won a contest for designing the U.S. Capitol. Like a Roman temple, his multistory design with columns in the center topped by a triangle pediment and a low dome evoked the symmetry of classical architecture. President Washington placed the cornerstone in 1793 and believed the U.S. Capitol "ought to be upon a scale far superior to anything in this country."

Yet, in 1813, the U.S. Capitol building had yet to reach its potential. Both wings were complete. Though elegant and graceful, the building relied upon a wooden walkway between the two wings. Missing was the dome, which had yet to be built. Also missing was a long, manicured mall. Though trees lined the wide Pennsylvania Avenue, dusty deep potholes and mud stole that street's elegance.

The swampy stick-in-the-mud capital couldn't compare in elegance and size to Senator King's beloved New York City. The nation's largest city boasted a population of more than 96,000 in the 1810 U.S. census while only 8,000 lived in or near Washington City. Where New York was old, founded by the Dutch and taken over by the English in 1664, thirteen-year-old Washington was an odd combination of classical man-made beauty and lopsided, untamed nature. This fledgling district's few taverns and boarding houses were spread out and stood out against the President's House and U.S. Capitol like a clothing line set in a palace garden. Washington was a poor man's town compared with cosmopolitan New York.

If King and others had their preference, the nation's capitol would return to New York or Philadelphia. Those places were better suited to a gentleman's sense of taste and refinement. Washington was as embarrassing as it was rustic. What good would ever come from this city? Nothing, at least to King and others like him.

While King did not love Washington City, he did love his country. And far more than elegance, he wanted peace for his nation and countrymen. They had neither. Without peace, there could be no prosperity. Without peace, there could be no pursuit of happiness.

━━━━━

While King publically questioned Madison in June 1813, Armstrong focused on Canada and one of his military generals, General Wilkinson, who had yet to arrive in Washington weeks after Armstrong had ordered him to do so. Wilkinson seemed to be snubbing him.

Armstrong badly needed a success in Canada to make up for the failed land campaign of 1812. Back then, William Hull, governor of the Michigan Territory, had led a combined force of 2,000 regulars and militia to defend Fort Detroit, secure Lake Erie, and invade Canada. Though he had successfully advanced into Canada and convinced 500 Canadians to desert, he became scared. Fearing that the British and their allied native tribes would cut off his supply lines around Lake Erie, he retreated back to Fort Detroit instead of advancing further into Canada as expected.

Sure enough, the British arrived with reinforcements and threatened to have their native tribe allies slaughter the Americans at Fort Detroit, where Hull's daughter and grandchildren were living. Soon Hull began displaying erratic behavior. Perhaps he was drunk or having a nervous breakdown, but his speech was slurred and he crouched in corners as if insane. Then suddenly, without consulting his officers or putting up a fight, he surrendered Fort Detroit on August 16, 1812. Hull's surrender was as humiliating as it was devastating.

Hull was court-martialed and sentenced to death. Madison commuted the execution because of the general's honorable service during the American Revolution.

Earlier in the spring of 1813, Armstrong had given Wilkinson a promotion to major general and ordered him to leave New Orleans and come to Washington City for further orders to go north. After all, why bother with continuing a large force in the South? Thanks to Wilkinson's success against the Spanish, the fort and bay in Mobile now belonged to the Mississippi territory and was on track to become a new state. Armstrong needed Wilkinson in Canada.

"Why should you remain in your land that grows the laurels?" Armstrong had written to Wilkinson. He'd reminded him of their joint service together during the American Revolution. They had been brothers in arms at the Battle of Saratoga in New York, a key turning point in the Revolutionary War.

"I speak to you with the frankness due to you and to myself," he concluded, "and again advise, come to the North and come quickly! If our cards are well played, we may renew the scenes of Saratoga."

For months Wilkinson had been aware of the government's desire to send him north. As he had complained to James Monroe, who was the acting war secretary until Armstrong assumed office, "My constitution will not bear a Northern climate, and...I do conceive my rank and service give me claim to a separate command."

Because he had taken possession of West Florida, Wilkinson did not receive Armstrong's instructions until May 19, when he had returned to New Orleans from Mobile. The exhausted and testy Wilkinson had written Armstrong that the delay had cost them precious time for a successful campaign in Canada. He was now facing a "sultry fatiguing, dilatory journey" that would "retard my arrival on the theatre where I am destined to take a part."

Indeed. Mid-June had arrived and Wilkinson was nowhere to be found in Washington City to receive his orders and march north. Armstrong fumed at Wilkinson's snub. He needed to instruct him to mount an attack in Canada before the fighting season closed. Time seemed to be ticking too fast for Armstrong's myopic plan to succeed. He was far less focused on word that the British were nearing Norfolk. After all, wasn't a Virginia seaport Navy Secretary Jones's turf?

CHAPTER SIX

Torpedo

"The boats of the *Victorious* picked up...one of the powder machines, commonly known by the name of Fulton's, made to explode underwater and thereby cause the immediate destruction to whatever it may come in contact with," Cockburn wrote on June 16, 1813, from his ship in the mouth of the Chesapeake.

They had found Elijah Mix's torpedo.

"This was no doubt destined for the *Victorious* or some other of our ships here. The American government intending thus to dispose of less by wholesale 600 [British sailors] at a time, without further trouble for risk," Cockburn complained, sarcastically calling the effort laudable.

Little caused Cockburn to flinch. Though his father, Sir James Cockburn, came from a wealthy Scottish landholding family, Admiral Cockburn was one of the most experienced seamen in the Royal Navy. His upper-middle-class mother was the daughter of a reverend who had tutored King George III when he was a boy.

Debts and poor decisions, however, had sent Cockburn's parents into poverty. The second of five boys and three half-sisters, George had no inheritance prospects. Already familiar with sea life, at age ten he began working as a captain's servant under the patronage of the admiralty's Lord Hood. Four years later, at age fourteen, he had entered naval service. By nineteen he'd become a lieutenant and received a commission as a third lieutenant a year later.

Though his marines had found only one torpedo that June day in 1813, they had rightly assumed that the Americans had built more than one. "I think it extremely probable others of a similar description have passed out to sea unobserved," the admiral observed.

Concealing his fear of a torpedo killing hundreds of his men, Cockburn kept his cool. He noted that because this weapon drifted as easily as a cut buoy, it could have destroyed an American ship as haphazardly as a British one.

He took comfort that if an atrocity like this had happened, the U.S. government, which boasted of "unvaried examples of humanity," would be blamed for its savage tactics.

"I have now closed with His Majesty's ships towards Hampton Roads, which will enable the enemy to try further humane experiments," he added sarcastically.

Cockburn was resolute. Once Warren returned, they would attack Craney Island and Norfolk. Little did he realize that soon his men, not the Americans, would be leaders of the most atrocious assault on the Atlantic coast since the start of the War of 1812.

Latrobe had written of Mix's mission, "If the enterprise miscarries it will be a consequence of its becoming the subject of conversation."

Conversation and loose lips had not sunk Mix's mission, however. Latrobe had written to Mix, "I watch the decline of the moon with more anxiety than I ever watched her increase."

Though Mix's timing with the tide and a dark moon had been good, his first attempt was unsuccessful because he had hooked the howser or thick tow rope of the British ship, a seventy-four-gun, instead of the rudder. Realizing his mistake but fearing detection, he had fled and left the torpedo behind, which the British found.

At this point Mix needed more money, which led Latrobe to give him a loan. Perhaps the next month, in July, when the moon grew dim, they would succeed.

Much was on the president's mind that June 1813. Madison swiftly and succinctly responded to the Senate's request. His annoyance flew faster than his pen: "The Senate are informed that the office of the secretary of the treasury is not vacated."

Why didn't they trust him? He'd deferred to their authority to consider the nomination. Why couldn't they understand? He couldn't control weather and risk waiting too long to send his peace commissioners to Russia. Now mischief makers in the Senate were using details to thwart a very important decision that was crucial to peace. What should he do? Madison decided to explain that the Treasury duties had been temporarily assigned to the navy secretary.

A clerk read Madison's reply to the Senate, which responded by sending the issue to a special five-member committee. King, of course, was one of the members.

In addition to Senate meddling, Madison was also worried about the English government's response to the Russian czar's mediation offer. He saw plausible reasons that Emperor Alexander's negotiation might lead to peace. Russia was "the only power in Europe which can command respect from both France and England." He was correct.

When it came to the mediation, Madison's deepest worry was "whether England will accede to the mediation, or do so with evasive purposes." While the Senate questioned Gallatin as a commissioner,

Madison correctly feared that the British government would torpedo the opportunity to treat for peace by rejecting Russia's mediation offer.

As worried as he was with state business that June, Madison was also proud of his wife for consenting to send her son Payne as an aide to Gallatin in Russia. He knew that the decision had required much courage on her part. Though he wasn't Payne's biological father, he treated him as such because he loved Dolley so much.

━━━━━

Many saw the Madisons as opposites in almost every way. One visitor described the president this way: "Mr. Madison reminded me of a schoolmaster dressed up for a funeral." In contrast, Dolley was the queen of hearts.

Some saw Mrs. Madison's appearance and manner of dressing to be a contradiction with the modesty of many Quakers. The night Mr. Hallowell, an old Quaker friend, visited the President's House, she raised her wine glass to her lips, bowed to her guest, and said cheerfully: "Here's to thy absent broad brim, Friend Hallowell."

"And here's to thy absent kerchief," he'd teased of her handsome evening gown that exposed her shoulders. He knew his friend's contradictions well. A modest Quaker she was not. A modern dresser in the low cut Empire style she was.

Dolley usually wore a plain housedress with a Quaker cap during the day, but chose stunning evening wear fitting a queen. Her friends often sent her turbans, hats, and other wardrobe niceties from Baltimore and Philadelphia. Phoebe, ever on the look out in Philadelphia, wrote Dolley whenever she found something likable. "Some splendid trimmings for dresses have just been opened for the brides they are about ten dollars a piece—If you would like some, I will endeavor to select the handsomest."

Dolley also sought fineries from clothing shops in Paris. Early in the administration, she wrote her friend Ruth Barlow: "Oh! I wish I was in France with you, for a little relaxation. . . . I will ask the favor of you to send me by safe vessels—large headdresses a few flowers, feathers, gloves and stockings [black and white] or any other pretty thing, suitable to an economist and draw on my husband for the amount."

In short, Mrs. Madison was a Quaker by day and queen by night. Though her extravagant style bucked the Quaker tradition of plainness and simplicity, she embodied Quakerism in one distinct way. She cordially welcomed her husband's political enemies to her house, even if she privately didn't like the aspersions they cast on James.

One reporter attending a drawing room for the first time observed, "There were many members of both houses of Congress present, both of the majority and minority, and I was told, some of the most acrimonious ones."

Each Wednesday, the Madisons held open parties that didn't require invitations. This gave both Federalists and Republicans a chance to talk in a relaxed atmosphere. Guests voluntarily risked sharing company with their opponents. The Madisons' approach was a contrast to the entertaining style of predecessor President Jefferson, who wouldn't invite members of opposite political parties to the same parties at the President's House. In an era where duels between angry men were common—including Jefferson's vice president Aaron Burr, who killed former Treasury secretary Alexander Hamilton in an 1804 duel—the Madisons saw an opportunity to change the culture of Washington. By mixing socially, politicians got to know each other as human beings, not as political enemies. They could talk politics, but social graces prevented them from getting too hot in the presence of ladies and cool ice cream.

"Everybody loves Mrs. Madison," Speaker of the House Henry Clay legendarily said.

"That's because Mrs. Madison loves everybody," she quipped.

By making everyone feel welcome in her house, Dolley nurtured good will for her husband. Mrs. William Seaton, sister of Joseph Gales, the editor of the *National Intelligencer*, made a similar observation: "I would describe the dignified appearance of Mrs. Madison, but I could not do her justice. 'Tis not her form, 'tis not her face, it is the woman altogether, whom I should wish you to see."

Though her clothing reflected sophistication, her character was warm and approachable: "But her demeanor is so far removed from the hauteur generally attendant on royalty, that your fancy can carry the resemblance no further than the headdress."

Her genuine love drew people to her. "I am by no means singular in the opinion, believe that Mrs. Madison's conduct would be graced by propriety were she placed in the most adverse circumstances of life."

Little did Mrs. Seaton know that her words were prophetic. The best way to understand Dolley's depth and complexity was to watch her handle pressure. Adversity would soon bring out the best in her.

━━━━━━━━

Dolley was not happy about the special session. In a letter to Edward, she confided that her servant Mitchell had abandoned them, forcing her to take on his duties, which created many new demands on her.

She had written on June 10 that "the city is more than ever crowded with strangers!! My head is dizzy." In an earlier letter to Phoebe, she had expressed a similar anxiety about staying in Washington, which attracted disease-carrying mosquitoes to the marshy Potomac River, instead of going to their Virginia mountain home for the season. "But this sad summer session, breaks up all my plans, unless it is made short by the fear of our unfinished canal or some other source of evil."

An epidemic was such an evil—as well as a visit by Cockburn.

Though she loved the vibe and vibrancy of a swinging social life that came when members of Congress were in town, she also often felt its downside: politics on Capitol Hill. "The mornings are devoted to Congress, where all delight to listen, to the violence of evil spirits—I stay quietly at home—as quietly as one can be, who has so much to feel at the expression, for and against their conduct," she had written to Phoebe of her observations.

With all that was going on there, and possibly a sense that James was feeling a little sickly, she needed her cousin Edward to return more than ever.

One piece of news, however, had encouraged her. Payne was doing well, in both health and spirits, as he had communicated in a letter. "I received one from my dear Payne, he is charmed with his voyage so far, and had escaped sea sickness, all the party except Mr. Bayard and himself were sick."

With Payne healthy and away and Edward still recovering in Philadelphia, James was her sole concern. She'd do anything for him, anything to help him succeed.

—————

As intriguing as a treasure chest to a pirate, so news of American politics left Cockburn wide eyed. He delighted at the latest jewel of gossip as he waited in Lynnhaven Bay for the return of Admiral Warren from Bermuda in June 1813.

"There was now only to be heard from one end of the country to the other lamentations of individuals who were now beginning to suffer from the effects of the war," he relayed of a report from a disgruntled merchant, whom he had met while surveying the nearby Elizabeth River.

This gentleman from Richmond was hardly a supporter of his fellow Virginian James Madison, for he "also added with much apparent pleasure that Mr. Madison had lost all the latter measures he had proposed to Congress [previous to its breaking up] for prosecuting the war with rancor."

The man was correct. The failures of the Twelfth Congress had become the top business of the Thirteenth Congress, which needed to raise revenue to fund a war sorely lacking in supplies and men. Would Madison resort to conscription, a draft to acquire more men? Doubtful. America relied on local militia. Besides, Madison was losing the inside game. The internal war with the Federalists could take him down before the British could get him." As Cockburn wrote, "And he assured me from the present state of the country, the president would neither be enabled nor permitted to continue it [the war]."

While Cockburn delighted at such golden treasure, other intelligence didn't bring him the same pleasure. Nearby, Americans had sunk three merchant ships with traditional weapons, which made it even more difficult to navigate his large British ships through the water for their next target.

Though rumors of his plan to attack Washington City had flown faster than his men could fire a rocket, Cockburn had decided that his next conquest instead would be Norfolk, Virginia. He had first eyed the magnificent USF *Constellation* not long after he arrived in Lynnhaven Bay in March.

Completed in Baltimore in 1797, this frigate was 164 feet long and 1,265 tons. The vessel featured thirty-eight 24-pounder long guns. After seeing action in the West Indies, the Mediterranean, Tunis, and Tripoli, the *Constellation* was docked at Craney Island off the Elizabeth River near Norfolk and Hampton, Virginia.

Cockburn took pleasure at his plan. What better way to further erode American public opinion and their confidence in President Madison's war than to capture one of America's finest and oldest warships? What better place to do it than Norfolk, the home of Gosport, the USA's oldest shipyard?

Founded in 1767 for the British crown on the Western shore of the Elizabeth River in Norfolk County, Gosport was transferred to the Commonwealth of Virginia at the beginning of the American Revolution. Two decades later, Congress leased the shipyard and ordered the construction of six frigates there. In 1801 the federal government purchased Gosport from Virginia.

The thirty-eight-gun USS *Chesapeake* was the first U.S. Navy ship built in Gosport. Ah, the *Chesapeake*! That's where all the latest trouble with the British and U.S. governments began.

CHAPTER SEVEN

Chesapeake Fever

O n the morning of June 22, 1807, the USS *Chesapeake* sailed from Hampton Roads. While it attempted to get off shore, the HMS *Leopard*, a fifty-gun British ship, hailed it. A British lieutenant boarded and demanded to search the *Chesapeake* for four British deserters. The U.S. commander refused, saying the British had no right to search a U.S. military ship. They argued for forty minutes before the British lieutenant rowed back to the *Leopard*, which soon opened fire on the *Chesapeake*.

The unprepared American crew hastily fired one shot before their commander offered to surrender. Three Americans were killed and eighteen were wounded. Instead of accepting surrender, the British commander demanded that the remaining sailors muster. Claiming they were deserters, he seized four of the men. One was later executed and three were imprisoned.

The *Chesapeake-Leopard* Affair ignited outrage in the USA. President Jefferson responded by issuing an embargo that prevented U.S. trade with other nations. A form of economic warfare that lasted fifteen months, the embargo hurt the U.S. economy more than British trade.

Repealing the Embargo Act shortly before Madison took office, Congress replaced it with the Non-Intercourse Act, which allowed trade with other countries, but continued prohibiting trade with England and France.

The Embargo and Non-Intercourse Acts were precursors of the war, as Dolley astutely knew. "Before this, you know of our embargo—to be followed by war! Yes—that terrible event is at hand, and yet England wants faith!" she'd written to a friend in France before the 1812 war declaration. The possibility had weighed on Dolley so much that she had written her sister, Anna Cutts, to prepare her Quaker heart for it, telling her, "I believe there will be a war as M[adison] sees no end to our perplexities without it—they are going on with the preparations to [g]reat extent."

———

Washington Irving knew what he had to do after he heard the most recent news about the USS *Chesapeake* in 1813. The battle gave him what he had been looking for, a compelling, resonate story for publishing in his *Analectic Magazine*.

Irving interviewed crewmembers from the *Chesapeake* and discovered the story of James Lawrence, the hero whom Madison had mentioned in his recent message to Congress.

After defeating the *Peacock* while leading the *Hornet*, Lawrence was promoted to captain and became commander of the famed USS *Chesapeake*. Sailing from Boston on June 1, 1813, Lawrence put the *Chesapeake* out to sea. Around 4:00 p.m. the British captain of the HMS *Shannon* spotted the *Chesapeake*. The vessels maneuvered until within pistol shot of each other. The *Shannon* fired and then both ships continued with broadside attacks.

Though a musket ball pierced Lawrence's leg, he continued to give orders. Three men were shot from the helm, each one taking over as the other was killed. Soon an anchor from the *Chesapeake* became stuck in the after port or behind the middle on the left side of the *Shannon*, prohibiting it from continuing to fire. The positioning, however, allowed the *Shannon* to continue to aim at the *Chesapeake*. Soon Captain Lawrence received a musket ball to his intestines. The wound was fatal.

"The brave Lawrence saw the overwhelming danger; his last words as he borne bleeding from the deck, were, 'don't surrender the ship,'" Irving wrote in his biography of Lawrence for the *Analectic*. The words became the immortal cry of "don't give up the ship."

Though one of Lawrence's men eventually had to surrender, a British sailor struck him in the head and killed him immediately afterward. The *Chesapeake*'s colors, however, were never struck or removed by the Americans, the universal sign of surrender. Instead the British sailors who boarded the ship removed the U.S. flag from its mast.

Irving's portrayal was as poetic as it was inspiring. "He [Lawrence] passed from the public eye like a star, just beaming on it for a moment, and falling in the midst of its brightness," Irving wrote.

Publishing articles about naval heroes had given Irving a new purpose. Because he could only base his stories on interviews with a handful of witnesses, he knew his accounts were journalistic, a first draft of history. He saw the opportunity to promote a spirit of patriotism. Irving hoped these hasty and imperfect sketches would "not merely to render a small tribute of gratitude to these intrepid champions of his country's honor…but to assist in promoting a higher tone of national feeling."

The war had turned Washington Irving from satire toward salutes, from comedy to biography. He never wrote the lampoon he had planned to pen after his visits to Washington City in 1811 and 1812. He never wrote a satire about the white house of the buxom dame married to the president.

Who would be the subject of his next biography? He didn't yet know but waited with great anticipation.

═══════

After receiving Madison's answers about who was in charge of the treasury in Gallatin's absence, a furious King gave a speech to the Senate.

He spoke with typical lawyerly logic combined with plainspoken pragmatism.

"Except in the case of inferior officers, Congress cannot by law authorize the President alone to make appointments. The question is a plain one—Can the secretary of the treasury be considered as [one of] the inferior officers?"

As a cabinet-level appointment, the Treasury secretary is one of the highest executive positions in the U.S. government. "We think not because the Constitution demonstrates him a principal officer, in whom may be vested the power of appointing the inferior officers of his own department. Indeed we hardly know where to look for superior officers, if the heads of the departments are to be considered as inferior ones."

As if fencing with a skilled opponent, King took a polite stab at those senators wanting to relinquish their appointment power. He noted the "increasing disposition in Congress to dispense with the consent of the Senate in the appointments of officers—a practice which unconstitutionally enlarges the power of the executive."

King had developed his debating skills over time after becoming an attorney, a profession that made his father proud and gave him an excuse not to serve during most of the Revolution. Born in Scarboro, Massachusetts, in 1755, King was a student at Harvard College when the British invaded Lexington and Concord. His father, Richard King, had been a successful landowner, merchant, and lumberman. Richard was also an ardent loyalist, someone who supported the British crown.

Knowing his father's loyalties and expectations, Rufus graduated from Harvard in 1777 and started his legal career with a successful Boston attorney instead of volunteering for military service. He couldn't avoid the war entirely. Despite his father's loyalty to the crown, Rufus decided to show his support for the patriots by joining a militia. He was part of the unsuccessful campaign to free Newport, Rhode Island, from British control.

Like Madison, Rufus King proved unsuited for military service, and he returned to his law practice within a year. He became one of New York's most successful attorneys. He was skilled in investigating a case or situation, documenting his conversations, and then asking questions to erode his opponent's argument.

Tapping his best talents, he took to the floor the first week of June 1813 to give his speech against Gallatin. What laws allowed the president to designate a temporary replacement at the treasury department without consent of the Senate?

"In the instance of Mr. Gallatin, does a case exist in which the president alone has power to appoint a person to discharge his duties?" The law was clear. The president had complete power of appointment when death or sickness caused the absence of a cabinet officer. "The cases described in the laws, in which the president has the sole power of appointment, are the death, absence from the seat of government, or sickness of the secretary of the treasury."

Mr. Gallatin was obviously not dead or seriously ill. "But is his appointment as an envoy to Russia, admitting its validity, and his consequent absence from the U.S., such an absence from the seat of government as the laws provide for?"

King thought not. The honorable senator from New York believed the law, and common sense, defined absence from the seat of government as an occasional, temporary measure, not another appointment. "His estate and private affairs at home may demand his attention, and other urgent duties may oblige him for a short time to be absent from the seat of government."

Absences because of circumstantial or private responsibilities were one thing. This was different. "Not an absence created by the President himself, nor one proceeding from the acceptance of another office, the duties whereof are incompatible with those of the secretary of the treasury."

King then put a little zing in his game: "If such be the construction, and especially if the substitute appointed by the president is to continue indefinitely, the heads of departments may all be converted into ambassadors, and the business of the nation conducted by undertakers or job men."

Such sarcasm showed King's fury. The mighty little Madison had blown it. Gallatin's appointment as a diplomat was invalid as long as he held the position of Treasury secretary, at least in the eyes of King. He would soon learn whether his arguments were strong enough to convince others to vote against Gallatin and ruin Madison's peace commission.

━━━━━━━━━━

From Philadelphia, Edward Coles responded to Dolley's request for him to remain as the president's secretary. He appreciated "the kind and affectionate assurances of the regard which you and Mr. Madison entertain for me, and of your wish that I should return and continue longer with you."

Though his health had improved, he was not yet strong enough to return to Washington. "I hope however it will not be very long before I shall have it in my power to be with you, and to attend to those duties which I fear will plague and embarrass Mr. M. in consequence of my absence."

He then gave his cousin an update on gossip. Mutual friends, Mr. and Mrs. Waddell, had recently moved to the country. Mrs. Waddell had bluntly asked Edward if she'd done something to offend Mrs. Madison.

"She was certain from your conduct that you were either offended, or had changed your former friendly opinion of her." Mrs. Elizabeth Pemberton Waddell complained that for years she'd carried on a correspondence with Dolley but that recently "she had written you four letters, two of which were on subjects interesting to her and required particular answers, neither of which you had noticed."

Edward then gave Dolley his blunt assessment of the woman's attitude. "I assure you the lady appears to be quite in a fit with you."

What to do? He sensed that this woman had no idea of the social responsibilities that pressed on Dolley as mistress of the President's House. Mrs. Waddell was simply being selfish. He tried to explain that as wife of the president, Dolley received numerous letters and could not possibly respond to them all. This only revealed that the woman's true feeling was jealousy. "When I attempted to apologize by reminding her of your incessant occupation, she said, you could find time enough to write to Miss Morris [Phoebe, who was the woman's niece] nearly every week who was a mere child."

The incident wasn't unique. Mrs. Waddell wasn't the only female seeking to boost her social status by claiming Mrs. Madison as a friend and correspondent. Many desired Dolley's attention.

"I have been so much mortified at not receiving one line from my dear Mrs. Madison, that under any other circumstances I should not presume to write again," Clara Baldwin Kennedy Bomford had written Dolley in February 1813.

She had good reason to try writing Dolley again. Her brother-in-law, Mr. Barlow, had been the U.S. minister to France after General Armstrong. Barlow had died while on a mission to Poland. Beyond the personal tragedy, Barlow's death had set back Madison's latest attempts to improve the U.S. relationship with Napoleon's France.

What women like Mrs. Waddell and Mrs. Bomford failed to understand is that family came first with Dolley. Phoebe was a daughter to her. She may have secretly hoped that a romance would develop with Phoebe and Payne. She would do anything for James, and give up anything for him—friends and correspondents included. She simply no longer had time to respond to every letter, no matter how many feelings she hurt in the process.

———

"Of all the situations Mr. Madison ever occupied, there was no one he was as fond of talking about, as the convention of 1787, which made the Constitution of the U.S. and of the one in 1788 which ratified it in Virginia. Of the acts and doings of these two bodies, he was as fond of talking, as some men are with their old schoolmates of their collegiate lives," Edward Coles reflected on James Madison.

Coles had heard the stories that the president told. Years earlier, in the summer of 1786, Madison had read numerous books on government. Sent by Thomas Jefferson, who was in Paris, he had pored through a thirteen-volume set on political history by Fortuné Barthelemy de Felice and an eleven-volume set of the history of humanity by Abbé Millot. Also reading Plutarch, Demosthenes, and Polybius, he studied ancient republics and what led to the fall of Greece and Rome, among other realms.

Absorbing this vast information about establishing and managing governments, he considered what worked and what didn't. He learned that weak federal governments made it easier for foreign entities to intrigue with forces within and overthrow empires. Then he wrote a paper called *Of Ancient and Modern Confederacies*, which included a section on the vices of the Articles of Confederation, the law governing the United States at the time. He also created a forty-page pocket-sized sheet of notes to carry with him as a resource for informal and formal debates.

In doing so he diagnosed the problems with America's government under the Articles. This affiliation of the states purposefully created a weak national government. Each state acted like an independent country more than a state within a nation. They had different currencies and standards of trade with each other and foreign countries. Not only that, all national authority—executive, legislative, and judicial—was held by one single body, Congress. This alone made it weak, in Madison's view.

Fearful that the current system was failing, Madison lobbied George Washington to meet for a convention in the summer of 1787. Publicly, the purpose was to consider revising the Articles of Confederation. Privately, Madison had another idea in mind. Revision wouldn't work. Replacing it just might. He used his in-depth study of governments to craft a new plan, which became known as the Virginia Plan.

"Having been lately led to revolve the subject which is to undergo the discussion of the convention, and formed in my mind some outlines of a new system, I take the liberty of submitting them without apology, to your eye," Madison wrote to Washington in the spring of 1787 as he submitted his ideas.

Because the Articles were "irreconcilable," Madison preferred to start over with a new constitution. "I have sought for some middle ground, which may at once support a due supremacy of the national authority, and not exclude the local authorities wherever they can be subordinately useful."

The heart of the new constitution would be a division of power in several ways. Authority would be divided between federal and state governments, with an eye for strengthening the federal side to provide a common currency, make all trade agreements with foreign nations, regulate trade between the states, and provide a tax system. He also believed the states needed a "disinterested," or impartial, federal government to serve as an umpire when conflicts arose between them.

The federal government would further divide its powers into three branches: the legislative, executive, and judicial. Not only that, but the power of the legislative would also be divided even further, into two houses. These branches would have the power to check one another and hold each other accountable in different ways.

"I would propose as the groundwork that a change be made in the principle of representation," Madison explained to Washington. Representation would replace royalty. *We the people* would replace *long live the king.*

Impressed with the thirty-six-year-old Madison and his thorough and well-reasoned plan, George Washington agreed to attend the convention in Philadelphia. He was elected president of this deliberative body, which later became known as the Constitutional Convention. Fifty-five men participated in the convention. Though many rotated in and out during the deliberations, about thirty attended on most days.

Because he had so thoroughly studied ancient governments and dissected their defects with the skill of a surgeon, Madison emerged as one of the most effective and important members of the Constitutional Convention. He had at his disposal historical evidence to refute arguments made by convention members opposed to entrusting a federal government with more power. Though a reserved man with an introverted nature, Madison used his skills of persuasion both on the floor of the convention and in small groups. He talked to men in relaxed settings about their concerns. They shared coffee or ale at the place where he boarded or other taverns in Philadelphia. Unlike some men, he knew how to disagree without being disagreeable. His quiet, reasoned, logical, and well-researched answers often overcame the loud, inflammatory rhetoric of more impassioned souls.

Madison didn't get everything he wanted, but that wasn't the point. The purpose was to create a stronger national government through compromise. The Virginia Plan morphed and changed, but its core of three branches and two legislative bodies remained intact. The result of their deliberations was the U.S. Constitution, approved by the convention on September 17, 1787.

Traveling to New York, Madison mapped a public relations effort with men such as Alexander Hamilton and Rufus King to motivate at least nine of the thirteen states to ratify the Constitution through special state conventions. His twenty-nine essays, along with those from Alexander Hamilton and John Jay, became known as the *Federalist Papers*, a total of eighty-five essays. Once again he used his research and reasoning to help reluctant Americans overcome their apprehensions about forming a more perfect union through the U.S. Constitution.

The *Federalist Papers* influenced many and created a foundational work of American political theory. The campaign worked. After the states adopted the U.S. Constitution, Madison emerged as a member of the new Congress from Virginia while George Washington became the first president in 1789.

Because Madison was a central figure in the greatest accomplishment of the century, men would later call him the Father of the Constitution, a title he rejected.

"You give me a credit to which I have no claim in calling me 'The writer of the Constitution of the U.S.' This was not, like the fabled Goddess of Wisdom, the offspring of a single brain. It ought to be regarded as the work of many heads and many hands."

Now, here he was in 1813, on the receiving end of the checks and balance system that he was most responsible for creating. Here he was leading the country under the Constitution in an unpopular war that had no end in sight. Peace, while vigorously prosecuting the war, was his best strategy. Why couldn't others see it his way and cooperate with him on the peace nominees and funding the war? Why couldn't Rufus King revive the cordiality they had experienced when lobbying the country to accept the Constitution? Humanity's minds and affections changed far more easily than the laws they created.

━━━━━━━━

The special Senate committee presented a resolution, which the full Senate accepted. They believed that the "the powers and duties" of the treasury secretary and of those of an envoy to a foreign power "are so incompatible, that they out not to be, and remain, united in the same power."

The committee chairman also sent Madison a letter asking him to meet with them "at such time as you may please to appoint."

What they didn't yet know was that Madison would not meet with them. Was he being defiant? Somewhat. More than that, the feverish president was ill—so ill that his wife feared his death was imminent.

CHAPTER EIGHT

Snubbed by Dolley

E arly in her husband's administration, Dolley had worried over "a bilious fever…caused by an unfinished canal." Bilious fever was a dreaded condition causing high fever, nausea, vomiting, and diarrhea. The mosquito-magnet of Washington City often bred disease, especially in the summer. One solution was to leave town when the heat set in, something many Washingtonians did each year. Though the Madisons loved to retreat to their mountain home, Montpelier, in Orange, Virginia, Congress's special summer session in 1813 prevented such flight.

Because she had lost her first husband to the yellow fever epidemic in Philadelphia twenty years earlier, Dolley understandably feared losing James in a similar way. In fact, several years before his presidency, when he had become very sick, Dolley had nightmares of his death, calling her visions painful and begging him to "think of thy wife! Who thinks and dreams of thee." Such words show how deep her love for James had grown since their marriage of seeming convenience.

Now in June 1813, bilious fever came upon James so seriously that her greatest fear struck her heart each time she wiped his fever-filled forehead or smelled the stench in overflowing chamber pots. Others quickly joined the melancholy chorus.

"Mr. Madison has been several days quite sick—is no better—has not been well enough to read the resolutions [of] the Senate," wrote Congressman Daniel Webster of New Hampshire, who delivered paperwork from Capitol Hill to Madison. Webster returned five days later and found Madison worse than before.

"I went to the palace to present the [House] resolutions—the president was in his bed, sick of a fever—his night cap on his head—his wife attending him." Because Webster was a foe of Madison's policies, he quipped: "I think he will find no relief from my prescription."

Ten days later, the president was even worse. James Monroe, the secretary of state, also visited his boss. Though several physicians had given Madison quinine, also called bark, and reported that he would recover, Monroe feared for Madison's life.

His fever "perhaps never left him, even for an hour." Unlike Webster and others, the secretary of state—who had known Madison for years—understood that the burdens of war and peace were too much to bring to his attention at the moment. Madison needed rest, not stress: "No pressure whatever should be made on him," Monroe concluded.

Soon those fears turned into rumors of his impending death. The French minister to the United States recorded his angst. "The thought of [Madison's] possible loss strikes everyone with consternation. His death, in the circumstances in which the republic is placed, would be a veritable national calamity."

No president had ever died in office, though the vice president, George Clinton, had died before the election the previous year. Elbridge Gerry was now vice president. Word of Madison's illness ignited a fire of panic, affecting anyone seeking Dolley's attention.

"I write to you in sincere anxiety for the health of the president … be assured my dearest Mrs. Madison of my sympathy and tenderness for every incident which interests you," Phoebe expressed her concern in a letter to Dolley as soon as she heard of the president's illness.

Not wanting to further burden Dolley, Phoebe updated her on Anthony's acceptance of his new post. "The anxiety of your mind must be so great on this subject that I only mention at Papa's request the determination he has made to leave us all here." Appointed by Madison as a special agent to Spain, Anthony Morris was leaving for Europe. For now, mother Dolley needn't worry about Anthony and Phoebe, who would attend a school in Philadelphia. James now consumed her entire existence.

His illness also made it impossible for Dolley to say good-bye to dear friends. "The dangerous sickness of the president at that moment prevented Mrs. Latrobe who called several times, from seeing you," Benjamin Latrobe explained to Dolley in a letter.

The need for the Latrobes to see the president and Mrs. Madison before they left was both personal and business. Mary desperately wanted to say goodbye to Dolley before they moved to Pittsburgh, while Benjamin needed an opportunity to remind the president that Congress still owed him $600 for his work on the President's House and the Marine hospital.

Too consumed with James's care, Dolley didn't answer Latrobe's letter, effectively snubbing them. Surely they would understand? She didn't have time to think too much about hurt feelings or consequences. Little did she realize that the depressed Latrobe would soon write to Robert Fulton, "Several times I had nearly thrown myself into the Potomac. I cannot receive $600 on two appropriations (the President's furniture and Marine hospital)."

With Madison too weak to write and Edward Coles's continuous absence, Dolley became secretary in chief. She wrote a letter for James on June 18 to inform the special senate committee that illness prohibited him from meeting with them to review the legalities of Gallatin's appointment. He was unavailable that day or "fixing a day when it will be in his power." She rightly suspected that his health was teetering between life and death.

While Dolley tended to James and carried on his correspondence in Edward's absence, she very likely read a resolution sent to James from the Society of Friends on June 17, 1813. Leaders of the Quakers had recently met at an annual assembly in Rhode Island and crafted a resolution for the president, Senate, and the House of Representatives.

Their concern was the war, proclaiming that "our minds have been affected with deep and serious consideration upon account of the national calamity of war, in which our once happy country is involved."

By reiterating a tenet of their beliefs—pacifism—they underscored the source of their opposition, saying that "it is well known that a fundamental principle of our faith leads us to believe that war of any kind is unlawful to us."

If they knew Madison's personal background well, then they would have known that as a young man right out of college, he had opposed the persecution of Baptist ministers by the royal government in Virginia. Within a few years, he was part of the 1776 Virginia Convention, which declared independence from England and also issued a declaration of rights. Among them was the right to the free exercise of religion, according to the dictates of conscience. As he expressed in Federalist 51, "If men were angels, no government would be necessary."

Years later as a congressman under the new Constitution, Madison had led the effort that resulted in the Bill of Rights to the Constitution. The first amendment began: "Congress shall make no law respecting an establishment of religion, or prohibiting the free exercise thereof." Madison had also proposed that "no person religiously scrupulous of bearing arms shall be compelled to render military service in person." While this amendment didn't make the final ten, Quakers hoped they had a friend in Madison.

Unanimous in their resolution, the Quakers concluded that they had a civic and religious duty to ask the president and Congress to end the war.

Dolley's reaction to Quakerism was often mixed. Years earlier she had gone to Philadelphia for medical treatment on her knee. When many of her family's old friends came by to see her, she remembered painful memories from her past, such as her father's excommunication for going into debt. Then at other times, when speaking with cousin Edward, a devout Quaker, or greeting someone like Mr. Hallowell at a party, she felt fondness and kinship.

On top of that, she couldn't argue with Scripture's reminder that peacemakers were a blessing to others and that peace on earth was an angelic hope. A few years earlier, Dolley had taken comfort in the hope of angels after the death of two of her nieces. She wrote her mother at the time. "They are now angels! And can never know evil or misery— ought we not to console ourselves with this reflection?"

Now, if her husband's peace commission succeeded, then Quakers would have an end to the war. For the moment she was doing all she could to make sure that James wasn't called to his heavenly home.

Unaware of Madison's illness, Admiral Warren returned from Bermuda to the Chesapeake Bay in mid-June 1813. He brought Cockburn the best possible gift: reinforcements. They now had enough men, more than 2,400, to launch a series of attacks. Two battalions of Royal marines made up most of these fighters, but 600 were true blue redcoats, regular British Army soldiers led by Colonel Sir Thomas Sidney Beckwith. A veteran of England's war against Napoleon, Beckwith was one of Britain's finest light troop leaders. Also among Beckwith's men were 300 Canadian Chasseurs.

In addition Warren brought several Royal Navy vessels for their disposal. Of that group, three were seventy-four-gun ships and one was a sixty-four-gun. Also included were four frigates and three transport barges. Attacking Norfolk and the USF *Constellation* had never seemed more promising. All they had to do was get past Craney Island, which guarded the mouth of the Elizabeth River.

As hungry as Cockburn was for another delectable victory, he made an interesting conclusion. His greatest obstacle just might be Admiral Warren, not the Americans. Warren's experience serving the British in the American colonies during the Revolutionary War gave him important know-how. But the sixty-year-old Warren hadn't seen much action since 1806 and experienced poor health. His lack of enthusiasm was as obvious to Cockburn as his overly cautious approach.

Nonetheless Admiral Cockburn was cavalier in his assessment of Craney, which he shared with Warren and others. Yes, he knew the water was shallow. Lieutenant Westphal had detected a shoal near the island that could cause trouble. But Cockburn was, well, cocky. He insisted on attacking Craney Island instead of invading Norfolk via an overland route. He believed the few Americans defending the place would flee in an instant and retreat toward Richmond.

"From what I have now seen and know of them, I have no doubt a larger proportion of their *now heroes* will be inclined to take advantage of such a circumstance," he wrote, invoking what he had learned at Havre de Grace and other places.

For all of Cockburn's recommendations about launching an invasion, Warren snubbed him. Beckwith had shared his ideas with Warren on how to best invade Craney Island during their voyage carrying reinforcements from Bermuda. Though Beckwith was highly experienced, he had not seen the terrain or investigated the waters like Cockburn had. Yet, Warren allowed Beckwith's strategy to prevail, much to Beckwith's delight and Cockburn's skepticism.

―――――――――

Illness, Senate opposition to Gallatin as a peace envoy, and rumors of a British attack against Washington were not Madison's only problems that summer. Some Federalists were seeking an opportunity to sever the Union and return New England to England.

Where did King stand on New England secession? Was he willing to go that far to embarrass Madison? Though he opposed the president at every turn, Senator Rufus King treaded carefully on this Federalist issue. The reason? A painful, personal past. Before the Revolutionary War, radical mobs burned portions of his Loyalist father's property. This destruction left him fearing radical factions throughout his life.

Once America became a united nation, King had worried that a runaway democracy would give way to violent mobs. Hence, he had often moderated his political views and snubbed extreme elements, such as those New England Federalists who were ready to secede from the Union to rejoin England or become their own nation.

King concluded that no thinking man with any clout should seriously consider secession.

Though he disagreed with secession as the solution, he believed that America was picking a fight with the wrong enemy. A devoted New Yorker, King had long bristled at the idea that England was America's true foe. In his mind, and in those of many Federalists, enemy number one spoke a different language: French. Napoleon Bonaparte had espoused disdain for monarchies only to make himself France's emperor. Napoleon's goal was to rule Europe and defeat England's economy and military any way he could.

"The only opposition will be from France: indeed the only serious danger to our country is from that quarter," King wrote.

To him, Madison's war was about politics, not America's national interests. "I regard the war, as a war of party and not of the country—those who have made the war will dread the unpopularity of French connection."

Not only did King think that Madison had gone to war against the wrong country, but he also thought war was impractical. He believed that U.S. military supplies were pathetically weak and the size of its force made it incapable of defending its shores, much less invading Canada. "The war cannot be carried on by the militia," he wrote. He also concluded that it was illegal for state governors to call up militia to defend their borders. A regular national army was the only way to properly defend America. Yet, that was problematic, too, because Congress couldn't legally draft men. He explained, "A regular army will be enlisted with the utmost difficulty; besides money cannot be raised by loans: and if taxes be collected, the popularity of the party according to Mr. Jefferson's former opinion, must be destroyed."

The fight and failure over establishing a national bank was shortsighted in King's opinion. He believed that America's financial situation, especially under Gallatin's leadership at Treasury, had been a disaster. He opposed sending Gallatin as a peace commissioner because he opposed Gallatin's financing methods. Blocking his nomination was a way to get rid of him from national politics once and for all.

All of these problems—the wrong enemy, a volunteer regular army, and no national bank—were recipes for failure to King. As a result he predicted that the war would be lengthy. "I infer that the war will drag on heavily; that it will become very, and extensively, unpopular; that the dread of French connection will greatly increase the mass of discontent."

Ah, but he had hope, and he found it in England. He placed more confidence in Britain's Parliament than he did in his own national government: "And if England have a wise ministry, we must soon return to peace."

Many believed that King had become too cozy with the British after serving as the U.S. minister to England. While there he had developed many friends and chums with Parliament and other prominent English gentlemen. At times his faith in Great Britain couldn't have been stronger had he been an English citizen. Ah. That was his problem.

"Notwithstanding the diplomatic quarrels and commercial regulations...I am not without hope that a final rupture will be avoided, and that things being left to the operation of time, temper and reflection, the former harmony and mutual intercourse of the two countries will be again restored and established," he had written to an English friend.

"The imbecility of Madison is daily more manifest, still his friends and party in general adhere to him," he had written to another.

He also dismissed his critics. "I know that our political adversaries will say that we aim at a monarchy....I am and shall always be ready to purge myself from this suspicion; I would lessen sooner than increase the presidential power."

Pleased that his opposition to Gallatin was injuring Madison politically, King hoped that England desired peace. "I am convinced that things cannot remain where they are if the war continues; a great change must happen."

Indeed. That great change wasn't England's quest for peace. Quite the opposite. It was Cockburn's lust for taunting and terrorizing his foes.

⸻

Madison had never been a fan of the U.S. Senate because of its composition and the equality it gave the states. Each state, regardless of population, boasted two representatives in the U.S. Senate. His initial vision had been different.

"The legislative department might be divided into two branches; one of them chosen every years [sic] by the people at large, or by the legislatures," he wrote to George Washington in the spring of 1787 as he referred to what became the House of Representatives, which was elected to two-year terms by the people.

Madison initially viewed the Senate as "the other to consist of fewer members, to hold their places for a longer term, and to go out in such a rotation as always to leave in office a large majority of old members."

But he opposed the composition of the Senate proposed by men from smaller states at the Constitutional Convention. They wanted the Senate to be limited to two members from every state. Focused on representation by population, Madison opposed giving equal weight to smaller populated states like Delaware compared to larger populated states, such as Virginia. Instead, in his proposal voters would have elected the House of Representatives, who would have used nominations from their states to elect the U.S. Senate.

Though it was easy to let many of the details change, the major loss for Madison during the Constitutional Convention was the composition of the U.S. Senate.

Gunning Bedford of Delaware soon fired off a volley against Madison and others that epitomized the venom between the smaller and larger states. He believed the bigger states would abuse their power. "I do not, gentlemen, trust you," he thundered in a rare personal attack. Until then, deliberations had been cordial in disagreements. He proclaimed that by giving each state equal representation, as they had under the Articles, the small states were protected. He warned of the dangers of failing to give them equal representation in the new constitution. "There are foreign powers who will take us by the hand."

The issue became a fear that larger states would intrigue with a foreign power to overthrow the government. Hence, the U.S. Senate needed equal representation to prevent this from happening and provide a check on the House of Representatives.

Indignant at the suggestion that a state would intrigue with a foreign power, Rufus King rose in defense and refuted Bedford.

"I am concerned for what fell from the gentleman from Delaware— 'Take a foreign power by the hand'! I am sorry he mentioned it, and I hope he is able to excuse it to himself on the score of passion."

King then made a pledge.

"Whatever may be my distress, I will never court a foreign power to assist in relieving myself from it."

The vote that followed on the composition of the Senate was deadlocked at five to five, with the representatives voting in blocks by states. The issue went to a committee, which came up with the Grand or Great Compromise. The House of Representatives would be based on population and each state would have two representatives in the U.S. Senate. After a weeklong intensive debate, the smaller states won in a five-to-four vote, with the representatives of Massachusetts divided.

The representatives of smaller states who had been tepid or reluctant to create a new Constitution now had vested stake in it. Though Madison opposed the Great Compromise and equal representation in the Senate, which he considered unjust, it gave him what he ultimately wanted—a new Constitution based on a stronger national government held accountable by checks and balances among the branches.

Now, here he was in 1813 battling the U.S. Senate over his nominees. He couldn't depend on Virginia's having more votes than New York or Delaware to support his commissioners.

Madison also couldn't depend on the very thing that had so often helped him: one-on-one conversations. His illness had prevented Dolley from entertaining, robbing him of the chance to speak and explain himself to members of the Senate in relaxed conversations over wine and ice cream. He had lost his best method for influencing the Senate. He had also lost his best technique for finding out just how cozy men like Rufus King were with Federal secessionists or others who would scheme against him and rejoin England or become their own new nation. Would he recover in time to save his nominees?

CHAPTER NINE

Washed Up at Craney

No one knows what Madison thought about as he fought the fever in June 1813. Before his illness, the gravity of his nation's situation had weighed heavily upon him.

Perhaps he thought about the issues and stakes of the war. In his heart, he fervently believed that he had exhausted all diplomatic attempts to solve America's problems with Great Britain. "On the issue of the war are staked our national sovereignty on the high seas," he had told the American people in his second inaugural address in March.

Depriving U.S. sailors and ship owners of the ability to sell their cargo in foreign ports was unjust. What angered Madison more than stealing livelihoods from sailors was depriving them of their liberty. Forcing them to serve in the Royal Army and Navy was appalling, as the *Chesapeake-Leopard* Affair and dozens of other instances had demonstrated.

"They have retained as prisoners of war citizens of the United States not liable to be so considered under the usages of war," he had said.

While England naturalized thousands of citizens each year from other countries, it refused to allow America to do the same thing.

Worse, the British were "compelling [naturalized U.S. citizens] to fight its battles against their native country."

As he tried to recover from his illness that summer, perhaps he thought about his recent special message to Congress on May 25, 1813, where he called for the end of impressment by the British. If he died now, it would be the last major message he would give them.

"The British cabinet also must be sensible that, with respect to the important question of impressment, on which the war so essentially turns, a search for or seizure of British persons or property on board neutral vessels on the high seas is not a belligerent right derived from the law of nations," he had declared.

The British government had recently issued an edict saying that it would accept merchant products from some U.S. ports, namely those in New England, but not the rest of the nation.

This also outraged Madison. "And now we find them, in further contempt of the modes of honorable warfare, supplying the place of a conquering force, by attempts to disorganize our political society, to dismember our confederated republic," he said.

Perhaps he thought about his enemies as his fever raged day in and day out. His internal political opponents had often expressed outrage at criticism that they were un-American because they opposed his war. Robert Troup of New York represented the sentiments of the antiwar Federalists when he wrote: "What is meant when we are told we must be Americans and support our government? What? Are we so blindly devoted to the measures of a government apparently bent on a system of policy that is likely to ruin, not only our commerce, our agriculture, and, I fear, our Constitution and our liberties?"

Madison was also well aware that the British were not the only ones trying to sever the United States by inducing New England to secede and rejoin Old England. The whispers of Federalists had reached his ears on many occasions. But the idea that New England would secede defied logic in his mind.

"I have never allowed myself to believe that the Union was in danger, or that a dissolution of it could be desired, unless by a few individuals, if such there be, in desperate situations or of unbridled passions," Madison wrote.

The president believed that every part of the nation had a vested interest in keeping the bond of states intact. He concluded that the East would "be the greatest loser, by such an event; and not likely therefore deliberately to rush into it."

Madison believed that New England needed the South more than it needed England. He saw little basis for commercial advantage if New England rejoined Old England, which had more to gain in an alliance with the South, in his view. "If there be links of common interest between the two countries, they connect the South and not the Northern States with that part of Europe."

Perhaps he thought about the irony of timing as he fought death. Congress had declared war a year earlier, on June 18, 1812. Unknown to America for weeks, Spencer Perceval, the cold, calculating British prime minister, had been assassinated by a deranged, disgruntled Englishman on May 11, 1812. Perceval had been the primary driver in Parliament behind the abusive trade policies against America.

Had Madison known of his assassination, he might have encouraged Congress to delay voting on war so they could wait and see if the new British prime minister would change England's policies toward America. Madison had responded: "The sword was scarcely out of the scabbard, before the enemy was apprized of the reasonable terms on which it would be re-sheathed." Yet, it was too late. The war had begun.

Perhaps he thought about faith as he fought illness that summer of 1813. Maybe he reflected on faith in God, which had been fed by his college mentor and minister, John Witherspoon, the only clergyman to sign the Declaration of Independence. Perhaps he also thought about his faith in the union of the states, in the patriotic spirit of every American bosom. He may have looked at the hope that individuals would fight for their turf, their homes, and their families. He may have been deathly ill, but he had not lost confidence in the American spirit.

Britain's intentions in June 1813 were no surprise to those at the Gosport Naval Yard, especially the crew of the *Constellation* and the local militia. Patriotic Americans they were. These men had been anticipating an attack since the English arrived near their shores in March 1813. Their fears increased in May after Cockburn terrorized many of Maryland's coastal towns. Unlike burning the houses of private citizens, an attack against Norfolk's Naval Yard fit the average American's expectations of warfare.

General Robert B. Taylor was in charge of Norfolk's defenses. He wrote General Armstrong a letter on June 18: "Should the enemy...attack Craney Island, it must fall unless we throw the greater part of our forces there."

Determined to prevent such a catastrophe, Taylor got to work. He ordered his men to erect a seven-gun battery, which included two twenty-four-pound guns, one eighteen-pound gun, and four six-pound guns. He placed another battery across the river. He also created a line of nineteen small gunboats. Taylor told Armstrong that he would try to trick the British by relocating tents from one side of the island to the other to hide their defensive capabilities.

Taylor couldn't have been more correct about the enemy's intentions. A newspaper later explained how the battle began.

"About daybreak the enemy were discovered with their barges pulling to shore about two and an half or three miles above the upper point of Craney Island," the *Boston Daily Advertiser* reported of the two-prong attack that started on June 22, 1813.

The British deployed a line of barges, including the fifty-foot long *Centipede*, directly against Craney Island. These vessels suddenly ran aground. They were stuck in the mud; several feet of it, in fact. Jumping out of the boats, the British invaders immediately discovered that the mud was multiple feet deep. They started sinking. Their timing proved all wrong. Because the tide was in, they couldn't safely wade through the water and mud to reach Craney Island.

About one hundred Americans commanded the U.S. artillery. Accurately aiming their weapons, they sank three of the enemy's large barges, including the *Centipede*.

British marines also landed on the mainland northwest of the island. At first they were out of reach of U.S. artillery. But as they armed at Wise Creek, which was opposite of Craney, the island's batteries also fired on them.

As the newspapers reported: "The batteries were manned with the troops stationed on the island, and a detachment of seamen commanded by the officers of the *Constellation*, who opened a heavy fire that compelled the enemy to retreat with great loss."

One U.S. captain proudly wrote that the sailors of the *Constellation* "fired their 18 pounders more like riflemen than artillerists. I never saw such shooting and seriously believe they saved the island."

Knowing that they had also captured eighteen enemy fighters, the captain continued his praise. "Our officers, soldiers, seamen, and marines exhibited the utmost coolness and enthusiasm." The British casualties included three killed, sixteen wounded, and sixty missing, likely from drowning.

The failed invasion left the British humiliated. The timing of the tides was a foolish and avoidable mistake, one certainly known to Admiral Cockburn, who suddenly took satisfaction that Warren had snubbed his strategy and favored Beckwith's. Now he couldn't be blamed.

Elijah Mix's torpedo may have failed earlier that month, but the victory the Americans felt after defending Craney Island was sweet retribution for Havre de Grace and other burned Chesapeake towns. Though a slingshot had yet to take out Cockburn or a cannonball decapitate him, they had defended Craney Island and the *Constellation* all the same. Surely the British would back off after being washed up. But they didn't know just how stubborn a pirate-like admiral could be.

Three days after their defeat at Craney Island, Cockburn and the other British officers made a choice. Norfolk and Portsmouth were too well protected to attack now. They needed a more vulnerable spot to gain momentum. From his own experience, Cockburn knew that they should aim for a soft target like Havre de Grace, which was full of private citizens and a disorganized militia. They should avoid a location filled with prepared military, multiple guns, and a warship. What place could that be? They quickly made a plan.

———

In his long hours of illness, Madison likely thought of Dolley.

True love bears each other's burdens. Dolley couldn't bear to see her husband suffer. Likewise James felt sad when Dolley was ill. Years earlier in 1805, Dolley had turned to James for comfort while she was ill in Philadelphia and he was in Washington serving as secretary of state.

"I was so unwell yesterday, my dearest husband, that I omitted writing," she'd explained.

He responded immediately after reading her words. "I have received my dearest yours begun on the 15th and continued on the 16th. The low spirits which pervade it affect mine."

Such a tender response revived her from the doldrums, as she conveyed in subsequent correspondence. "The letters of my beloved husband are always a cordial to my heart—particularly the one received yesterday which breathes that affection so precious that I wept over it in joy."

On another occasion Dolley had written him, "Your charming letter my beloved has revived my spirit and made me feel like another human being—so much does my health, peace, and everything else, depend on your affection and goodness."

That June of 1813, as he fought fever and felt her wipe wet washcloths on his face or clean his legs and remove his soiled sheets, he knew how much she loved him. More than ever, her love was his balm.

Meanwhile Benjamin Latrobe realized he would not be able to say good-bye to Dolley or the president in person as he left the city for his new life in Pittsburgh.

"It is not probable that I shall ever have the honor again to see you," Latrobe wrote to her. Melancholy mastered his mind, preventing him from seeing the fruits of his success in Washington, such as the renovation of the President's House or the completion of the House of Representatives wing at the Capitol.

"For the waste of life, of reputation, and of fortune which my ten years of public service have brought upon me...my greatest consolation will always be, that I have not forfeited the personal respect and friendship of the president and yourself."

Meanwhile, as Madison fought death, the British were ready to turn their redcoats, and Canadian green coats, into pirates once again. The atrocities these buccaneers would soon commit, including violence against women, would surpass their arson against Havre de Grace. Their wake of infamy would horrify Americans from the East Coast all the way to New Orleans.

CHAPTER TEN

Atrocious Hampton

The "unfortunate females of Hampton who could not leave the town were suffered to be abused in the most shameful manner," Major Stapleton Crutchfield, a U.S. commander, wrote to the governor of Virginia about the British attack on Hampton, Virginia, on June 25, 1813.

Founded in 1610 at the mouth of the James River, Hampton—which means "homestead"—was one of the oldest seaports in the United States. Those who settled Jamestown, Virginia, in 1607 identified the spot where three rivers came together: the Elizabeth, Nansemond, and James Rivers. They called the area Hampton Roads after Henry Wriothesley, Third Earl of Southampton. Henry was a patron of Shakespeare and an important leader of London's Virginia Company that sponsored early settlements in Virginia. In 1610 the colonists established Hampton as a small town with a church.

Two hundred years later, in 1810, Hampton was part of Elizabeth City County, whose population of 3,600 was nearly three times smaller than Norfolk's population of 9,190. Because cotton was its dominant crop and manufacture, Hampton was an agrarian hamlet, and thus perfect prey for what the British needed after Craney Island—a quick and easy victory.

Just as Blackbeard and other pirates had easily attacked the area in the 1700s, so Cockburn swaggered into Hampton with little opposition. This time the admiral had more authority. He sent his marines and green-coated Canadians under the leadership of Colonel Beckwith. Outnumbering the Americans, the British approached from the rear and met about 450 local Virginia militia, who soon fled, just as Cockburn predicted. What was next for the admiral? Burning, of course.

Cockburn and Beckwith confiscated a house in town, kicked back, and let the fun unfold under the leadership of their officers. By delegating their authority, they had what they needed most: cover from responsibility. What mischief was made could be blamed on others. Cockburn also allowed Beckwith to issue the official report, which he did.

"The gallantry of Captain Smith, the officers, and men of the two companies Canadian Chasseurs who led the attack was highly conspicuous and praiseworthy," Colonel Beckwith soon praised in a letter to Admiral Warren, adding, "as well steadiness and good conduct of the officers, and men of the hundred second regiment and the Royal Marines."

Why did he report such admiration? Bravado. After their failure a few days earlier, Beckwith longed to impress Warren with news of their successful conquest. The *Baltimore Patriot* printed a very different account of what happened at Hampton.

"Our sod must be purified from the pollution of these miscreants, who do not bear the attributes of an honorable enemy, but are more cruel than savages, and more rapacious than pirates," the editors described of Cockburn's and Beckwith's men.

The truth about Hampton was so vile and atrocious that newspapers throughout the U.S. soon revealed the details—though hesitantly because of concerns of propriety.

The *National Intelligencer* in Washington City was one such newspaper. Like many others, editor Joseph Gales reprinted an investigative reporter's account, which broke the bounds of social mores of what was acceptable to publish at the time.

"We copy from the [*Richmond*] *Enquirer,* the following extracts of a letter to the editor of that paper. We almost shrink from the task of recording such atrocities. But our public duty and the present circumstances of this district require it," he explained of his decision to print something so shocking.

Didn't he have an obligation to warn Americans, especially the ladies of East Coast towns, about what might happen to them if the British attacked their city? Yes, he did.

"It may be soon our turn to encounter this band of blood hounds, whose course is marked by fire and sword and brutal violence. Let every man remember the sad fate of Hampton, and prepare to take a signal revenge on the ruthless despoilers of female innocence."

"Having just returned from Hampton, where I made myself acquainted with all the particulars of British outrage, whilst that place was in their possession," the reporter began in his letter to the editor in Richmond. "That the town and country adjacent was given up to the indiscriminate plunder of a licentious soldiery, except perhaps the house where the headquarters were fixed, is an undeniable truth."

Stripping windmills of their sails, the British looted the homes of local residents. They also plundered stores, pharmacies, and churches.

"Several gentlemen informed me that much of their plunder was brought into the backyard of Mrs. Westood's house, where Sir Sydney Beckwith and Admiral Cockburn resided."

Dr. Colton shared his story with the investigative reporter. After British soldiers destroyed his private property, he approached Cockburn and Beckwith. Instead of taking responsibility for their men, Cockburn and Beckwith blamed Colton for daring to leave his house.

"'Why did you quit your house?' they replied. 'I remained in my house,' answered Doctor Colton, and have found no better treatment.'"

The investigative journalist also reported the horrible murder of a senior citizen, Mr. Kirby, by British soldiers, who also shot his wife and dog. The British claimed this was payback for Craney Island and "revenge for the refusal of the militia to give quarters to some Frenchmen (Canadian Chasseurs)."

The atrocities were so great that some in Hampton were afraid to share their experiences with the reporter. One woman's "story was too shocking in its details to meet the public eye."

By explaining that he wanted the public to know the whole truth "to do justice even to an enemy" and also "electrify my countrymen with the recital of her suffering," the reporter convinced her to share her story. And so she did—anonymously.

"This woman was seized by five or six ruffians—some of them dressed in red, and speaking correctly the English language—and stripped naked.

"Her cries and her prayers were disregarded, and her body became the subject of the most abominable indecencies."

At one point the woman escaped and ran into a nearby creek but was caught: "Whence she was dragged by the monsters in human shape to experience new and aggravated sufferings. In this situation she was kept the whole night, whilst her screams were heard at intervals by some of the Americans in town, who could only clasp their hands in hopeless agony."

Another woman came to Hampton to visit her husband, who was one of the captured American militia. Soldiers, who were dressed in green not red, took her and her daughter, in spite of their screams.

"They had previously robbed them of their rings and attempted to tear open their bosoms. A Mrs. Hopkins, who was not in town when I was there, obtained assistance of an officer and rescued the woman from her ravishers; but not until one had gratified his abominable desires."

This same Mrs. Hopkins testified to similar treatment of at least two other women, but would not give up the names of any of them to protect their privacy.

The green uniformed soldiers also stripped another man, Mr. Hope, age sixty-five, of his clothing and pointed bayonets at his breast. They spared him from further torture after realizing that a woman had taken refuge in his house. "They followed her into the kitchen, whither she had run for safety." Then "Mr. Hope made off amidst her agonizing screams, and when he returned to his house, he was told by his domestics that their horrid purposes were accomplished [against the woman who'd taken refuge]—this I had from him."

Such testimonies led the investigative reporter to draw a clear conclusion: "But the enemy are convicted of robbery, rape, and murder."

Though the reporter didn't know it at the time, the culprits were part of the green-uniformed Canadian Chasseurs or Chasseurs Britanniques. They were not Canadians as their name suggested. Instead they were French prisoners who chose to enlist in the Royal Army rather than rot in prison. They had given the British officers trouble from the start by threatening mutiny upon occasion.

The reporter ended his newspaper account with a call to arms and a plea. "Men of Virginia! Will you permit all this?—Fathers and brothers, and husbands! Will you fold your arms in apathy, and only curse your despoilers?—No—You will fly with generous emulation to the unfurled standard of your country."

He wanted people to support President Madison and solicit the enemy "wherever he dares to show his face." He called on them to put aside civil pursuits, such as making a living, to oppose the enemy instead.

"And devote yourselves, to the art and knowledge of which the enemy has made necessary—You will learn to command; to obey, and with 'Hampton' as your watchword—to conquer."

While U.S. government agents also investigated what happened at Hampton, the governor of Virginia formally protested the soldiers' actions to Admiral Warren. Did he take responsibility? Hardly. Warren claimed the acts at Hampton were revenge for the American militia who shot at helpless British troops floundering in the mud at Craney Island. Dismissing the assaults against women as meaningless and blaming the

French Chasseurs as wayward, Warren only admitted that some plundering had taken place.

Lieutenant Colonel Charles Napier, who was a British officer and part of the attack on Hampton, years later confessed that "every horror was perpetrated with impunity [by our troops]—rape, murder, pillage—and not a one was punished."

▬▬▬▬

Two days after Hampton, on June 27, 1813, King and Armstrong met face to face, but not to talk about invasions or terrorism or even military strategy. Politics topped their priorities.

Perhaps they shared some ale at a boardinghouse tavern or took an afternoon stroll along the banks of the Potomac and the green concourse near the Capitol that would one day become the National Mall.

Though they shared a bond as New Yorkers, they'd chosen different political parties and affiliations. But that didn't stop Armstrong from revealing sensitive political information to his boss's fiercest opponent in the Senate.

"Armstrong said Daschkoff, Gallatin, and Parish intrigued to have Gallatin appointed to Russia—that Daschkoff had a slice in the loan," King wrote in his notes of their conversation.

Daschkoff was the diplomat from Russia assigned to the United States. Armstrong suggested that Daschkoff was benefiting financially from the multimillion-dollar loan to fund the war that Gallatin had negotiated with Mr. Parish, a foreign-born American banker and uncle of an assistant to the war secretary. Though Armstrong accused Parish of intriguing to send Gallatin to St. Petersburg, wasn't Armstrong intriguing or conniving with King? Yes, without a doubt.

King also learned from Armstrong that another U.S. senator had arrived in town. But not to worry. This man wouldn't vote for Gallatin as a peace envoy. Armstrong also conveyed that Secretary of State James Monroe wanted to become head of the army, a move that Gallatin had supported. Nothing could have disgusted Armstrong more. He complained "that [Monroe] knew nothing of war and was without experience."

They discussed another issue: Madison's nomination of Jonathan Russell, who was born in Rhode Island, as an envoy to Sweden. This, too, was critical to the vote on Gallatin. Why? Tit for tat politics. Senator Jeremiah Howell of Rhode Island would vote for Russell, his state's native son, in exchange for voting against Gallatin.

Oh how King hummed along as he drank in the news and gossip that Armstrong shared with him that summer's day. He soon just might have what he most wanted before the session ended—embarrassing Madison by blocking Gallatin's nomination as an envoy, and, eventually, pushing Gallatin out as Treasury secretary. Which did he want more? To damage Madison or to secure peace? Didn't he long for peace above all else? Wasn't he undermining peace by leading the charge against Gallatin? He didn't see it that way. Sometimes the best of minds fail to see reality when ambition blinds them.

———

Not long after the invasion of Hampton, Sally Stevenson wrote her cousin Dolley and shared her concerns about the health of her brother, Edward Coles: "Would to Heaven my dear Edward was with you, he writes us that he is rather better."

Also pressing on Sally's mind was the fallout from Hampton and its impact on her town. "You can form no idea of the spirit that has been excited in Virginia by the late invasion—it transformed all our young men into heroes. They waited not for the 'spirit stirring drum' to call them to their duty."

Sally explained that her neighborhood had sent a company of fifty volunteers, who gathered over a two-day time period, to defend their shores. Even old men in Richmond were joining the preparations to resist the enemy if they came. "They will find it no easy task to conquer Virginians, even the ladies show a Spartan courage."

In contrast to many others, Sally understood the stress and demands facing her cousin Dolley. "But I forget how many cares you have to occupy you at this time, soon may they be dispelled by the perfect restoration of your husband's health."

What would happen if Madison were to die during such duress? The president needed a breakthrough more than ever.

CHAPTER ELEVEN

Dear Dolley

A few days after Hampton's turmoil, Dolley had great news to report. James's fever had broken on July 2, as she wrote Edward: "I have the happiness to assure you my dear cousin that Mr. Madison recovers, for the last three days, his fever has been so slight as to permit him to take bark [quinine] every hour, and with good effect."

The ordeal had nearly killed her. "It has been three weeks since I have nursed him night and day—sometimes in despair! But now that I see he will get well. I feel as if I should die myself, with fatigue."

Cousin Sally again wrote Dolley after she heard of James's recovery. "Rumor with her hundred tongues had circulated at least a hundred reports about your dear husband.... And most fervently do I thank Heaven for granting to our prayers one who is not only necessary to the happiness of those who 'love him best' but to the prosperity and welfare of his country."

A tall gallant man, John Peter Van Ness had come to Washington in its very early days as a member of Congress from New York. When Thomas Jefferson appointed him to the Washington militia, Congress would not allow him to simultaneously hold two federal offices. Van Ness chose the militia. Over ten years he rose to the position of major general, the rank he held at the time of Cockburn's raids in 1813. His longevity was the best evidence that he couldn't have been a better supporter of the militia system. From the days of the revolution, Americans had embraced local militias to protect and defend their hometowns. In an era when the average man relied on firearms for hunting, militias made sense. Van Ness's loyalty to the militia was a prime example.

His ties to Washington were not only martial, but they were also marital. He had married Marcia Burnes, the daughter of an original landowner in the area. Now a banker who owned a large estate, General Van Ness had the money to be a patron to the Washington theatre and other entities. With money in one pocket and loyalty in the other, he had emerged as a local leader who maintained ties with New York friends, such as Washington Irving.

Though he had settled in Washington City, the forty-four-year-old Van Ness still had something in common with General Armstrong: New York. Would that tie be enough to bridge their opposing views? Only time would tell.

Because of Cockburn's raids, Van Ness had experienced many encounters with the new war secretary. He'd been more than willing to comply with the War Department's request to call up part of the militia earlier in the summer of 1813. Because locals had seen the enemy's ships in the Potomac, the request made sense. Van Ness had complied with promptness, diligence, and urgency.

Soon it was clear that the U.S. government had few resources to help his men. Where were the arms? Ammunition? Camp equipment? Provisions? Constant delay and confusion proved that the militia didn't have what they needed from the federal government to repel the British from the nation's capital city. The deficiencies were as obvious as they were painful. When the British ships left the Potomac, instead of making a plan to stand watch, the militia was ordered to disband.

Worried about these inadequacies, Van Ness had approached Armstrong several times. They needed to bolster the incompetent Fort Washington, which was located on the Potomac River's East bank below the city of Alexandria. Armstrong himself had spoken on the topic. Van Ness and other local leaders had suggested erecting a new battery, one that could seal off the river if the enemy approached again. So far nothing had been done, even though the horrors of Hampton were becoming known.

Once again Van Ness approached Armstrong. With earnestness and urgency, he pressed the issue: What of erecting a battery? Armstrong replied that he "was about to execute it." He explained that he "was only balancing between several different points which had been proposed or presented to his view, and he believed he must go down himself to reconnoiter and select."

Though Armstrong said the words Van Ness wanted to hear, something bothered him. Armstrong appeared rather indifferent. The war secretary's tone conveyed little emotion and no passion. Armstrong then expressed his opinion that the enemy would not come, or even seriously attempt to come, to the district.

Van Ness was as stunned as he was worried. What if Armstrong was wrong? Why was he so certain? Did he possess intelligence that he wasn't sharing, something that indicated Warren's or Cockburn's true intentions? But why wouldn't the British come to Washington? Though deficient in grandeur and lacking in culture, the seat of government symbolized representation, not royalty.

Van Ness left Armstrong as he always did, with more promises than payoffs.

━━━━━━━

Soon the president's recovery was widely known. The chairman of the Senate select committee sent Madison another letter on July 12, 1813.

"The committee sincerely laments that your indisposition for some time past has been such as would have rendered it improper to have addressed you upon this subject." They were glad to learn of Madison's "restored health."

Would they now trust his judgment and join with him to accomplish his greatest need and want, peace? All he could do was defer to their decision-making timetable.

On July 19, 1813, the Senate voted on the nominations for a peace mediation with Britain. As the Senate reported, "That the Senate do advise and consent to the appointments of John Q. Adams and James A. Bayard agreeably to their nominations, respectively." Adams received thirty yeas and four nays. Bayard's tally was twenty-seven yeas and six nays.

As for Gallatin, the Senate did not "advise and consent to the appointment of Albert Gallatin." He received seventeen yeas and eighteen nays. That was it. One vote separated Gallatin from approval.

Not only did the Senate vote against Gallatin, but they also reprimanded Madison for nominating him. They didn't believe the president had the power to appoint envoys during the Senate recess, because these were new positions, not vacancies. They concluded that the president could fill a vacancy during a Senate recess but not create a new position without their consent.

"That the granting of commissions...to negotiate and sign a treaty of peace...during the late recess of the Senate...was not in the opinion of the Senate, authorized by the Constitution, inasmuch as a vacancy in that office did not happen during such recess of the Senate."

While venerating the authority of the president, the Senate also accused him of exceeding his power. The "rights of the Senate have been infringed."

The Senate trampled on Madison's choices and used the moment to embarrass both him and Mr. Gallatin. For all his anger and disappointment at their decision and politicking, Madison had a strong balm. He'd prefer this checks and balances system, the one he designed, over the other extremes: rule by tyranny or a mob.

Elijah Mix tried the torpedo again when the moon was growing dark starting on July 18. After several attempts he finally thought he was in reach of *Plantagenet*, a British ship. But the tide blew the torpedo and it exploded too soon and too far from the ship to seriously damage it. The explosion primarily threw a column of water onto the ship's deck and blew over a small boat next to it.

"Had you been twenty feet nearer her, she must no doubt had been destroyed," Latrobe later wrote to Mix about seeing the episode in the newspaper. Mix, the navy secretary, Latrobe, and Fulton were all disappointed with the experiment, but grateful that no American had been killed in the process of trying. The torpedo had yet to come of age.

Mary Sumner Blount wrote to her friend, dearest Dolley, from North Carolina, on July 18, 1813. As with many others before her, she shared her disappointment that Dolley had stopped writing to her.

"If I reproached you for not writing it was not that I wished to hurt your feelings, know that I could never do intentionally? But from my great affection, I felt mortified at being slighted by one I loved so much one that I had cause to look at as a dear friend."

Though she confessed that she'd felt Dolley had forgotten her—a polite way of saying she felt snubbed—Mrs. Blount expressed understanding that "every hour of your life is and ought to be devoted to your husband, who is one of the best of men."

She acknowledged that many longed for Dolley's attention and time. "And that the public have a claim on you also, but still I hoped that you would sometimes write a few lines to one who loved you so much, to let her know you had not forgotten her entirely."

Mary also had a public safety reason for writing. Along with many families, she was leaving town. "We are in hourly expectation of the British coming up here." She relayed that one friend had died just from the fright. "Poor Mr. Gaston has had the misfortune to lose his lady, she was so frightened [being in a family way] when she was told the British was coming up the river that she was taken with fits in which she never recovered."

What fear she relayed! Mrs. Blount then shared her deepest emotions. "Oh my friend what distressing times every moment we have fresh news of the British depredations...I am so frightened that I scarce can write, the men flying to arms and the drums beating."

As these letters, and many others, showed, Dolley was a leader among women everywhere. These ladies looked to her for hope.

━━━━━

Now it was time to talk, face to face. General Armstrong greeted General Wilkinson, who had finally arrived in Washington City on July 31. The pair discussed several possibilities for attacking key Canadian locations. The leading option was to move U.S. forces from Fort George to Sackets Harbor and then attack Kingston.

Alternatives included a simultaneous movement from Lake Champlain to Montreal, where they might attack instead if the enemy weakened its forces at Montreal to save Kingston. Still a third option was to occupy a point on the St. Lawrence twenty miles below Ogdensburg. Then they could move at the same time as General Wade Hampton's attack on Montreal.

Wilkinson opposed Armstrong's plans. Instead he suggested that operations should begin near Fort George. General Hampton should harass Montreal. If they were successful in those places, then they would be in a stronger position to attack Kingston.

Armstrong disagreed. "Kingston, therefore...as well on grounds of policy as of military principle, presents the first and great object of the campaign."

Yes. No. Yes. No. The duo dueled in disagreement. Wilkinson later expressed contempt for the secretary and his plan, calling it "a pleasant work, to a minister in his closet, and quite easy of execution, on paper:

where we find neither ditches, nor ramparts, nor parapets, nor artillery, nor small arms."

The battle for Canada was in jeopardy, but not only from the British. The internal squabbles of America's generals were just as great a threat.

━━━━━━

There was one thing President Madison absolutely had to do before departing for Montpelier as the summer of 1813 ended. He had to write Albert Gallatin.

"You will learn from the secretary of state the painful manner in which the Senate have mutilated the mission to St. Petersburg," Madison penned, revealing his deepest regret. "It is not easy to express the mixed feelings produced by the disappointment or the painfulness of my own in particular."

He confessed that he had no indication before nominating him that the Senate would reject him. Sure, he knew that extreme Federalists would oppose it, but they didn't have enough votes to kill it without moderates. He didn't anticipate that Senator King would convince others to oppose the nomination on the grounds of incompatibility with Gallatin's cabinet post.

Madison explained to Gallatin why he didn't pull him as Treasury secretary and re-nominate him as an envoy to the mediation: timing. Gallatin and the others had departed Washington in April and likely had reached St. Petersburg by July. If the mediation had taken place within a month, then they could be on their way home by now with a peace treaty in hand. So he hoped.

"It was calculated, that the mediation, if accepted by Great Britain, would be over, and the envoys on their way home, before the decision of the Senate could reach St. Petersburg."

If so, then Gallatin deserved to remain as Treasury secretary when he returned. But Madison had good reason to fear that the envoys were headed home for a different reason. The possibility of Britain's Parliament rejecting Russia's mediation offer was increasingly worrisome.

"*Should the mediation* be rejected *as was becoming more and more probable*," he wrote, partially in cipher or secret code. There was "a *temper in the body capable of going* very great *lengths*" to degrade the executive.

Then, as if communicating to a close friend, not an advisor, Madison also told Gallatin about his illness. "I have just recovered strength enough after a severe and tedious attack of bilious fever, to bear a journey to the mountains whither I am about setting out."

The president appreciated his mountain home of Montpelier in Orange County, Virginia, and admired those who had created it. John Madison, his great-great-grandfather, had come to the tidewater area of Virginia from England in 1653. John's grandson, Ambrose Madison, was James's grandfather. Ambrose patented 2,650 acres west of the tidewater in the area of Virginia known as the Piedmont. There his son James Sr. built the mansion called Montpelier, which held a spectacular view of the nearby Blue Ridge Mountains. The family moved into the house when James Madison Jr. was eleven.

A sickly boy, the president had heard many doctors over the years suggest that the mountain air benefited his health. As he wrote Gallatin in 1813, he knew that he needed his mountain refreshment more than ever. "The physicians prescribe it as essential to my thorough recovery, and security against a relapse at the present season."

As Madison closed his letter, he worried that it would "be intercepted on its passage." He rightly feared that English or French captains would capture the ship carrying his letter and prevent its arrival.

For now it was off to Montpelier, which he had inherited after his father died in 1801. Born in 1751 as the oldest of twelve children, Madison also held the responsibility of overseeing the family plantation and caring for his mother, Nelly. He'd retreated there before, after falling ill while a student at Princeton College. Respite was what he needed then, and what he needed now. He would defer to his cabinet members to do their jobs in his absence. What he didn't realize was that not everyone in his inner circle could be trusted.

Mrs. Blount's fears of Cockburn attacking North Carolina were well founded. Indeed. Cockburn completed a successful mission at Ocracoke, one of the most remote outer banks islands of North Carolina. The locale had been a favorite hangout for the pirate Blackbeard. Cockburn and his men had captured an eighteen-gun brig and taken the inlet. "I feel it right to state to you that the blockade of the Chesapeake is very materially, if not entirely frustrated at the port of Beaufort and the Ocracoke inlet," he reported to Admiral Warren.

One thing had changed under his command. Gone were the green coats or the French prisoners disguised as Canadian soldiers. While failing to acknowledge the extent of this unit's atrocities at Hampton, Cockburn and other British officers nonetheless recognized the risk in keeping them. They put them on a ship and sent them away.

By the end of summer, Cockburn had made his choice for winter quarters. He left the Chesapeake for the waters of Bermuda. There he could rest, recover, and revel in the glory he had attained by raiding innocent towns on the East Coast. He couldn't have asked for better evidence of his capabilities. Surely the admiralty would notice, be pleased, and entrust him with attacking larger cities of even more importance. While merely fulfilling his orders, Cockburn was on his way to the promotions and future positions that he longed for.

Armstrong also decided to leave Washington City. He wrote Wilkinson that he would soon join him at the front to "furnish with promptitude, whatever might be necessary." Wilkinson, no doubt, hated the idea.

Not only was he leaving Washington City to join his Northern army, but by doing so, he was also abandoning his responsibility to oversee the president's policies for troops everywhere else, including the West, East, and South. He hoped his presence would finally lead to success in Canada, where it mattered.

Meanwhile Madison remained confident in Armstrong. He had told Congress in May that "under a wise organization and efficient direction, the Army is destined to a glory not less brilliant than that which already encircles the Navy."

Would that glory come? If so, how?

_____

While Madison looked to the mountains for renewal and Armstrong looked to Canada for glory, Benjamin Latrobe said good-bye to Washington City.

"Bidding adieu to the malice, backbiting, and slander, trickery, fraud, and hypocrisy, lofty pretensions and scanty means, boasts of patriotism and bargaining of conscience, pretense of religion and breach of her laws," he wrote to a friend.

Pained by the jealous maneuvers of rival architect Dr. Thornton, he continued his rant: "Starving doctors, thriving attorneys, whitewashing jail oaths, upstart haughtiness and depressed merit, and five thousand other nuisances that constitute the very essence of this community."

He was convinced that "the more you stir it, the more it stinketh."

Latrobe's friend had asked a favor of him to pass along to Madison. Stung by Madison's unwillingness to hire him as a military engineer and by Dolley's refusal to say good-bye to them when they'd called on her during Madison's sickness, Latrobe responded with equal parts bitterness and sarcasm. "So you really think that my good word would be of promise to you with the President. Wonderfully sagacious...what pray, does Mr. Madison care for you or for me? Every dog has his day, and ours is past."

Latrobe had concluded that Madison was stubborn. Because he was moving to Pittsburgh, he would never see the president again. This freed him to let loose with his pen, albeit privately to a friend. The words are among the strongest criticism that Latrobe ever wrote about the president.

"As general, honest and right intentioned is our cold-blooded President, you might as well stroke an armadillo with a feather by way of making the animal feel, as try to move him by words from any of his opinions or purposes," Latrobe concluded.

He would miss seeing his accomplishments—the south wing of the Capitol, the interior of the President's House, the Navy Yard arch, and others. Yet he couldn't imagine any scenario that would cause him to return.

———

Rufus King couldn't have ended the summer of 1813 happier had he been elected president. The *Maryland Gazette* printed a column praising his return to the U.S. Senate and his recent leadership in that body.

"All who have had an opportunity of witnessing any important discussion in the Senate, in which Mr. King has taken a part, have almost universally assigned him the palm," the article began.

His role in speaking truth to power, namely against Madison, had caught this newspaper editor's attention. He saw King as a bipartisan man, capable of attracting praise from both parties. "His talents are spoken of in more exalted terms, even by his political opponents, than any other member of that body.... But since all parties now unite in speaking his praise, it is sincerely to be wished that his councils may produce that effect, which they so eminently deserve."

Then the editorialist took a veiled stab, an undercut, at the president: "And we do not think it would be too much to say, that he [King] is superior at this time to any other man of which the United States can boast."

King couldn't help but feel uplifted. This editorialist noted his public service, honesty, and reputation for justice. More than anything, the fact that the *Maryland Gazette* was a southern newspaper made his Northerner heart sing. After all, if hundreds of others joined this editorialist, their combined chorus could send him to the President's House one day.

"With such a man at the head of our government, we might soon expect to witness a change in the gloomy aspect of our affairs, and that scene of prosperity again restored which formerly spread its blessings around us."

Perhaps after learning of the forty burned houses in Havre de Grace and reading of the lost dignity of the feminine souls in Hampton, this editorialist concluded that the people had been misled by wild opinions. King could be the answer to the nation's woes. So they hoped.

"If ever there is a time when honest men come again into fashion, it would be the pride of our nation to have a statesman like him to direct its affairs."

Thus, King ended the summer with a proverbial crown on his head— a fitting image for a man named *King*.

―――――

"One thousand dollars reward will be given...for the head of the notorious, incendiary, and infamous scoundrel, the violator of all laws, human and divine, the British Admiral George Cockburn," James O. Boyle had offered.

As the summer ended, Philadelphia's *Democratic Press* wasn't the only publication to advertise a call for Cockburn's assassination in August 1813. Many around the country read that ad in their newspapers and felt similar sentiments about this ravaging pirate disguised as an honorable British admiral. Some called him a burglar and other names for his wake of destruction. Yet, no slingshot or torpedo had struck Goliath. No sword had yet to cut off his head. No Peter sliced his ears. At the end of summer in 1813, he simply slipped away to Bermuda for the winter.

What would happen next? Would America's second war with England return to traditional fighting between armies and navies, or would terrorism worsen? Indeed. Cockburn wanted to take a bow at the President's House.

In fact, he was so confident of his charming abilities that he was sure he could set one of Dolley's parties ablaze by his very presence. Yet he didn't have what he needed most to accomplish such a feat at a fête. He still needed something he didn't have—a superabundant force of multiple thousands. Something big would have to happen. Something really big.

PART II

1814: White House Ablaze

There is a secret in life, better than anything a fortune teller can reveal. We all have a great hand in the forming of our own destiny.
—Dolley Madison

This illustration shows the charred walls of the White House after the British military burned it on August 24, 1814. *Courtesy Library of Congress, from an engraving by William Strickland after a watercolor by George Munger*

CHAPTER TWELVE

The White House

The term *White House* appears to have started as a slur, at least in the newspapers.

"I will turn Jefferson out 'of that white house and hang him' and that 'congress I will pack off,'" Vice President Aaron Burr told a general. Burr's quotation was printed in New York's *Republican Watch-Tower* on January 30, 1807.

This was one of the first—if not the first—newspaper references to the term *White House*. Burr was later tried and then acquitted for treason.

The origin of the President's House dates to 1792, when President George Washington held a contest to select the design for the mansion. The winner was James Hoban, an Irish-American architect and builder whose classical, stately drawing had impressed Washington. Unlike then-secretary of state Thomas Jefferson, who preferred a red brick building and submitted his own secret contest entry, Washington believed the executive leader of a republic deserved a grand, sturdy house made of stone.

The choice made sense. Washington had used white paint and sand to make his private pinewood house, Mount Vernon, resemble stone. For the president's palace in Washington City, Hoban used the finest cut of masonry, called ashlar, to build a bona fide stone house. The intricate scalloped carvings above the north door added elegance and beauty.

While George Washington never lived in the President's House and died in 1799 before its completion, the executive mansion embodied his ideas as much as the city that carried his name. Though made of white-washed stone, the residence was initially called the President's House or President's Palace, not the White House.

As "White House" had been hurled against Jefferson, so it was used to attack Madison. "If the dispatches from France and the news from the Chesapeake and Virginia don't drive the poor little viceroy in the white house crazy, he must be as tough as a pine knot," reported George-town's *Federal-Republican* newspaper.

Another Baltimore editorialist, who claimed to be a friend of the president's, admonished him, saying, "The American people placed you at the helm of government" and you have a "duty to steer it aright."

A Maine editorialist warned Madison that if he didn't take greater control of his cabinet, the American people would replace him: "The next presidential period shall bring a more energetic and manly tenant into the white house."

Speaking truth to power, the Baltimore editorialist angrily concurred: "You hear no language like this at the drawing room parties of 'the white house.'" This was not the only time that Dolley's parties were used to criticize the president.

"Dazzled with the blaze" is how a Maine editor described the figurative effect of one of Dolley's open house gatherings on her husband. Not only that, but because of these events, the president was also "enveloped in the smoke…or turned giddy with the flattery." In this man's view, Madison was a lightweight because he engaged in too much frivolity. What a contrast this was to those who saw Madison as a shriveled man lacking passion.

With so much animosity, how did "White House" become a term of endearment? Though it's impossible to know for sure, Dolley Madison, whether consciously or unconsciously, intentionally or unintentionally, may be responsible. One party of hers in particular appears to be the start of turning a slur into a salute of pride.

After a refreshing break at Montpelier, James and Dolley returned to Washington City in the autumn of 1813. In many ways, life now seemed much brighter. Madison's health was restored and Edward Coles had resumed his secretarial duties.

Best of all, the social season was starting. Dolley couldn't contain her exuberance as she soon wrote to Thomas Jefferson's daughter. "We have ladies from almost every state in the union, and the city was never known so thronged with strangers—Thus, it is a pleasing and instructive scene for the young."

On December 20, 1813, Dolley set the White House ablaze with a glow and merriment that caught the eye of an influential Philadelphia reporter visiting Washington City. Once again, the *Democratic Press* created a sensation. This time, the wave of excitement centered not on an advertisement seeking Cockburn's head on a plate, but on the novelty that this reporter, using the pseudonym Tyro, found at "*the White House.*"

"You can little imagine how great a privation it is to a stranger in this place, to be shut out of the capital for four days in succession," Tyro began, writing of the Thirteenth Congress's short break.

Tyro was disappointed that Congress had taken a few days off in December following a vote for another embargo restricting trade. After all, they had only just begun their new session. How would he spend his time? "There is an utter absence of all amusement here, except what is derived from seeing the proceedings of the legislative bodies."

He was correct. Washington City had few sources of entertainment. With so little commerce and so few mansions—the "splendor of the wealthy"—little attracted his fancy. He was bored. "There are no muse-ums of things curious in nature or art, and I have been so unfortunate as not to have an opportunity of even seeing the ladies of this place 'swell the mazy dance.'" Soon, however, something more enchanting than dancing caught his fancy.

"I must not forget, however, to mention that Mrs. Madison, the President's Lady, gives a tea party every Wednesday evening." Most intriguing to him was the openness of the occasion. Anyone could attend. That meant him. "It was a novelty to me to find that these parties were not assembled by cards of invitation, but that everybody was free to appear there, and that all were received with hospitality, politeness, and attention. Finding access so easy, I wished to attend last Wednesday evening."

Because he was a little nervous, he convinced an old college friend to accompany him. As it turned out, he didn't need a human crutch after all. "It was with much satisfaction I found everything more easy than I had anticipated, ceremony and formality were observed no further than decorum required."

Coffee. Cakes. Nuts. Fruit. Whiskey punch. Much tempted his taste buds. "Refreshments were very liberally handed round, and all partook freely and cheerfully. I understood it was a pretty full assembly: there might have been from one to 200 persons present of both sexes."

Unlike modern tours where visitors pass through State Floor rooms without meeting the president or first lady, guests in 1813 received a huge bonus for stepping inside the President's House.

"The president, Mr. Madison, mixed with the company all the eve-ning, and talked by times with everybody; even I claimed some notice where I looked for nothing but a common salutation."

This reporter wisely observed that he wouldn't meet the shortest but most monumental politician in Washington by hanging out at the Cap-itol. He would only find the president at the President's House. "But for the drawing room I might have dragged out the whole winter here and not have beheld the man whom the American people have twice called on to preside over them, much less have spoken with him."

Tyro told his readers that even "the men who slander him with the most reprobate license seek his hospitality." Dolley's charisma was a huge factor in making them feel welcome and comfortable. Thus, "by appropriating two or three hours of an evening every week the executive can, in the most affable manner, mix with his fellow-citizens and neither subject himself nor others to the insupportable drudgery of receiving a hundred formal visits a day."

Another thrill came from meeting the guest of honor. "General [William Henry] Harrison was there, and there were more eyes than mine who surveyed the Hero of the West with interest." He wasn't sure which was better, shaking Madison's hand or the palm of the military hero.

A few months earlier, General Harrison had defeated British forces on the Thames River in Ontario. Not only that, but Harrison and his men had also killed the native leader and British ally, Tecumseh. Harrison's victory was important because it had ended British superiority in the Northwest, especially in Detroit, and driven the action squarely back to the Niagara frontier on the New York–Canadian border, precisely where General Armstrong had wanted it.

Tyro also told his *Democratic Press* readers that the President's House was far grander than he expected. "If you have not seen it you can hardly form an idea of the scale on which this house is built."

The rectangle-shaped mansion featured two stories over a basement. With steps leading to the North entrance, visitors had the sense of stepping up to power as they entered the entrance hall of the main or State Floor. Tyro wrote, "My observations at 'the White house' (for so it is called here) have satisfied me that its economy is well regulated and that it is kept as becomes the chief executive officer of a free people."

Thus this reporter put in writing the most important detail of his article. The White House was no longer a term of editorial derision in newspapers. Dolley's warmth and hospitality had led to a cultural change in Washington.

"The little president is back and game as ever." So observed Richard Rush, who would soon become Madison's attorney general. Madison had returned to Washington healthier and more optimistic about the country than he had left it.

The president had shared his confidence in a message to Congress on December 7, 1813. "In fine, the war, with all its vicissitudes, is illustrating the capacity and the destiny of the United States to be a great, a flourishing, and a powerful nation, worthy of the friendship which it is disposed to cultivate with all others."

He had good reasons to be hopeful about the nation's future. Earlier in September, after spending the summer building several ships for battle, Commander Oliver Perry and his sailors had put their new ships to the test and soundly beaten the British. As Perry had reported to General Harrison: "We have met the enemy and they are ours." They had captured two British ships, two brigs, one schooner, and one sloop. The Battle of Lake Erie was the first time a fleet of British ships had surrendered to an American. Perry's success on the lake had led to Harrison's victory on land.

The politics, however, were not lost on Madison. He knew that Federalists like Senator King continued to oppose the war and refused to support robust measures to bolster resources for the supplies and men necessary to win it. Many extremists whispered of their desire to break away from America. In his message to Congress that December of 1813, Madison made his point clear: "That the union of these states, the guardian of the freedom and safety of all and of each, is strengthened by every occasion that puts it to the test."

But he also had disappointing news to report to Congress. Without giving an official response to the Russian government, the British government had rejected the mediation offered by Czar Alexander. Madison had hoped for a better outcome. Yet he believed it was not in the British nature to consent "to the decisions of an umpire."

Though optimistic, he knew great challenges faced him in 1814. He had two priorities: prosecuting a war with limited money and men while obtaining peace with a foe unwilling to submit to a mediation by another country. Madison needed Congress to increase recruits for the upcoming summer campaign in Canada against the British. He needed to find a way to achieve a successful peace. Until then, Canada was still the eye of the American target.

―――――――

In his role as editor of the *Analectic Magazine*, Washington Irving wrote a biographical sketch of Oliver Perry. He described the happenings of September 10, 1813, on the great lake. Perry commanded a ship he had newly built, which was named *Lawrence* after James Lawrence, the deceased commander of the USS *Chesapeake*.

"At 10 a.m. the wind hailed to the southeast and brought our squadron to windward," Irving wrote of the U.S. squadron's movements. Then he described how Commodore Perry hoisted a flag on the *Lawrence* and recalled "the dying words of the valiant Lawrence, 'Don't give up the ship!' It was received with repeated cheering by the officers and crews." (While Lawrence's last words were "Don't surrender the ship!" Irving changed them to "Don't give up the ship!" The phrase has been a part of American culture ever since.)

Irving chronicled that Perry continued to fight and boarded another boat with calmness, even after the *Lawrence* and much of its crew were lost. Irving saw Perry's victory as one for the ages, something that people living in the area in the future would not forget. He wrote his prediction in colorful, poetic terms.

"In future times, when the shores of Erie shall hum with busy population; when towns and cities shall brighten where now extend the dark and angled forest...then will the inhabitants of Canada look back to this battle we record, as one of the romantic achievements of the days of yore," he wrote.

Dreaming that historical markers and artifacts would one day mark the spot, he added this to his conclusion of Perry's victory.

"The fisherman, as he loiters along the beach, will point to some half buried cannon, corroded with the rust of time, and will speak of ocean warriors that came from the shores of the Atlantic—while the boatman, as he trims his sail to the breeze, will chant in rude ditties the name of Perry—the early hero of Lake Erie."

Irving was no longer a satirist; he was a storyteller. He was also no longer just a journalist but also a commentator. Concerned about the outcome of the war, he sent a warning to those who prioritized their opinions over the best interests and longevity of America.

"Whatever we may think of the expediency or inexpediency of the present war, we cannot feel indifferent to its operations," he wrote, taking an indirect swipe at Federalists such as Rufus King who publicly decried the war. "He who fancies he can stand aloof in interest, and by condemning the present war, can exonerate himself from the shame of its disasters, is woefully mistaken."

Irving put unity of the nation above all else. He was no New England separatist and focused on the bigger picture of America's story. "Whenever our arms come in competition with those of the enemy, jealousy for our country's honor will swallow up every other consideration—our feelings will ever accompany the flag of our country to battle, rejoicing in its glory, lamenting over its defeat," he continued.

He believed that in a time of war, party politics and infighting were destructive. "Other nations will not trouble themselves about our internal wrangling and party questions; they will not ask who among us fought, or why we fought, but how we fought."

He didn't believe that defeat would disgrace only those who started the war or those who fought it "but will extend to the whole nation, and come home to every individual. If the name of American is to be rendered honorable in the fight, we shall each participate in the honor; if otherwise, we must inevitably support our share of the ignominy."

Would Washington heed Irving's warning? Would party infighting lead to Washington's destruction or would patriotism lead the nation to peace?

CHAPTER THIRTEEN

Hospitality and Hostility

"Messrs. King and Gore and their wives are the best people I have found here. I see them pretty frequently and the more I see of them the better I like them. Mr. King is a very great man; Mr. Gore great enough."

So wrote Congressman Jeremiah Mason, who was supremely impressed with the honorable senators from New York and Massachusetts and their hospitality that winter.

Senator King had also returned to Washington in December 1813. Either at the Capitol or his boardinghouse in Washington, King sat a desk or table. The date was December 19, 1813, the day before Dolley's big White House bash. He picked up a pen, swished it in ink and wrote his friend Gouverneur Morris. With the peace mission a failure, King knew that the war he so vehemently opposed would continue. Military strategy for the upcoming summer campaign was on everyone's mind.

"We may conclude that our session will be consumed in giving authority to the plan of the next campaign. What this plan will be, we are not informed, indeed as the secretary at war has not returned, it is probable that the plan is not yet fully prepared," King wrote.

Armstrong had yet to arrive from overseeing military operations in New York along the Canadian border. Nonetheless, talk of implementing a draft drifted throughout the halls of Congress. This would be "a revision of the militia laws, and such a modification of them, as will enable the president to raise by draft or otherwise 50- or 60,000 men."

The number was ambitious. King fully pegged the war secretary as the source of the idea, as he told Morris. "With sixty thousand men all Canada may be conquered, says General Armstrong (who would be named Lieutenant General, if he could), in a single campaign."

Federalists thought that Armstrong's strategy for the war was strange and pointed to his vanity as a reason for his lack of practicality. Arrogance, vanity, and ambition were Armstrong's weaknesses.

The senator from New York knew that Mr. Morris didn't approve of Armstrong and considered the administration to be tyrannical. Morris had earlier written, "The report of the Secretary at War will do no credit to the administration or to the country." Indeed, once he arrived in Washington, Armstrong would submit a report of the recently failed campaign to capture Montreal.

King doubted the nation could afford to recruit 60,000 men or that Americans had the stomach for husbands and fathers to be forced to fight. Volunteering was patriotic; compulsion was tyrannical, wasn't it? What would differentiate America from England if men were forced into military service in the USA? Isn't that impressment? Wouldn't it turn the war into hypocrisy? Where would it end?

Also bothering King was the federal budget. The nation's finances were in shambles. Before Gallatin had left for Europe in April 1813, he had secured a $16 million loan from mostly foreign-born American bankers to fund the war through the end of the year. New England banks, which held most of the nation's hard money or specie, had refused to provide more than 3 percent of Gallatin's loan.

Now the Treasury would soon be empty with a gap between incoming income and outgoing expenses. How many more banks would dare loan the government more money to prosecute such a futile war? King didn't think many, if any.

Like Madison, King wanted peace. Unlike the president, King didn't want to prosecute the war with vigor. In his view, the best solution was to wait for news from Europe. Napoleon's recent losses there hinted that his time as France's emperor would soon be over. If he fell from power, then England would have no more need to impress U.S. sailors into British military service and continue a war with America. So he optimistically thought.

———

Commodore Joshua Barney was a regular American with a patriotic soul. At age fifty-four in the winter of 1813–14, he was also a Revolutionary War veteran, master sailor, and privateer. Where James Boyle's ad calling for Cockburn's head had failed and Elisha Mix's torpedo had yet to come of age, Barney's boats just might be the remedy that America needed to rid itself of redcoats raiding the Chesapeake Bay.

Barney's idea was to build and buy a fleet of flying gunboats and shallow-water barges to patrol the Chesapeake and its rivers. Properly supplied, manned, and armed, this flying squadron would distract Cockburn's attention from raids and attacks on local fishing towns and force him to fight or flee. This patriot's plan caught the attention of Navy Secretary William Jones. From his post in Baltimore, Barney joyfully read Jones's assessment.

"We shall expect you to keep the enemy below the Potomac, and then the whole force can unite," Jones wrote. "I am clearly of the opinion your force will be fully competent to repel any force the enemy can put in boats."

What stood out to Barney was Jones's worry over their foe's target. Unlike his counterpart, Secretary Armstrong, Jones voiced concern that the British sought to destroy the Chesapeake region.

"The enemy has a strong desire to destroy this place, and will assuredly make an effort for that purpose, your force is our principal shield, and all eyes will be upon you."

Though Jones didn't specify what he meant by "this place," any number of nearby cities could be a target, including Baltimore, Annapolis, and Washington. How Barney hoped his flying squadron would do just that, be a shield, a sword of protection for his beloved country!

———

Dolley wasn't hospitable only to her husband's political foes; she could also welcome the nation's leading antagonists. The relationship she had once developed with the wife of a British diplomat years earlier showed that while Dolley often dressed a step above most women in Washington City, her wardrobe wouldn't have fit in with royalty in England.

A decade earlier Anthony and Elizabeth Merry had arrived in Washington City after a voyage from England. Assigned as the top diplomat from Great Britain, Mr. Merry had worn his finest, gaudiest embroidered clothing, duds fit for a king, and called upon President Thomas Jefferson. With then–secretary of state James Madison escorting him, Merry had walked down the hall toward Jefferson's office on the west end of the White House. Before Merry had arrived to make his bow, Jefferson had appeared in the hallway. Why not accept the credential rights then and there, on the spot?

Merry couldn't believe it. Not only was he performing his rehearsed lines in the hallway and not in a formal drawing room, but President Jefferson had also been wearing threadbare informal clothing and tattered shoes instead of proper heeled men's shoes and formal clothing. Because Jefferson had known that Merry was coming, the British diplomat had taken the president's casual attire as an insult. Jefferson had just been himself. Disdaining any hint of monarchy, he had greeted the British diplomat the same way and considered his attire the cloth of simple republicanism.

The Merry affair was just beginning, however. In early December 1803, Jefferson had invited the Merrys to dinner. While knowing full well that France and England were at war, he had also invited a French diplomat, which was an insult. Before dinner, the guests had gathered outside of the dining room for informal conversation.

Believing the dinner was in their honor, the Merrys had worn full formal attire. Clad in a white satin dress, Mrs. Merry had also been covered in diamonds, attire appropriate for a royal court.

Dolley, though also in attendance, had not dressed as lavishly. She hadn't worn diamonds then. Years later for her husband's inaugural ball, she had worn pearls, not diamonds, to match her velvet buff gown. Though fancier than most women's clothing, Dolley's dresses hadn't been queenly by European standards.

At that 1803 dinner, when the food was ready, President Jefferson had asked to take Dolley's hand to escort her to the table instead of Mrs. Merry's. Why? She may have been the closest woman to him, making it easy to take her hand, but she had also often served as the widower Jefferson's hostess. Everyone else had taken the first seat they saw, leaving Mr. Merry to escort Mrs. Merry to a seat at the table. This every-man-and-woman-for-themselves approach had been such a sharp contrast with the formalities of dining in a royal court that the Merrys had been highly insulted. They'd taken such offense that Mr. Merry complained about the matter to his superiors in England.

Madison had the Merrys to dinner a few days later. Still smarting from Jefferson's snub, Mrs. Merry had described the meal as "more like a harvest-home supper, than the entertainment of a secretary of state."

According to a favorable account written decades later, Dolley had stood up for herself and her country and replied that "she thought abundance preferable to elegance." She had explained that circumstances created customs, which led to preferences for food and drink. America wasn't a replica of England and took pride in avoiding repugnant foreign customs. Their customs "arouse from the happy circumstance of the superabundance and prosperity of our country." Dolley would give up the delicacy of European style cooking and clothing in exchange for plainer but more abundant Virginia food and customs.

Soon, however, the Madisons realized that the Merrys had been so insulted that the problem was leading to a rift in foreign relations with

England. What to do? Madison had encouraged Jefferson to put into writing his new form of etiquette, which was based on the principle that all were equal when it came to sitting at the table. Madison had also written letters to try to smooth the ruffled feathers of his English goose and gander.

What did Dolley do? She had reached out to Mrs. Merry by inviting her over for intimate social chats and perhaps by giving her small gifts or tokens. Mrs. Merry had never been warm to America. She had often kept to herself and rode on horseback alone. But over a two-year period, Dolley had developed enough of a relationship with her that Mrs. Merry called upon Dolley. One incident showed Mrs. Madison's ability to be cordial in the face of animosity.

"The other evening she [Mrs. Merry] came in high good humor to pass three hours with her patient, as she styled me," Dolley shared with her sister Anna in a letter. Then one of the servants had called and "mentioned that the General [French diplomat] and his family were walking near the house."

Though she had been there three hours and had enjoyed the time, Mrs. Merry didn't take the news well. "Mrs. M instantly took the alarm said they were waiting for her to depart in order to come in, seized her shawl and in spite of all I could say marched off with great dignity and more passion, you know when she chooses she can get angry with persons as well as circumstances."

Many women shunned Mrs. Merry for her strange behavior, but not Mrs. Madison. The overdressed, dripping with diamonds Mrs. Merry had acted like a prized show horse among plain working mares. Dolley had handled her well. Her genuine love of people and her ability to both laugh and love had brought great good to her husband's reputation and to her country.

Rear Admiral George Cockburn also knew the Merrys quite well. He had escorted them to America on his ship in the autumn of 1803.

When his ship needed repairs for its return voyage, bankers in New York had refused to grant him credit, because he was an officer in the Royal Navy. They forced him to pay cash. Worse, some of his men deserted and claimed U.S. citizenship. Finding their hiding places, he forced them to return to his service. After all, he needed a crew to sail with him and didn't have the authority or desire to recruit Americans for his next mission, escorting hard money or specie from New York to India for later deposit into the English crown's treasury. The money was payment from America to England stemming from the peace treaty ending the American Revolution decades earlier.

Though he wasn't as easily insulted as the Merrys and had a good sense of humor, Cockburn believed the bankers and authorities concealing the whereabouts of his deserters should have treated him better. Thus, his first trip to America hadn't been a good one and hardened his anti-American views. The intervening eleven years had not softened Cockburn, as his raids in 1813 had shown.

After spending the winter in Bermuda, Cockburn returned to Lynnhaven Bay on February 23, 1814. Though this rear admiral had borne confidence on his shoulders as easily as epaulettes, one of his subordinates, Captain Robert Barrie, had little hope in Cockburn's ability to fulfill any bold initiatives. The reason? The British admiralty had confined the rear admiral's mission in 1814 to raids, not full-scale attacks. "I fear he is cramped in his orders," the captain wrote to his mother. Barrie had been successfully holding down the fort, or the sea as it were, in Cockburn's absence. From September 1813 to December 1813, Barrie's squadron captured or destroyed seventy-two U.S. merchant vessels trying to slip past the British blockade of the East coast.

Upon his return to the Chesapeake, Cockburn kept a low profile by sending out crews, such as Barrie's, to survey rivers and take the war pulse of the Americans. He also scouted Tangier, an island in the Chesapeake Bay, to set up British headquarters. Dutiful diligence to details was important to earning the admiralty's respect.

But without a robust commander in Admiral Warren, Cockburn had little hope of doing much more than casting nets and poles to fish for fun and burning a few American homes here and there. Though he was supremely confident in his own capabilities, he was frustrated at his superior admiral's lack of bold initiatives. Warren seemed to want nothing more than to go home to England. How Cockburn longed for a bigger strategy, one that would culminate in a large-scale attack, and a better commander.

━━━━━━━

"Have you quite forgotten me? I would not write a second time could I imagine for a moment that you received my letter from Washington," Mary Latrobe wrote Dolley again from her new Pittsburgh home. She referred to the letter that she had sent during James's illness the previous summer.

"I wrote a few hasty lines previous to our removal...to acknowledge the many, many proofs of kindness I had received from you," Mary explained. Despite Mrs. Madison's snub, Mary gave her the benefit of the doubt and still wished Dolley well. She knew her favorite time of the year was about to start.

"Your winter campaign has again commenced, I think of you every Wednesday evening particularly! I see you surrounded by friends and enemies! How undeserving are you of the latter!"

Upon her return to Washington, Dolley needed to make amends with friends like Mary whom she had ignored or understandably snubbed while James was ill. Her outreach reflected her renewed desire to foster goodwill for her husband and his presidency. Another lady who needed Dolley's attention was Ruth Barlow, whose husband had died while serving as Madison's top diplomat to France. Dolly wrote Ruth a letter in December 1813.

"My husband desires to be presented to you in the kindest manner," she passed along. Best of all, James was doing much better. "His health is more perfect than ever, but his cares and confinement, I fear will soon impair it."

Ruth responded, swiftly confessing, "Having met with such severe affliction and needing so much the tender consolation of my friends that, not receiving a line from dear Mrs. Madison, led me to fear I had been so unfortunate as to lose her friendship." Ruth added, "to know that is not the case, and that she still regards me with affection is very solacing to my wounded heart."

Dolley's campaign to soothe ruffled feathers among prominent ladies was working. She had another reason to rejoice that winter. Her married sisters, Anna and Lucy, had joined her for the social swirl. In 1812 Lucy had married a Supreme Court justice, Thomas Todd, and moved to his native Kentucky. Married to former congressman Richard Cutts, Anna trekked back and forth from Maine, which was part of Massachusetts, to their home in Washington City. Cutts, who had lost his seat in the last election, now served as superintendent general of military supplies.

With her husband's health improved, Dolley turned her attention outward. The year of 1814 would provide opportunities to influence others in ways she never expected or wanted. She would also soon welcome the most uninvited guests ever to step into the White House. In doing so, this lady of many firsts would have a hand in determining her own destiny.

CHAPTER FOURTEEN

Noses for News

In the spring and summer of 1814, rumors and news turned Washington City inside out.

"Armstrong was decided to have his just weight in the cabinet, or to throw up his office," Senator King wrote of the secret information he'd received. "That an understanding with the Federalists in Congress was his wish; that he desired nothing on their part in respect to himself."

Sympathetic to Armstrong's preference of New England over the South, King wasn't completely surprised at Armstrong's recent proposition to him. "That he was willing to co-operate against Virginia, leaving men and things to take their course when the Presidential election comes on."

When Armstrong arrived in Washington from the New York–Canadian war front after the new year began in 1814, he'd brought with him the reality of defeat. For months he and Wilkinson had argued over whether to target Kingston first and then Montreal or to skip Kingston and target Montreal directly with the aid of General Wade Hampton's troops. Finally, in mid-October 1813, they had abandoned plans for Kingston and determined to strike Montreal. In early November, Wilkinson led a force down the Saint Lawrence River while Hampton moved from Lake Champlain. This uncooperative pair sent each other testy letters questioning each other's authority and supply lines. The result was disastrous. Wilkinson lost a battle at Chrysler's Farm on November 11, 1813, which ended the campaign to take Montreal. The British reoccupied York, Canada, and ravaged Buffalo, New York. Hampton blamed Wilkinson, while Wilkinson blamed Hampton, who resigned in protest. Wilkinson wrote Armstrong: "What a golden glorious opportunity has been lost by the caprice of Major General Hampton."

Armstrong had had enough of both men, both of whom had been born in the South. Wilkinson hailed originally from Maryland, while Hampton was a wealthy plantation owner in South Carolina. Armstrong was tired of dealing with southerners, especially Secretary Monroe, who had fulfilled some of Armstrong's duties in Washington City while Armstrong was away on the Northern frontier. By the winter of 1814, enough was enough.

The war secretary made a key decision, but he had to be careful. So he sent an intermediary, Colonel Swift, to hold several conversations with another intermediary, Jeremiah Mason of New Hampshire. Mason relayed their conversation to Rufus King, who recorded what he learned about Armstrong's determination in his diary: "Their tenor was that the Virginia dynasty must be broken; that state must not furnish the next president. The policy has been to divide the Eastern States, to exclude from every public office of distinction Eastern men."

Armstrong had become so distrustful of President Madison and Secretary Monroe that he was willing to secretly join forces with the Federalists to make sure that Monroe or any other Virginian or southerner did not win the presidency in 1816. As Swift relayed, General Armstrong "speaks respectfully of Mr. King, wishes to open himself upon these topics to the Federalists."

Armstrong called upon Mr. King in a few days. He was ready to rid the military of his disappointing generals.

"Wilkinson and Hampton will be brought to trial and crushed," Armstrong assured King.

Armstrong's unauthorized plan for drafting 60,000 men soon failed in Congress. Instead, lawmakers decided to increase the size of bounty offerings, making them five times higher for recruiting volunteers. They also funded war operations at the same level as previous years and authorized borrowing to cover any differences between money coming in and expenditures going out.

King was pleased with Armstrong's decision to break with the administration and support someone from New York or the North in the next presidential election. Yet the outcome from Congress wasn't what he wanted. King wanted peace and an end to the war. Nothing else would do.

━━━━━━

Gossip was the news that most concerned Dolley Madison in January 1814. Needing to quell it, she wrote to former President Jefferson's daughter, Martha Jefferson Randolph, about the social swirl of the winter of 1814. Up first was flattery. She invited her cousin Sally Coles and one of Martha's teenage daughters to come for the social season, saying if "you could possibly spare Ellen, it would delight us to receive her—S. Coles (who is a lovely girl) would be her companion, and together they would enjoy a large and enlightened society."

Dolley knew that the New Year had started off well. She had heard others say so. Mrs. Seaton, the sister of the Mr. Gales the newspaper editor, wrote of the sparkling New Year's Day open house at the White House. As usual, foes and friends alike came. Mrs. Seaton explained that "everybody, affected or disaffected was truly regal towards the government, attended to pay Mrs. Madison the compliments of the season."

Dolley especially had caught Mrs. Seaton's eye. "Her majesty's appearance was truly regal—dressed in a robe of pink satin, trimmed elaborately with ermine, a white velvet and satin turban, with nodding ostrich plumes and a crescent in front, gold chain and clasps around the waist and wrists."

Mrs. Madison was clearly back on her game. Her feathers stood high and tall, which made it easier for guests to spot her from a distance. Though the social season was off to a good start, the politics needed help.

Dolley continued her letter to Jefferson's daughter by explaining the latest political problem. "The members of Congress seem a good deal occupied at present in dispute about French influence, some of them desire to impeach the president, in order that he may come forward and manifest his innocence of the charge."

She then arrived at the real reason for her letter. Fishing for news from Martha, she added, "They have a report among them that your dear father has consented, again to tempt the ocean for the great object of making a peace."

Was it true? Was Thomas Jefferson planning to go to Europe to negotiate a peace treaty with the British? Dolley doubted it but needed to send a signal for her husband nonetheless. Mr. Jefferson need not insert himself in the mix of peace. Madison hadn't given up hope that Mr. Gallatin and the others might still negotiate for peace, even though the Russian mediation was off.

"Should Mr. G. remain with Mr. Bayard [in Europe] he would still make the third negotiator," she told Martha.

If the rumor was true, Dolley's dabble in politics worked. Martha got the message about her father. Jefferson did not go to Europe.

President Madison, however, issued good news in February 1814. He resubmitted Albert Gallatin's name to the Senate as a peace commissioner because the peace process was officially back on track. The president couldn't have been happier.

England had offered to negotiate directly with the United States. Eschewing Russia's mediation offer, one English lord considered the conflict a family quarrel, a matter between brothers. The British government proposed a meeting in Europe, perhaps in Sweden, between a British delegation and an American one. No third party was allowed.

Because Gallatin was still in Europe and had been absent from America for eight months, it was fruitless for him to continue to hold his cabinet post. Declaring the Treasury secretary position vacant, the Senate confirmed Mr. Gallatin as a peace commissioner. They again approved James Bayard and John Quincy Adams. This time they also named Speaker of the House Henry Clay and Jonathan Russell to the team.

Now, Madison's job was to give instructions to his peace team. Crafting diplomatic directions was very much like a dance. He had to give enough form and structure to conform to the rhythm and rules of the dance, while also providing his emissaries with enough flexibility to improvise. Because communication was slow and time-consuming, he must strike just the right tempo.

His commissioners agreed. At a dinner before he left for Europe, Clay best expressed his boss's expectations and strategy in a toast: "The policy which looks to peace as the end of war—and to the war as the means of peace."

———

Not long after this, on February 25, Secretary Armstrong gave Senator King the news or gossip that he most wanted to hear about Madison's instructions to the commissioners. As King recorded: "Armstrong said that there would be peace; they would give up everything."

Giving up everything meant that the reasons for the war—ending England's abusive trade policies and stopping impressment—would be tabled in favor of peace on any terms. Victory would mean ending the war, not gaining any progress on why the war was fought in the first place.

The news left King a little puzzled. By giving up the moral reason for the war, going to war in the first place seemed even more senseless. He had to wonder, was Armstrong correct? Was Madison willing to give up everything?

He also had to wonder whether Madison would give away land to acquire peace. It was one thing to give up the reason for the war and to let go of a desire to gain new territory in Canada. But would Madison give up existing U.S. territory or give away America's right to fish in the waters between Canada and America? Would he let go of the right to sell goods along the Mississippi River or claims to the land around it? What could the president do to keep this from happening? Many questions remained as Armstrong continued to intrigue with King and plot against the administration he served.

Cockburn couldn't believe his eyes as he read the news in his hands. He had a new boss. Gone was Admiral Warren, dismissed from his command by the admiralty in London. Replacing him was sixty-two-year-old Admiral Alexander F. Cochrane, a veteran of the American Revolution on the British side.

Cockburn was as surprised as he was pleased. Maybe, just maybe, Cochrane would give him what Warren could never fully provide: energy and resolve. Warren lacked passion and authority to prosecute an attack on the Americans with utmost vigor. Cockburn respected enthusiasm, especially Cochrane's orders: "You are at perfect liberty as soon as you can muster a sufficient force to act with the utmost hostility against the shores of the United States."

He agreed to Cochrane's assessment of the Americans. "Their government authorizes and directs a most destructive war to be carried on against our commerce and we have no means of retaliating but on shore."

Cockburn loved Cochrane's desire for retribution because he shared it wholeheartedly: Cochrane had written, "They must be made to feel in their property, what our merchants do in having their ships destroyed at sea; and taught to know that they are at the mercy of an invading foe."

Cockburn fully agreed. If they could keep the enemy in constant alarm through raids and create a considerable diversion in the Chesapeake Bay, then the U.S. government would be unable to recruit soldiers from the Eastern states or send them to the border. "This is now more necessary in order to draw off their attention from Canada, where I am told they are sending their whole military force," Cochrane had relayed.

What stood out was Cochrane's motive. While the strategy was to distract the U.S. military's attention from Canada, the British now claimed a new reason for doing so: retribution.

Just a few months earlier, Admiral Warren had called the burning of Newark in Upper Canada a "system of retaliation threatened by King Madison." A wide-eyed Cockburn read Cochrane's latest assessment. "Their seaport towns laid in ashes and the country wasted will be some sort of a retaliation for their savage conduct in Canada; where they have destroyed our towns, in the most inclement seasons of the year."

Then Cockburn read the words he most longed to hear. His new boss shared his longing to attack Washington City. "It is therefore but just, that retaliation shall be made near to the seat of their government from whence those orders emanated."

Cockburn couldn't have agreed more. He used flattery to win over his new boss. "Allow me in the first instance to offer you my congratulations on your appointment to this command," he responded.

One question worried him, though. Would he get to join in the fun? Did the admiralty intend to relieve him of his post, as they had done to Warren? Fretting about the very real possibility, he picked up his pen and asked Cochrane. Did the admiralty intend to give him leave to visit his family? Or was he to stay and serve? He promised to maintain "all your views and wishes so long as I continue on this station." Though he wanted to stay, Warren's removal worried him.

"But the conduct of the admiralty towards me, inclines me rather to think that they are not very anxious I should remain here." Then Cockburn used a face-saving technique by saying, "and induces me to take the liberty of asking you direct whether they have not empowered you to make arrangements for me to return home in the event of my wishing it?"

Another question, even more critical to the cause, surfaced in his mind. Where would he get more men to accomplish their ambitious plans? The answer would soon take everyone, both the British and the Americans, by surprise.

========

National and local news in the spring of 1814 stalled Joshua Barney's plans to build a fleet of barges to protect the Chesapeake Bay. Solomon Frazier, his lieutenant tasked with recruiting men and boats for what was nicknamed the mosquito fleet, gave him a discouraging report, which Barney conveyed to Secretary Jones.

"I have just heard from Mr. Frazier, he complains that men cannot be procured on the Eastern shore for that both parties discourage enlistments."

What was the reason for weak recruiting? Local party politics were interfering: "Each wishing to keep the men, for the next elections, as they are so equally divided, that the loss of a few votes would throw the balance into the hands of the other party."

Barney did his best by assuring leaders of small Maryland towns that their men would be available to vote in the upcoming local October elections. Local politics were not the only pests, however. National politics also plagued him and stalled his recruiting efforts. As Barney said, "We were doing very well in procuring men, until the news of raising the embargo arrived."

Deciding that the plan wasn't working, Madison had asked Congress to repeal a recent trade embargo. Little did they know that the embargo had negatively affected the British military's ability to acquire rope, cotton, and other supplies. Admiral Warren in Bermuda had secretly called the embargo "severe" in a letter to a captain tasked with blockading the U.S. coast: "I suppose whatever supplies you now procure as the embargo is so severe must be by force."

As Barney absorbed the news of Congress lifting the latest embargo, he realized that sailors now preferred making money over serving their country in his fleet. Yet, he had recruited some thirty men to aid him.

Two weeks later, Barney tapped additional political power to help his efforts. "I enclose you the copy of a letter from Governor Wright to the secretary at war respecting the sea fencibles," he explained to Navy Secretary Jones of the Maryland governor's efforts asking the War Department for help. "I do not know what effect it will have, but I wish to leave no stone unturned to obtain men; after this effort I am done, and the blame will lay on the right person."

He seemed skeptical that Armstrong would respond favorably. Though Barney's recruits increased—including the addition of former slave Charles Ball who had walked from Georgia to Baltimore to regain his freedom—failures by the War Department were problematic. Blame would become the name of the political game infesting not just Barney but, soon, all of those living in the swamp known as Washington City.

CHAPTER FIFTEEN

Not Your Average News Day

"There will be no peace," Armstrong boldly proclaimed. A shocked Senator King recorded their April 5, 1814, conversation into his journal.

"You have then changed your opinion which was lately favorable to the expectation of an early peace?" King challenged.

This time the pair discussed politics in Europe, where the allies of six nations were successfully pushing Napoleon and his Grande Armée back to Paris. Senator King believed that if Napoleon lost, then the British government's need to impress or take American sailors from ships and force them to fight in the Royal Navy would be gone.

Armstrong disagreed, telling King, "I have altered my opinion. I think the late and great success of the allies will indispose Britain; their terms will be too hard." He believed that Parliament wouldn't make peace with the United States even if England and the allies defeated Napoleon. He concluded that the peace talks between the U.S. and Britain scheduled to take place in Sweden would break off and "a war pulse will be excited" in Britain. His resolve of what America should do was clear: prosecute the war in the North with vigor.

"In this case we must take Canada and Nova Scotia," Armstrong declared.

"Are you not mistaken about your expected war pulse?" King replied with as much shock as anger. "What reason have you to conclude that your cabinet will not descend as G.B. [Great Britain] rises? And in case of a failure at Göteborg [Sweden], is it not probable that another mission will be dispatched to sue again for peace?"

"It cannot, or rather ought not to be expected."

Unhappy with what he was hearing, King challenged Armstrong further, hitting him in the gut with a direct salvo, one that struck Armstrong's greatest desire—military glory in Canada. He also struck at Armstrong's greatest insecurity—his distrust of Virginian politicians Madison and Monroe.

"Do you believe, and if you do, are you not deceived, that you or any other man of talents from the East will be permitted to acquire the credit of conquering Canada, or of rendering any other important service to the country?" Though seeing Armstrong's temper rise, King did not give him a chance to respond.

"I do not wait for a reply, but express my own opinion that the Virginia dynasty will never allow to you an opportunity to take Canada. Peace is the order, and the object, of the day," King said. "It is to be sought for, and accepted upon the best terms which can be attained. But peace must be had upon any terms."

Armstrong's anger over the insult was so obvious that the senator abruptly ended their conversation. King wrote that he "was at no loss to interpret the feelings of the S.W. [secretary of war] and broke off the conference."

King was incredulous. Why couldn't the administration see that it needed to end the war, and end it quickly, not escalate it? Madison's imbecility continued, in his view. What to do? He decided to push his views with another member of the cabinet.

The next day King held a conversation with Secretary Monroe. As he did with Armstrong, he pressed the secretary of state on the effect of Napoleon's demise on America's war with England.

"If there be a reasonable hope of peace, why proceed immediately to fill up the army—Why invade Canada, when the status quo ante bellum will restore it, should you have taken it?" the prying senator asked. He saw no reason to go after Canada if its prewar—*antebellum*—boundaries with the United States would be restored anyway.

"If Congress remain two or three weeks in session, something important from Europe may be expected," Monroe replied, hinting that big news was coming from Paris.

Monroe explained that the president had sent instructions to Gallatin through a ship that should have arrived in Europe by now. The hope was that England would follow through on negotiating directly with America in Sweden by appointing delegates or ministers. "If ministers be immediately appointed to proceed to Göteborg, [Sweden], and evidence shows itself of the expectation of an early peace, we shall learn it. We shall know it shortly."

Secretary Monroe then shared his hopes that the news about Napoleon would soon provide a positive change for America. "Moreover dispatches from the continent may be soon expected."

"I hope that if peace be expected the evils of war may be diminished as much as possible," King replied, strongly expressing his displeasure over the administration's myopic focus on Canada.

While the senator was cordial with Monroe, he knew that this Virginian had his eye on the presidency. After all, though he hadn't received any electoral votes, Monroe had been on the ballot for president in the 1808 election. It was up to King and the Federalists to stop a southerner from winning the 1816 election. Oh how they must defeat Madison's plans, and in so doing, defeat Monroe's candidacy.

More than preventing Monroe from becoming president and trying to defeat Madison every chance he got, King hoped an armistice would soon arrive. Instead, word came of another proclamation, one designed to shake up Marylanders and Virginians up and down the coast.

Montpelier had been many things to James Madison. First and foremost, it had been his family's home for more than fifty years. Many memories filled his mind when he thought of Montpelier. This estate was the place where he had made the decision as a teenager to defy expectations for a male of his family's founding stature. Instead of attending the College of William and Mary in Williamsburg, Virginia, Madison opted for the faraway college later known as Princeton, in New Jersey.

Influenced by his tutors who had gone to school there, he paved his own path, which paid off. The ties Madison made with college men from Pennsylvania and New Jersey broadened his perspective beyond Virginia, which gave him an advantage when he was a member of the Continental Congress. Though pro-Virginia, he became pro-Union above all else.

Montpelier had also been the place he had in mind when, years earlier, Madison had worried over Spain's attempt to keep America from navigating and trading at the mouth of the Mississippi River at New Orleans. With such a grand view of the West and the mountains of the Blue Ridge at Montpelier, he knew that trade out West and along the Mississippi was vital to the financial future of Virginia and America. In fact, he had been fearful when John Jay nearly negotiated these rights away in a treaty with Spain years earlier. U.S. rights to the Mississippi prevailed then, and Madison was as firm now on the subject as Blue Ridge mountain rock.

Montpelier had also been the place where, in 1786, he had read the great works of history that led him to create the framework behind the U.S. Constitution. Here he'd studied the Netherlands, where jealousies among the provinces had led to foreign intrigue and influence. Indeed the Netherlands had recently given itself up to Napoleon. These and other similar governmental failures led Madison to conclude that a weak union of states would only lead to disaster. Hence, he favored the stronger Union outlined by the U.S. Constitution. How he hoped the United States would write a different story now, and would survive the current war as a united country.

While at Montpelier in May 1814, Madison learned of the biggest event to take place on the globe in years. Printed in newspapers around the world, the news came while he relaxed during a brief break after Congress's winter session ended. Napoleon had unconditionally abdicated his empire and gone into exile to Elba, an Italian island. Europe was at peace.

A thrilled Madison optimistically wrote Thomas Jefferson, his neighbor, of the news on May 10, 1814. "The turn of recent events in Europe, if truly represented, must sharpen the motives [of the British government] to get rid of the war with us; and their hopes by continuance of it to break down our government must now be more and more damped by occurrence now as they become known there."

Oh, how the president hoped that the British negotiators would be willing to treat for a quick peace with the American delegation.

———

Within ten days, more news arrived on the steps of Montpelier. "I am just possessed of the intelligence... of the proclamation of Cochrane addressed to the blacks," Madison replied by firing off a letter on May 20, 1814, to General Armstrong.

Admiral Cochrane had issued a proclamation on April 2, 1814, to encourage slaves to leave their masters and migrate from the United States to England. Those slaves who joined the British would have a choice of entering the king's military or being sent as free settlers to British territory in North America or the West Indies.

Madison wasn't shocked at the news. He had seen the tactic during the American Revolution. Back then the strategy led to both sides creating black corps of fighters. What did surprise him was the timing. If the British intended to treat for peace, as they had signaled and surely would because Napoleon was in exile, why were they now encouraging slaves to join the British and fight against their previous masters?

"They admonish us to be prepared for the worst, the enemy may be able to effect against us," a highly concerned Madison warned Armstrong.

The proclamation seemed "to indicate the most inveterate spirit against the Southern States...within reach of vindictive enterprise."

Madison also wasn't shocked at the tactic because he had proposed a similar measure years earlier during the Revolution. "Would it not be to depend as well to liberate and make soldiers of the blacks themselves as to make them instruments for enlisting white soldiers? It would certainly be more consonant to the principles of liberty which ought never be lost sight of in a contest for liberty."

Not only that, but in 1785 Madison had also supported Jefferson's bill in the Virginia Assembly to follow the example of Pennsylvania and gradually abolish slavery. He had written a relative that he wished "to depend as little as possible on the labor of slaves." While living in Pennsylvania in the 1780s, he had sold his favored slave Billy because he knew it would lead to his freedom within seven years. If he took him back to Virginia, he would be a slave forever. Yet, despite these acts, he had been unable to overcome the system of slavery and the dependence Montpelier had on it.

Now the issue factored into the schemes of the British military in the War of 1812. Did they really want peace? Was their goal to sever America from within? Did they want to turn southerners and northerners against each other so New England would secede and rejoin Britain? He knew the slave proclamation had been issued a few days before Napoleon's abdication and weeks before the news arrived in America. Perhaps the misplaced timing led to a mistake by the British signaling more war instead of peace.

Nonetheless, Madison couldn't take any chances. He conveyed to Armstrong his most ominous concern about the British military's intended target: "among those the seat of government cannot fail to be a favorite one."

Though a scholarly man without significant military experience who had served only briefly in a local militia, Madison knew that capturing a capital city fit within the framework of war. He also knew that Armstrong had ignored requests in 1813 by town leaders, such as John Van Ness, to bolster military defenses along the Potomac south of Washington City.

Surely this proclamation was all the proof that Armstrong now needed to get moving on fortifying the nation's capital as a precaution against invasion. Surely. The question was simple. Did Armstrong see it the same way? Deferring to his cabinet member's judgment, honor, and patriotism, Madison assumed he did.

Joseph Gales was literally an average Joe. Though born in Britain, by 1813 this twenty-seven-year-old was living the American dream in Washington City, where he operated his own newspaper business, the *National Intelligencer*. Gales had learned the trade from his father, who brought Joseph and his family to North Carolina after fleeing Britain.

Gales came to Washington City in 1807 and began reporting on Congress for the *National Intelligencer*. Three years later he bought the newspaper and managed it with his tall, handsome brother-in-law, William Seaton. Gales was a short chubby cheeked man, but what he lacked in good looks he overcame with manners, warmth, and insight. He often drew people to him by taking an interest in them and asking intelligent questions.

There was an exception, a limit to his affability. Gales had often raised the ire of Admiral Cockburn, who disdainfully called him "Dear Josey." Cockburn didn't understand the concept of freedom of the press. The English crown controlled newspapers in London. Napoleon had controlled newspapers in Paris. How could America be any different?

Gales lived that difference. Though a friend of the Jefferson administration and favorable to Madison's, Gales didn't run an official state or government paper. The thought was repulsive. After all, his father had fled Britain because he wasn't free to criticize authority.

Over the years, Gales had freely published his opinion and those of others. May 1814 was no different, as he wrote in this analysis: "What, though the enemy has taken possession of some islands in the Chesapeake? It is absurd to suppose that government can fortify every point, island, or nook along an extensive coast." He concluded that "the neighboring militia must protect them; and though their officers are principally federalists, yet they are not of the Boston stamp."

Some editors in the Baltimore press evoked a similar sentiment and determination: "We have powder and ball, muskets and prepared ammunition enough to kill all the Englishmen in or coming to America. Madison's capital may be threatened, or the destruction of Baltimore talked of, but we guess they will not be burnt at present."

Gales proclaimed: "As to his near approach to the capital, which has been hinted at, we have no idea of his attempting to reach this vicinity; and if he does, we have no doubt he will meet such a reception as he did at Craney Island. The enemy knows better what he is about than to trust himself abreast or on this side of Fort Washington."

Many hoped that Gales was right.

━━━━━━━

Pesky politics also continued to infect Barney as he sought to build his fleet. He reported to Secretary Jones from St. Leonard's Creek. "Yesterday a gentleman of this county by the name of Parren (a violent Federalist) who lives at the mouth of the creek, came up, and said that himself and [a] brother had been taken and carried on board Commodore Barrie's ship."

Parren's politics were obviously pro-British. He may have been on Cockburn's spy payroll. His mission was to inform Barney and the local inhabitants of the British admiral's demands, which were straight from Cockburn's Havre de Grace playbook: "That if they remained at home quietly they should not be molested, but if on landing he found their houses deserted he would burn them all."

Barney was furious because Parren had the audacity to brag that he planned to return to the enemy ship after leaving Barney. What did the commodore do? He had the traitor arrested.

Barney also learned from Parren that several other Americans had voluntarily boarded enemy ships. Nothing infuriated him more than this lack of patriotism goaded by a payoff for pocketbooks.

The commodore perceived that he was outnumbered nearly two to one, with the British having 800 to 900 men and Barney having only 450. Once again the problem was politics. Most of the officers of the local militia were Federalists who were unwilling to help Madison's Republican war.

"The militia have all been discharged, except one company, the fact is, their officers (mostly feds.) did not encourage their men to act, and such conduct only encouraged the enemy to commit depredations along the river."

A few days later, Barney reported to Jones of another incident. "The enemy has come up the creek once or twice after dark, threw a few rockets and shot, and retired, but with no effect."

How Barney needed help! Without it, would he ever break through the stalemate and accomplish his mission to be a shield for the Chesapeake? Would he have to abandon his barges and make a land trek to safety? How he hoped not. If only reinforcements would come!

Drat those American papers. Was it true? Had Cochrane taken his eye off the target? Was he now aiming for New Hampshire instead of Washington City? Cockburn had to do something.

"The American papers tell me you have determined in the first instance to attack Portsmouth and they add that they are quite prepared to receive you there, I doubt their being so anywhere," Cockburn wrote to Cochrane. He lobbied his cause. "I am sure they are not equal to defend themselves against a determined attack in any part of this neighborhood."

Bolstering his argument, Cockburn cited Madison's lack of finances and America's weak militia system, saying, "and the government not being able to obtain money to go on with is not likely to improve their means of resistance."

He had at least one good reason to smile. The admiralty wanted him to stay in the Chesapeake, as he added in a postscript. "I am rather surprised at learning by your letter that my ideas were erroneous respecting your having brought permission from the admiralty for my return to England."

Cockburn was more than happy to stay. Maybe, just maybe, with a little more convincing, he could finally seize the best treasure of all: Washington City.

CHAPTER SIXTEEN

Superabundant Force

The summer of 1814 would bring the biggest and worst news ever to hit the newspapers of Washington City and every city in America.

Before that news arrived, however, General John Van Ness decided that the time was right to make a bold move. He approached General Armstrong and again pressed him on the issue of defending Washington City. Constructing a battery to protect the Potomac south of Washington was essential, as he conveyed. But he believed they needed more. Who knows where Cockburn would send his raiders next?

Why not set up "the convenience and importance of a central camp, intermediate between Baltimore, Annapolis, Washington, Alexandria, Georgetown, and the neighboring towns and country?" Van Ness asked.

He waited for a reply. Once again Armstrong offered assurances, though orally, not in writing. Despite his words, his tone was as indifferent and dismissive as ever.

Van Ness left the war secretary more frustrated and angry than when he'd come. He knew he wasn't alone. He had heard several civic leaders, local business people, and militia members express similar sentiments. Many were losing confidence in Secretary Armstrong. Why didn't he do more? Was Canadian glory to blame? Was Armstrong so focused on the Canadian campaign that he failed to see what was right in front of him? So it seemed.

A recent example had rankled Van Ness. Several weeks earlier, in April, Colonel Clinch had arrived in Washington with regular troops. Thrilled to see members of the U.S. military on the town's green, Van Ness had hoped that they would stay. They didn't. Instead, Armstrong sent them to the northern front.

Why was the war secretary failing to bolster Washington City's defenses? Was the problem something deep, such as a bias against the South? Was Armstrong too much of a New Yorker to believe that the British would care much for a fledgling southern city, no matter that it was the nation's capital? Had he never fully accepted the relocation of the capital from New York to Philadelphia and now here?

As Van Ness battled Armstrong's indifferent attitude, he had one hope. Local bankers had recently approached the war secretary with a plan. They would pool their money and offer the U.S. government a loan of $200,000 to use for building defenses for Washington. Armstrong had agreed. Knowing the money was coming, surely this would spur the War Department to act decisively to fortify Washington City. Surely.

But as Van Ness thought about it, he wondered if he should try someone else. Perhaps he should also approach Monroe, who had been warm to him on previous occasions when the two had discussed the topic. A Revolutionary War veteran and a Virginian, Monroe seemed to better understand. Too bad he wasn't war secretary instead of Armstrong.

Having returned from a brief break at Montpelier, Madison knew it was time to get down to the business of the war as summer began in

1814. He held many cabinet meetings in the East Room, the room adjacent to his office. When John and Abigail Adams had moved into the White House in 1800, they had found this room unfinished and in need of plastering. Abigail also discovered that the house lacked a fenced-in area necessary for drying laundry. Hence, she had used this room to hang the president's underwear and conceal it from public view.

Jefferson then divided the room, with part of it for storage and the other part serving as the sleeping quarters of Meriwether Lewis, the man whom he groomed to lead the first U.S. Western expedition. When Madison took over the White House, he had the East Room split into two spaces, with a space for Edward Coles's sleeping quarters and the other as a cabinet room. His cabinet deliberated among wallpapered, plastered walls with a window that overlooked the expansive South Lawn.

Within this comfortable setting and a great view, their first meeting that summer took place on June 7, where they debated several strategies for the summer campaign in Canada. As usual, the challenge of creating an effective supply line made plans as difficult as they were costly.

Remembering the success of Commander Perry, who had built several vessels the previous summer, they decided to order the construction of fourteen to fifteen new armed ships to patrol the St. Lawrence River. They hoped an advance toward Montreal would force the British to abandon Lake Champlain.

The cabinet gatherings continued. On June 23 and June 24, Madison held his most important meeting since launching the war, on the topic of impressment. Though Armstrong had told King months earlier that Madison had given up everything in the instructions he'd given to his peace commissioners, it wasn't true.

While Madison didn't need the vote or consent of his cabinet to draft new instructions for peace to his commissioners—who were now going to meet in Ghent, Belgium, instead of Sweden—and could have taken charge on his own, he deferred to their judgment on this issue. Was it time to remove impressment from the demands for peace with the British? This led to a robust debate of several observations and questions.

Because the British no longer needed men to fight Napoleon, would they now continue impressing U.S. sailors? If Madison took the issue off the table as a condition for peace, would their commissioners have a greater chance of getting a peace treaty? Would the American people understand his choice?

The president put forth the question to his cabinet. "Shall a treaty of peace, silent on the subject of impressment be authorized?"

His cabinet struck down the idea in a three-to-two vote, with Secretary of State James Monroe, Attorney General Richard Rush, and Treasury Secretary George Campbell voting no and General Armstrong and Navy Secretary Jones voting aye.

Little did they know that Albert Gallatin's vote, far away in Europe, would soon count more than any other.

━━━━━━━

Because he first went to sea as a child and commanded his first boat as a teen, Joshua Barney had a bit in common with Cockburn, whose naval career began in a similar fashion. But that's where their commonalities ended. Barney, a native of Maryland, had commanded privateers during the American Revolution for the Continental Navy.

He had even served in the French Navy and received a snuffbox from Napoleon with allegorical images of flags. By 1802 he had returned to America as a commodore. With a flair for wearing long hair and bearing a dashing demeanor, he also carried with him some charm.

As the summer of 1814 progressed, Barney knew that his flying squadron had accomplished at least one goal: distracting the enemy. The first distraction had come on June 1 at the Patuxent River's Cedar Point. There Barney had played hide and seek with British Captain Barrie's boats.

Just the day before, Cockburn had "received intelligence that Commodore Barney has again come down with his flotilla to the neighborhood of the Potomac." Cockburn had responded by sending an auxiliary unit to Barrie, whose force included the seventy-four-gun *St. Lawrence* and other, smaller ships.

Barney's force was by no means equal, but it was respectable none-theless. By this time he had twenty-five vessels and 450 men. When Barrie spotted Barney's fleet, he chased them. Soon Barney saw that the *St. Lawrence* had grounded because of its size. Ever the dashing captain, he took advantage and chased Barrie's smaller boats.

The winds varied throughout the day, favoring both sides at alternating times. Rain soon poured and troubled both. Yet, as Barney's boats closed in, he discovered that the British had another sizable armed ship, the British *Dragon*, which featured seventy-four guns. Quickly realizing that he was no match, Barney turned his squadron into the Patuxent River between Drum Point and Cedar Point. Though firing at the British boats that followed him, he was too far away to successfully hit them.

Known as the Battle of Cedar Point, this contest was a draw and a test for both sides. Barney, however, made an astute observation, which he shared with Secretary Jones. Their rockets "will be their mode of warfare against the flotilla."

What would happen next? Could he keep up the game of cat and mouse, of swordfish to Cockburn's hammerhead shark? Would that at least distract Cockburn from whatever he had planned? Playing prey to Cockburn's jaws wasn't the scenario Barney longed for, but it was a plan B, an alternative that would help the cause.

━━━━━━

With Napoleon out of power, King was convinced that England would make a quick peace with America. Because the U.S. Senate was out of session, King couldn't discuss the issue with his fellow senators in person. Hence, he wrote letters from his home on Long Island. He chose to share his view that the war would end soon in a letter to Senator Gore. He also complained about the extreme factions who disagreed with them. "It is manifest that the democratic party are disappointed, and con-founded, by the overthrow of Bonaparte—they affect to be, and perhaps are, alarmed at the politics of England, and assert that she will be indis-posed to peace with us."

Trusting Parliament more than Madison's ability, King explained why he thought that peace with Britain was coming quickly. Yet, he feared that the president would ruin a peace treaty by tying the hands of his commissioners through overly restrictive instructions and demands. As he explained, "I am of a different opinion, and still believe that we shall have peace, provided that the envoys are not limited in their powers."

His confidence in Britain was based on Parliament's economic motives. "I think England, as well as the maritime allies, must desire peace between America and England—the market of the U.S. is of more value to England than that of all Europe."

England's need for raw goods, such as cotton supplied by American farmers, was not the only factor. All of Europe needed U.S. trade to recover from the Napoleonic wars. "The continent is impoverished and cannot pay for the supplies England could furnish."

With Napoleon out of power, other countries should jump at the chance to buy goods from America. "Spain, Portugal, France, Holland, Russia and perhaps others will want our ships and services in resuming their trade, into which, at least temporarily, we should immediately enter, were we not involved in a foolish and unprofitable war."

Though King doubted Madison and his cabinet's competence, he, too, didn't want peace on just any terms. "I mean peace consistent with the just rights of the country. I cannot desire peace on other terms."

Tapping his diplomatic and legal expertise, King figured out what those terms should be. "We must not relinquish territory (the Louisiana boundary is an open question), we must not yield any maritime rights appertaining to the sovereignty; we must therefore retain the right to use the ocean for navigation and fishery."

He also recognized that it shouldn't require much time to figure out if true peace was obtainable, as he wrote to Senator Gore. "A long time cannot be wanted to ascertain whether a peace can be made—so that the result will, in all probability be known here before October."

King believed that continuing the war was futile and that America should pull back its plans against Canada. "The president must now be convinced that he can gain nothing by prosecuting the war; his tone may continue to be lofty, but his terms will lower."

Finances once again surfaced in King's assessment. "Not only can nothing be gained by prosecuting the war, but the present administration cannot go on with it if they would, because they have omitted to lay taxes, and will be unable to make loans."

―――――――――

Meanwhile Cockburn's desire to hit Washington received a boost. The news came from one of his most enthusiastic and reliable officers, Captain Barrie. "I pushed on towards Marlborough, where I understood there were several stores of tobacco and other property," Barrie began in his latest letter to Cockburn, "and as Marlborough is near the seat of government, I thought an attack on this town would be a sad annoyance to the enemy."

Instead of fighting, the militia and inhabitants of Marlborough fled to the woods. From Barrie's perspective, seizing Marlborough was as easy as fishing for flounder in the Chesapeake: "And we were allowed to take quiet possession of a town admirably situated for defense, here we passed the night without molestation though only eighteen miles from Washington."

The admiral couldn't have been more delighted to read Barrie's report. If Marlborough was that easy to capture, once enough reinforcements arrived, nothing could stop them from capturing the ultimate prize.

Within days, Cockburn picked up his pen and wrote to Admiral Cochrane. "I am decidedly of opinion that about the seat of government and in the upper parts of the Chesapeake is where your operations may be commenced to most effect."

He added with great assurance: "But the country is in general in a horrible state. It only requires a little firm and steady conduct to have it completely at our mercy."

Then he noted his pleasure with his newest recruits. These runaway slaves, about 300, continued to train at Tangier Island. After organizing them into different tasks and conducting drills, Cockburn's views had improved. "They have induced me to alter the bad opinion I had of the whole of their race and I now really believe these we are training, will neither show want of zeal or courage when employed by us in attacking their old masters."

Though they'd given the runaway slaves red uniforms in hopes that the brilliant jackets would attract more to join them, Cockburn knew their numbers weren't strong enough. Hence he put in a plug for what he longed for more than anything: regular British soldiers. "And [I] can truly assure you that every man has done his best, had I had more force at my disposal more should have been done."

He had one major military obstacle, Barney. "But should you have any hopes of an army arriving, that could attack their capital, it would be very necessary that Barney's flotilla should be pent up the creek."

——

At this time, Barney was up a creek. Literally. His fleet was stuck in St. Leonard's Creek, hemmed in by the British. He'd seen the futility of trying to win by attacking the British. "This kind of warfare is much against us, as they can reach us, when we cannot reach them, and when we pursue them, their light boats fly before us."

Worse, his provisions would last only twelve days. But when the British ship *Narcissus* replaced another ship in their blockade, Barney gained an opportunity for learning intelligence.

"Deserters, of whom I have had six from the *Narcissus* say they [the British] will wait for troops from Bermuda, but little dependence can be placed in such information, at all events they have kept pretty well out of this creek for some days past," Barney wrote to Jones.

While Cockburn acquired runaway slaves for soldiers, Barney acquired British deserters. Ironically, both ran from tyranny to freedom. British deserters often gave Barney what he most needed: intelligence.

From these departed Englishmen, he had learned that Cockburn's captains continued to raid towns along the river, which was the very reason Barney had created his flying squadron in the first place. Questions arose. Wasn't he forcing the British to use valuable resources to blockade him? And yet, wasn't he also failing his countrymen by not preventing the British raids? He fretted over the likelihood.

Would he ever break through the stalemate and accomplish his mission to be a shield for the Chesapeake? With more men, maybe. While Barney put his hopes in reinforcements for getting him out of the creek, Jones sent him a most sobering letter. He wrote, "The force of the enemy present and accumulating in and near the Patuxent, either for the real or ostensible purpose of destroying or blockading the flotilla under your command, calls for a deliberate view of the motive and object of the enemy."

Jones doubted that the British truly cared about the flotilla. What if their attention on it was nothing more than a ruse, a distraction from a planned attack? He posed the possibility this way in his letter to Barney: "Such a force will either accomplish his object, if the destruction of the flotilla be in reality the object."

Jones concluded that Barney's flotilla wasn't that important to Cockburn. "Hence I believe he has other and greater designs."

———

"A well-organized and large army is at once liberated from any European employment, and ready, together with a superabundant naval force to act immediately against us," Albert Gallatin had written from his post in London.

He was correct. After the fall of Napoleon, instead of sending many of its troops home to their families, the British government decided to send thousands of them to America.

No sooner had Madison's cabinet voted against taking impressment off the table as instructions for the peace commissioners than Secretary of State Monroe received this alarming information from Gallatin.

Understanding its significance as a game changer, he shared it with Madison.

The news hit the president in the gut. Gallatin's assessment was quite the opposite of what he'd shared with Jefferson a few weeks earlier. Instead of moving toward a swift peace with America following Napoleon's demise, the British were bolstering their troops in North America.

Superabundant was the key word, as Gallatin conveyed: "And they will also turn against us as much of their superabundant naval forces as they may think adequate to any object they have in view."

Madison reviewed the letter. Gallatin's fears for his country were obvious. "How ill-prepared we are to meet it (it is well known); but, above all, our own divisions and the hostile attitude of the Eastern states give room to apprehend that a continuance of the war might prove vitally fatal to the United States," the former Treasury secretary wrote.

Many questions emerged, but one stood out. What was the end game for the British? Gallatin doubted that the British intended to conquer all of America, only part of it.

Madison understood Gallatin's words. The British were strategizing that Federalists in New England would break off and rejoin England or that a Federalist would become president in 1816. Revenge was a motive, though not fully revenge for the American Revolution but revenge for having the audacity to declare war against England in 1812 in the first place. Gallatin put it this way: "In the intoxication of an unexpected success, which they ascribe to themselves, the English people eagerly with that their pride may be fully gratified by what they call the 'punishment of America.'"

He continued, "To use their own language they mean to inflict on America a chastisement that will teach her that war is not to be declared on Great Britain with impunity." The British authorities had used newspapers, which they controlled, as propaganda to deceive the English people. "They do not suspect that we had any just cause of war, and ascribe it solely to a premeditated concert with Bonaparte at a time when we thought him triumphant and their cause desperate."

The British government now had thousands of battle-hardened soldiers and sailors at its disposal. Why send them home to their families when they could use them for the good of Britain? What could be better than to use their experience and cause great mischief and harm to the United States? As Gallatin explained, "The numerous English forces in France, Italy, Holland, and Portugal ready for immediate service, and for which there is no further employment in Europe, afford to this government the means of sending both to Canada and to the United States a very formidable army, which we are not prepared to meet with any regular, well-organized force."

Gallatin's words sobered Madison more than any other correspondence he'd received that summer. If he was correct, redcoats by the thousands could target American cities. The numbers were against them. In August of 1813, the British had 75,000 soldiers serving in Europe outside of the British Isles and Ireland. In contrast, they had fewer than 20,000 soldiers scattered in North America, from Bermuda to Nova Scotia. They now had the capacity to increase the number of their soldiers in North America to 40,000, double its previous number.

Madison's optimism was diminished. After defeating Napoleon, the English were intoxicated by success, puffed up and prideful about their capabilities. They deeply desired to fully gratify that pride by punishing America.

What was the president to do with such threatening news? A day after receiving Gallatin's dispatches, on June 27, Madison called the cabinet to another meeting. Within the plastered walls of the East Room, they voted once more on whether to strike impressment as a condition for peace. The measure was now unanimous, "agreed to by Monroe, Campbell, Armstrong and Jones; Rush being absent."

With this vote, Madison had new instructions to send to his peace commissioners. They could abandon impressment as a requirement for peace. Oh, how he needed peace. Now he was facing the worst problem of his administration: a possible invasion by the British somewhere on the East Coast. There was more he needed to do. Much more. But first he needed some time to think.

======

While Madison contemplated Gallatin's ominous news, Barney was so happy that he could hardly wait to share the news with Navy Secretary Jones. Colonel Wadsworth had come! Reinforcements had saved them from the enemy blockade!

"This morning at 4 AM, a combined attack of the artillery, marine corps, and flotilla, was made upon the enemy's two frigates at the mouth of the creek," Barney wrote to Jones on Sunday morning, June 26.

Colonel Decius Wadsworth of the U.S. Army created a battery on a high bluff that overlooked the Patuxent River to the right and St. Leonard's Creek to the left. This commanding position stunned Captain Brown, who had replaced Barrie as leader of the British blockade.

"After two hours engagement, they got under way and made sail down the river," Barney explained of Brown's decision to move his ships.

Brown figured that Barney would chase him to Point Patience. Instead, Barney and his men rowed away. "I am moving up the Patuxent," the commodore wrote to Jones of his decision to head toward Benedict, Maryland.

Though six of Barney's men were killed and four wounded, the rest had escaped. After swiftly signing his name, Barney handed his message to a militia member, who hurried to Washington City and delivered the good news to Jones.

Barney, however, wasn't the only commander to receive reinforcements.

CHAPTER SEVENTEEN

Twenty Thousand Reinforcements

"**L**ord Hill and 15,000 men are said to be coming out from Bordeaux and several regiments from England and Ireland," Admiral Cockburn read with excitement in a letter from Cochrane, dated July 1, 1814, "by the account I have received from England that a considerable body of troops are under orders for this country."

Cochrane believed that the combination of regular British soldiers and slave recruits seeking revenge on their masters was enough to conquer the Americans.

Cockburn couldn't have been happier with Cochrane's news. After all, fifteen to twenty thousand reinforcements were enough to conquer several cities, much less Washington City's unprotected hamlet of 8,000.

While he waited for reinforcements, Cockburn deployed the 900 marines and a company of Royal Marine artillery that Cochrane had sent him. He formed two squadrons, one led by Captain Barrie to command attacks along the Potomac and the other by Captain Joseph Nourse to chart the Patuxent River and raid towns along its banks. Then he gave instructions.

"Barney had got above Benedict and that it was useless to endeavor to follow him up this river affording him such facility of retreat to so great a distance from our shipping," Cockburn wrote to Captain Barrie, noting that Barney was hemmed in again, this time at the head of the Patuxent River in Maryland.

In the meantime, Cockburn would play pirate and visit as many points as he could to distract the enemy. Divert he did. Without opposition his men burned courthouses and homes and seized vast quantities of tobacco in more than fifteen towns.

In a letter to Barrie, he also took a jab at the president: "Mr. Madison must certainly be either in confident expectation of immediate peace, or preparing to abdicate the chair."

Peace, yes. Abdication? Hardly.

———

After receiving Gallatin's warning, Madison took a few days to think. Then he took action. It was time to assert his authority.

He held another cabinet meeting. The date was July 1. This time Washington City was the focus, not Canada. This scholarly president asked for an assessment of the number of forces available to defend the nation's capital. Drawing from cavalry units, infantry, marines, artillery, and Barney's flotilla, Armstrong dutifully reported that the estimated number of defenders was 3,500.

Worried that the British could send three times as many men, Madison gave the order for "10,000 militia to be designated and held in readiness. 10,000 Arms and camp equipage to be brought forward for use."

His cabinet chose sides. Rush, Campbell, and Monroe agreed with Madison, who also appointed General William Winder as commander of the new military district in Washington. Taken as a prisoner of war in Canada in June 1813, Winder had recently returned to America after a prisoner exchange. He was also the nephew of Levin Winder, the

Federalist governor of Maryland. The Republican Madison needed the political alliance that Winder's Federalist family connections brought.

Whether Armstrong asserted his weight in the cabinet by expressing his displeasure that day is not known. Did he cast a look of contempt or keep his reserve in check?

Madison likely detected something in Armstrong's demeanor, because he didn't stop there. The next day, July 2, he took another step to strengthen compliance with his orders. As if giving instructions to a student, he sent Armstrong a memorandum. "The secretary of war will digest and report to the president corresponding precautionary means of defense" for Washington City and "the other more important and exposed places along the Atlantic frontier; particularly Boston, New York, Wilmington, Norfolk, Charleston, Savannah, and New Orleans."

He also ordered Armstrong to distribute and report on "a circular communication to the governors of the several states" to determine "adequate portions of their militia." He wanted "them in the best readiness for actual service in cases of emergency."

Was the president's accountability of Armstrong robust? Yes. Would it work? Possibly. One thing was certain. Madison's prior deference to his advisors was giving way to assertive executive decision-making.

Van Ness was also highly concerned about the news from Europe. Armstrong had given him some false hope the previous month when he called up the district militia at sightings of the enemy along the Potomac. No sooner had the war secretary called up the militia than he dismissed them, a measure Van Ness strongly opposed. Much good could come of keeping them on duty twenty-four hours a day, seven days a week in a rotating system. Thinking the idea too costly, Armstrong sent them home instead.

After hearing rumors about the cabinet's decision to create a new military district, Van Ness took his concerns to Monroe. Was it "the intention of the government to abandon and sacrifice the district or not?"

Before Monroe could fully answer, Van Ness added, "If it were so, it would be well for us, at least, to know it."

As far as Monroe was concerned, "Every inch of ground about it [the city] was determined to be contested, and the last drop of blood to be spilt in its defense." Monroe, who held the rank of colonel, continued, "It was decided...to form a camp of regular troops, say between 2- and 3,000, at a central position."

Van Ness couldn't have been happier. This was the plan he had put forward many times to Armstrong, and also, in limited opportunities, to the president. He believed that "together with the local troops, [they] would constitute an adequate defense for the surrounding points, to either of which they might be promptly and conveniently drawn."

How Van Ness hoped these men would come soon! As much as he loved the militia, they needed the discipline and experience of a troop of regular U.S. soldiers.

<hr>

Though Armstrong felt that those who wanted the federal government to build batteries and other fortifications below Fort Washington near Alexandria on the Potomac had good intentions, he also thought they were misplaced. He believed that "a small work would be unavailing, and that, to erect one of sufficient size and strength, was impracticable, for want of money."

No matter how much money Van Ness and bankers offered to pay from their own pockets, they just didn't understand. Where they took pride in the crude capital city, Armstrong saw a rustic town of little value.

He later reflected: "To put Washington...by means of fortifications, would, from physical causes, among which is the remoteness from each other of the several points to be defended, have exhausted the treasury."

Now Madison had joined their chorus. The president had the ineptitude to choose General Winder, who was younger than many of the militia he would command, for the leader of a new military district in

Washington. Armstrong was reluctant to spend money by calling up the militia to defend the district. Wasn't Washington relatively safe because it wasn't a military post or a military objective of great importance?

Besides, as Armstrong saw it, locals and their knife-tipped muskets would be sufficient defense. He wrote, "Bayonets are known to form the most efficient barriers; and that's there was no reason, in this case, to doubt beforehand the willingness of the country to defend it."

Strategy topped Armstrong's mind as he read General Winder's latest letter, dated July 9. Armstrong had agreed to call up the local militia to comply with the president's order. But now Winder, like Van Ness, had the expensive idea to call them up for large blocks of time. Winder thought that the militia "should be called out for one, two or three months."

Armstrong disagreed. He believed "that the most advantageous mode of using the militia was upon the spur of the occasion, and bring them to fight as soon as called out." After all, it was costly to call up the militia and fruitless to do so too soon.

Now Winder recommended that 4,000 men be placed around the regions. "Should Washington, Baltimore, or Annapolis, be their object, what possible chance will there be collecting a force, after the arrival of the enemy, to interpose between them in either of those places?" Winder asked.

He concluded that sufficient numbers of militia "could not be warned and run together, even as a disorderly crowd, without arms, ammunition, or organization, before the enemy would have already given his blow."

What to do? Armstrong had Madison's approval of this notion, of calling up the militia only as needed. He knew that the president had written the governor of Virginia as recently as June to explain that the task was to discover the objectives of the enemy, then apply resources and militia accordingly.

Armstrong wrote Winder on July 12. He instructed him to call for militia only "in case of actual or minutes to invasion of the district." He wanted to avoid unnecessary calls. The number of militia should correlate to the emergency—"her proportion the call to the exigency."

By July 17, 1814, Cockburn had concluded that "it is quite impossible for any country to be in a more unfit state for war than this now is."

While aboard the *Albion* off Jerome's Point in the Patuxent River, which ran through Maryland from the Chesapeake Bay, he boasted to Cochrane about the region's demise. "I can only say the whole of the country around here (excepting a few of the towns most exposed like Norfolk etcetera) is in as defenseless or indeed in a more defenseless state than it was at the commencement of the war."

He added boldly: "I have no hesitation in saying they have not a place on the seaboard which can hold out any length of time against the force I understand you expect."

Cockburn was ready for the arrival of 20,000 reinforcements. He had mapped a plan in expectation. From the scouting of his captains, he was confident that they could find good quarters in Benedict, Maryland, near the river's mouth, and take advantage of the rich countryside for obtaining supplies and horses. He believed these "advantages might certainly now be obtained without meeting with the slightest opposition or requiring any sacrifice from us whatever."

The best advantage was Benedict's location and close proximity to Washington, a mere forty-five miles away, as he understood it. A fine high road connected them. Cockburn's eye was squarely focused on the seat of government as the first great objective, as he confidently boasted: "I therefore most firmly believe that within forty-eight hours after the arrival in the Patuxent of such a force as you expect, the city of Washington might be possessed without difficulty or opposition of any kind."

The admiral believed that possessing a capital city was "always so great a blow to the government of a country as well on account of the resources, as of the documents and records the invading army is almost sure to obtain thereby."

James Madison by Gilbert Stuart, c. 1821. *Courtesy the National Gallery of Art, Ailsa Mellon Bruce Fund*

Dolley Madison by Gilbert Stuart, 1804. *Wikimedia Commons*

Painting of Rear Admiral Sir George Cockburn with buildings in Washington burning behind him, by John James Halls, 1817. © *National Maritime Museum, Greenwich, London*

Rufus King, U.S. Senator from New York during the Thirteenth Congress, by Gilbert Stuart. *Wikimedia Commons*

Architect Benjamin Latrobe by Charles Willson Peale. *Wikimedia Commons*

John Armstrong Madison Administration by Daniel Huntington after John Vanderl (1775–1852). *Courtesy U.S. Army*

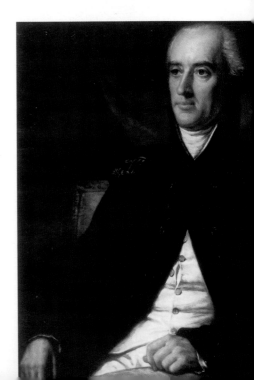

Portrait of James Monroe by Samuel Morse. *Wikimedia Commons*

Commodore Joshua Barney. *Courtesy the Library of Congress*

Author Washington Irving in 1809 by John Wesley Jarvis. *Courtesy of the University of Texas Libraries, The University of Texas at Austin*

The Splendid Mrs. Madison by artist Peter Waddell for the White House Historical Association. This shows Mrs. Madison's levees in the oval drawing room in the White House during the Madison administration. *Courtesy the White House Historical Association*

Image of the dome-less U.S. Capitol after the British military burned it in 1814. *Courtesy the Library of Congress*

Dolley Madison sacrificed most of her wardrobe, including beautiful gowns, when the White House was burned. She later wore this ivory satin gown, embroidered with butterflies, dragonflies, and phoenixes—the mythological symbol of rebirth after a fire. This gown is part of the highly popular First Ladies exhibit at the Smithsonian's National Museum of American History. *Courtesy Division of Political History, National Museum of American History, Smithsonian Institution*

Dolley and James Madison portrayed at Montpelier, the Madisons' historic home and museum in Orange, VA. *Courtesy Kenton Rowe for The Montpelier Foundation*

The Madisons lived in the Octagon House, the finest house in Washington, following the burning of the White House. *Courtesy the Octagon Museum/AIA Foundation*

James Madison signed the Treaty of Ghent that ended the War of 1812 at the Octagon in February 1814. *Courtesy the Octagon Museum/AIA Foundation*

Dolley Madison's portrait by Gilbert Stuart hangs in the Red Room, which is the site of her yellow music room. This photo is taken underneath where her portrait hangs. From this positioning, the Dolley portrait faces the George Washington portrait in the East Room. In this way, Dolley Madison still keeps her eye on Washington.

Strongly urging the adoption of his plan over the Eastern cities in discussion, he continued, "As the other places you have mentioned will be more likely to fall after the occupation of Washington, than that city would be after their capture."

He anticipated questions from Cochrane. How about Annapolis? No. "Annapolis is tolerably well fortified, and is the spot from whence the American government has always felt Washington would be threatened, if at all, it is natural therefore to suppose precautions have been taken to frustrate and impede our advance in that direction."

What about Baltimore? "Baltimore is likewise extremely difficult of access to us from sea, we cannot in ships drawing above sixteen feet, approach nearer even to the mouth of the Patapsco [River] than 7 or 8 miles and Baltimore is situated twelve miles up it, having an extensive population mostly armed."

On top of that, Fort McHenry guarded Baltimore: "And a fort for its protection about a mile advanced from it on a projecting point where the river is so narrow as to admit of people conversing across it." Capturing this brick star-shaped fortress, built by French engineers, would require time and land forces.

In Cockburn's assessment, "Both Annapolis and Baltimore are to be taken without difficulty from the land side, that is coming down upon them from the Washington road."

Yet, Cockburn knew his place and deferred to Cochrane, at least in writing: "And from the moment of your arrival in the Chesapeake, let the plan adopted be what it may."

He also recommended landing the main force in the Patuxent River and sending a bomb ship division up the Potomac to confuse the Americans as to their intended target.

Unknown to Cockburn at that moment, Cochrane wrote a letter the same day, July 17, 1814, from Bermuda. He gave his assessment to his superior, Lord Melville of the admiralty. "Boston, and New York, and I may add Philadelphia—ought not to be attacked by a force under 12,000 men."

Cochrane also wrote that Philadelphia could be reached within fifteen miles by ship, if accompanied by a land attack. Like Cockburn, he also concluded that Baltimore would be difficult to approach by water alone and required land forces.

Cochrane didn't disagree with Cockburn that Washington should be a target. He just didn't think it should be the first one. Washington should be taken after seizing a larger city. "After leaving Baltimore, the army ought to march upon Washington, Georgetown, and Alexandria," Cochrane told the admiralty.

Success depended on reinforcements. "If troops arrive soon and the point of attack is directed towards Baltimore, I have every prospect of success and Washington will be equally accessible. They may be either destroyed or laid under contribution, as the occasion may require."

Cochrane concluded that large ships couldn't easily reach Annapolis, but that Richmond in Virginia could be easily destroyed. With the right lightweight ships, North Carolina could also be attacked with ease. The next day he issued general orders to all of the British commanders in North America. "You are hereby required and directed to destroy and lay waste such towns and districts upon the coast as you may find assailable." Specifics would come soon.

━━━━━━━

Armstrong was aware of criticism coming his direction. He'd recently received a letter from William Tatham, who had created topographical maps of the region and accompanied General Winder on his visits to different Chesapeake locales.

"My belief is we cannot defend Washington, because Congress have such a mistaken notion of public economy that they will not allow us the wherewithal!" Tatham had confided in Armstrong. His fury was unmistakable. "Thus, I foresee, if they are in a condition to make a push from the enemy's fleet, as policy will direct them to do if we are not the peculiar favorites of heaven, the result will be that, we shall fail."

Tatham's most stinging jab was directed squarely at the war secretary: "And popular clamor will shelter the real pitiful cause, by an abuse of John Armstrong, for being less than on to it."

Once the United States won a large victory in Canada, Armstrong knew all of this talk of an invasion of Washington would disappear. Regret would take hold. Wasn't Winder Madison's choice? Wasn't it up to the commander in chief to follow through? Worse, wasn't it Monroe who was whispering in the president's ear? Armstrong's hands were washed of responsibility for the Chesapeake. If it was Monroe who was behind it, it was Monroe who should take any fall.

General Armstrong also received a letter from General Philip Stuart of the Maryland militia. Stuart told of a specific instance of Cockburn visiting a household on one of his raids. "He consoled the suffering individual, whom he had stripped of his property."

Stuart believed the moment provided insight that Armstrong should be aware of "by an assurance that he should not visit him again, as the reinforcement so long expected, had arrived and he should proceed on against Washington."

Armstrong didn't doubt Stuart's sincerity or accuracy of the incident. He just doubted the intent of the British. Yes, British reinforcements would come, but why would they land in the Chesapeake? Canada was much more valuable to them. Wasn't it?

If the Americans could take Kingston or Montreal, then they would have every military advantage and a strong position at the peace table. He must prosecute the war with vigor, not defend a region of little military value to the British. New York and Boston, northern cities, were more symbolic and valuable for their large populations.

If the British sent a large force to Canada, 22,000 or more, and won, wouldn't they march southward city by city? Armstrong knew that people like Van Ness considered him indifferent. He was myopic, focused on the initial strategy of the war.

Besides. Washington City was sandwiched between two southern states, including the one Armstrong most loathed, Virginia, the birthplace of three of the first four presidents.

Thus, under these circumstances, Armstrong's fate was sealed, while others would try to take out Madison.

CHAPTER EIGHTEEN

Hanging Madison

The time had come to hang James Madison. Yet, an ordinary noose of rope wouldn't do. Something else—something more feminine—was in order.

"One day a lady drove up to the President's House, loosened her long beautiful hair and standing up in her carriage, shouted that she'd be happy to let someone cut it off and hang the president," Dolley's niece later reflected of the most unusual war protestor that Washington City had yet seen.

Admiral Cockburn, it seems, was not the only one who longed to witness the president's execution. James Madison's political foes could be nearly as vicious.

"We have been in a state of perturbation here, for a long time—The depredations of the enemy approaching within 20 miles of the city,"

Dolley confessed to Hannah Nicholson Gallatin, wife of Albert Gallatin, on July 28, 1814, of her concerns over threats against James. Not having any new reports from Europe, she conveyed her worry about Washington City to her friend.

Perhaps she had in mind the woman with the long hair who'd threatened James's life when she added," And the disaffected, making incessant difficulties for the government."

Even her sunny side saw a cloud over the nation's capital. "Such a place as this has become I can not describe it."

Then she made a startling confession, especially for the wife of the former congressman who had helped secure the Potomac River as the site of the nation's seat of government.

"I wish (for my own part) we were at Philadelphia. The people here, do not deserve that I should prefer it."

Knowing that her desire to leave Washington City might surprise Hannah, Dolley shared some of the worst rumors, the ones most threatening to her and her husband: "Among other exclamations and threats they say if Mr. M. attempts to move from this house, in case of an attack, they will stop him and that he shall fall with it."

Courage isn't the absence of fear, it's the presence of determination in spite of the unknown. Dolley put it this way: "I am not the least alarmed at these things, but entirely disgusted, and determined to stay with him."

Mindful of her need to be a leader and defuse others' fearmongering, she also revealed her confidence in the military, writing that "our preparations for defense by some means or other, is constantly retarded but the small force the British have on the Bay will never venture nearer than at present 23 miles."

In that letter to Hannah, she also had a job to do on behalf of James. She had to reprimand her friend for stirring up alarm in New York. "I desired Mr. Astor [the banker] to tell you the strange story they made, about your having received a letter from Mr. G. full of alarming information, such, as his having no prospect of making peace and urging you for your personal safety to quit New York and reside in Philadelphia."

Dolley was worried that if Hannah kept talking, Gallatin's advice for her to evacuate would launch a panic in Washington as well as New York. "It had a distressing effect on our loan and threw many into consternation for awhile but we were able to contradict and soften consequences."

How did Dolley soften the consequences? Perhaps she'd called on several friends, which was part of her habits, and calmed their nerves over a cup of afternoon tea. Maybe she told them of her husband's efforts to call up 10,000 militiamen to protect the district. Whatever she said or did, she took a leadership role among women on behalf of her husband. The ladies must show a brave front, no matter what happened.

———

The president was hot at General Armstrong. As Madison had recently discovered, perhaps from the whispers of Monroe, the war secretary had failed to communicate with him on many occasions even though the law required the president's approval for specific military decisions, especially major ones.

While Madison was at Montpelier in May 1814, Armstrong had concealed information from him. He'd written unauthorized dispatches to urge General Harrison—one of America's greatest war heroes—to retire. He'd also made it look like the president was blocking a promotion for General Andrew Jackson, when, in fact, Armstrong was the one blocking it. Despite Madison's instructions, the commanding officers were sending all of their correspondence to Armstrong, and not to Madison. Without consultation, Armstrong had also reorganized army regiments, which by law was the president's responsibility.

Realizing that he was learning more about Armstrong's activities and decisions from newspapers and his cabinet members than from Armstrong himself, Madison decided to take action. As if reprimanding a wayward student, he took on the role of schoolmaster yet again and sent Armstrong another memorandum on August 13, 1814.

It began, "I find that I owe it to my own responsibility as well as to other considerations, to make some remarks on the relations in which the head of the department stands to the president, and to lay down some rules for conducting the business of the department."

First he outlined the offenses. Armstrong had consolidated regiments "without the knowledge or sanction of the president." This infuriated him because it was "subsequently made known to him otherwise than through the publication of the act in the newspapers." No leader appreciates being embarrassed in this way, especially a president.

By issuing several new rules to follow, Madison was as stern as he was methodical. The war secretary was to communicate to him on all orders relating to dismissing and transferring officers, consolidating corps, requisitioning militia, instructing officers about military operations, and changing the boundaries of military districts.

He wasn't done. Spymaster was part of the president's job. "All letters giving military intelligence or containing other matters intended or proper for the knowledge of the president will of course be immediately communicated to him."

Madison had been too trusting for too long. He'd deferred to Armstrong's judgment too often. While the war secretary was blinded by the glory that victory in Canada would bring, the president had failed to see the consequences of Armstrong's contemptuous attitude. He was trying to take charge of his rebellious subordinate, but would it be enough to make a difference before it was too late?

———

The First Amendment right to free speech is a cherished principle in our country, but it can also create dilemmas in controversial situations. For example, what if America's enemies twisted American citizens' opposition to a war as justification to oppose the U.S. government? This is precisely what happened during the War of 1812.

Senator King was a prime example of someone who opposed the war and President Madison at every chance he got. The British Parliament used the sentiments of American Federalists like King to its advantage by showing people in England that America wasn't united and, thus, that the war should continue.

In August 1814, Senator King was hotter than the summer sun beaming on his Long Island estate. He had just read reports from Europe about Albert Gallatin's letters, which accused the British government of using American Federalists' opposition to the war as justification to the English people for continuing the war instead of making peace.

King was so angry that he penned his thoughts as robustly as if preparing a rebuttal for a case before the Supreme Court. The question was a tricky one for a government based on representation, not royalty.

"The charge that opposition encourages the enemy and injures the cause, has at all times been made as an excuse for the failure and defeat of a weak administration," King wrote.

Albert Gallatin had complained in a letter that the English people didn't have all of the facts. They'd falsely believed that Madison was on Napoleon's side. The people in England had only been given one side of the story. Some government-run newspapers served as propaganda. "That such opinions should be almost universally entertained here by the great body of the people is not at all astonishing," Gallatin had fumed.

The British government had help from reliable sources: Federalists like Rufus King. Gallatin explained: "To produce such an effect, and thereby render the American war popular, the ministerial papers have had nothing more to do than to transcribe American Federal speeches and newspapers."

King responded to Gallatin's assertions by defending his right to speak against Madison's policies: "If war suppresses opposition, the public liberties could not endure."

He was angry and explained that: "Neither the administration, nor its supporters will doubt, what no one can do, that the friends of peace, including the Federalists...have as much honor and integrity and as deep a stake in the preservation of the liberties and just rights of their country, as any other description of citizens."

King believed that those who "have no confidence in the measures or the ability of the present weak and dangerous administration" were just as willing to shed blood for their country as those who supported Madison's war.

Gallatin believed that the Federalists had been too publicly vocal in their opposition. He thought their views had hurt America as a whole. If the Federalists "have not brought a majority of the American people to their side, they have at least fully succeeded here [in England], and had no difficulty in convincing all [in England]...that we had no cause of complaint, and acted only as allies of Bonaparte."

In contrast, King believed that Madison's preference for France had led to war with England. He concluded that embargos and trade restrictions had done little to inflict harm against the enemy and more to ruin America's prosperity.

King believed the conquest of Canada had backfired and preferred a different strategy, one focused on defending America's shores and waters. "If you prosecute the war.... You must abandon the project of free conquest, and preparing to defend your frontiers, cast your whole strength upon the ocean: here, if anywhere you will make your power felt."

Gallatin believed the Federalists were plotting to secede from the Union. He wrote, "A belief is said to be entertained that a continuance of the war would produce a separation of the Union, and perhaps a return of the New England States to the mother-country."

Though King opposed secession, many Federalists supported it. The contrasting views of Gallatin and King show the challenges that this new republic faced during war. For the first time, Americans wrestled with the dilemma of supporting free speech, which included opposition to the war, in the context of needing to show a united front against an enemy. This was the first generation to grapple with such questions of liberty. It was also the first to confront a terrorizing enemy on U.S. shores.

CHAPTER NINETEEN

Invasion

O n August 17, 1814, Admiral Cockburn finally received what he had been longing for: regular British reinforcements. The gift, however, came with as much shock as disappointment. Instead of twenty or thirty thousand British soldiers and marines, only about 3,700 arrived in ships on the Patuxent River. Combined with the men Cockburn already had, the English forces on America's mid-Atlantic coast totaled roughly 4,500.

What Cockburn didn't anticipate was the conservatism of the admiralty. First Secretary of the Admiralty John Crocker had sent instructions, written weeks earlier, to the general leading the soldiers aboard the ships. The orders started ideally: "Their lordships entrust to your judgment the choice of the objects on which you may employ this force."

Then came the hitch. No land invasion. Stay close to the ship, "as it will rarely if ever be necessary to advance so far into the country as to risk its power of retreating to its embarkation."

In other words, the admiralty didn't want the force to embark too far from their best means of escaping. "You will also consider yourself authorized to decline engaging in any operation which you have reason to apprehend will lead from the probability of its failure to the discredit of the troops under your command."

The commanding officer receiving the order was forty-seven-year-old Major General Robert Ross, a veteran of the Napoleonic wars. Arriving in advance of his convoy of soldiers and marines, Ross came to the Patuxent River on August 14 to meet Cockburn. Cochrane was also present. Ross and Cochrane were not in complete agreement on the target that Cockburn had in mind.

The trio huddled aboard the flagship and discussed their options. Cockburn was intent on Washington. Cochrane still wanted to go north to Rhode Island. Ross was concerned that his men were physically unfit for an attack anywhere after being confined to ship travel for so many weeks.

Cockburn put forward his best arguments, logic, and evidence. In the past twenty-five days he had conducted nine successful raids and his captains had easily landed eighteen miles from Washington at Marlborough, where the locals had fled to the woods rather than defend their town.

Despite his experience and expertise in the region, Cockburn held the inferior position among the trio. Cochrane was his commanding admiral, while Ross had the full backing of the British government to make command decisions while the force was on land.

Cockburn knew the best evidence was to show Ross in particular the lackluster American spirit.

Early the next morning, on August 15, a small unit led by Cockburn landed on shore at St. Mary's River. They easily attacked and destroyed a factory five miles from the river. No one fired a shot at them. A surprised Ross was much more open to Cockburn's plan for invading Washington as a result. They agreed to take it one target at a time. What to strike first?

That was an easy decision. Barney's flotilla was holed up at the top of the Patuxent. Success there was essential in this first act. Without it, the second act would be impossible, especially with the less-than-expected numbers of reinforcements.

On August 19 in the middle of the night, the British force disembarked at Benedict, Maryland. They included the 4th, 21st, 44th, and 85th Regiments. Each man carried sixty rounds of ball cartridge, a knapsack of clothing, a blanket, a drinking canteen, and a haversack for provisions lasting three days. Men, not beasts, hauled supplies and weapons from the ships.

Under such burdensome conditions, Cockburn gave James Scott, his aide de camp, an important job.

"Rear Admiral Cockburn had directed me to land on the left bank of the river, to obtain, if possible, a supply of horses for the officers and artillery," Scott wrote. "I came upon a farm, which the proprietor had abandoned, better stocked than usual with these useful quadrupeds, but all young, and apparently never broken in."

Knowing that acquiring horses was essential for his commander's success, Scott pressed on with steely determination. "They were as wild as deer; but, having finally succeeded in driving them into the farmyard, and thence into a stable."

Within an hour, he bragged that his marines, who had spent as much if not more time at sea as on land, had conquered the horses. "It is a singular fact, that not one of the riders was unshipped; though I firmly believe it was the first time they had ever bestrode a horse."

The British now had enough horses to do the job. Cockburn couldn't have been more pleased.

Major General Van Ness called on Armstrong again. With all that was known, the reinforced British fleet and its troops entering the Patuxent River, surely General Armstrong was ready to do more.

With great apprehension of the secretary's answer, Van Ness pressed his case. He knew they weren't prepared for an attack, and he had many questions. How will the enemy be repulsed? By land? By sea? What to do about Washington City? How should the locals prepare? What of the militia?

This banker argued with the vigor of the best of attorneys, yet it wasn't enough. A steaming Van Ness couldn't believe Armstrong's indifferent attitude. Didn't he think the enemy intended a serious blow to Washington City?

"Oh yes! by God, they would not come with such a fleet without meaning to strike somewhere," Armstrong replied.

Van Ness felt slightly relieved. At least Armstrong was acknowledging a threat.

Then the war secretary added, "But they certainly will not come here; what the devil will they do here?"

The words were as shocking as they were devastating. How could Armstrong come to that conclusion? Not even their shared ties to New York were enough to find common ground. Clearly Armstrong's preference for larger more established cities had blinded him to reality. Completely disagreeing, Van Ness made no effort to hide anger over the danger. His tone of voice, words, and body language conveyed the injustice he felt for both his neighbors and his nation.

What if the enemy intended to attack the seat of government? Capturing a capital city would place a crown in their caps.

"No, no! Baltimore is the place, sir; that is of so much more consequence!" Armstrong replied without hesitation.

Van Ness couldn't believe it. What would happen if Armstrong was wrong? He knew the answer. Catastrophe. Conflagration. Capitulation.

Twenty minutes after receiving a letter from Secretary Monroe on August 21, 1814, Madison wasted no time and sent him a reply via an express messenger. He had no time to deliberate or defer to others' assessments.

"If the force of the enemy be not greater than yet appears, and he be without cavalry, it seems extraordinary that he should venture on an enterprise this distance from his shipping," he wrote Monroe.

The day after the British disembarked at Benedict, the secretary of state went scouting. Pointing his spyglass toward the river, he estimated that the size of the enemy's force was around 6,000 men and nearly two dozen ships. Missing were enough reliable spies. He hadn't discovered anything of consequence about the enemy's intentions.

Madison weighed the balance. Would the brashness and boldness of the British emerge, or would caution guide them? More than anything, with Armstrong's leadership, he was concerned about the lack or "want of precaution on ours."

Many questions pulsed with the speed of a tropical summer downpour. What were the redcoats' orders? Who was more conservative, the British admiralty or the officers in charge of the campaign? Who was more brazen? The answer would matter most. Having watched many a horse race, the president knew which way to bet. Madison wrote Monroe and mused about the British commander's intentions. "He may be bound also to do something, and therefore to risk everything."

At this point the president had little information about what was happening elsewhere, especially along the southern portion of the Potomac River. He had no news from the northern campaign along the Canadian border in New York or the peace negotiations in Europe. If word of a peace treaty arrived soon, then the British would back off. Such was the hope. What he needed were Noah's dove and Gabriel's miracle.

―――――――

Van Ness complied immediately with his orders on August 18. Armstrong had asked him to provide Secretary Monroe with two small troops of horse "to accompany him to the Patuxent."

General Winder was also hesitating on the size of the force he wanted from the District of Columbia. Van Ness strongly advised him to call up the whole division. Winder ultimately agreed.

As Van Ness gave orders for the Washington militia to aid Winder, many questions lingered in his mind. Who was in charge? Was he still their commander or did General Winder now command the Washington militia? After all, Madison had appointed Winder to lead the tenth military district.

Perhaps Van Ness should approach Armstrong or maybe the president. Not wanting to distract attention from the rising emergency at hand, he would wait to ask.

On August 21, Barney found himself holding a position near Pig Point in the Patuxent River. He had long worried that this day would come. From the moment he had received Jones's warning back in June, he'd felt anguished over the fatal command given to him should certain conditions arise.

"I acknowledge the justness of the reasoning, and the precaution in your orders, but I feel a depression of spirits on the occasion, indescribable," Barney had replied to Jones.

The commodore had explained that if the conditions arose, he must be cautious in how he went about implementing Jones's orders because his officers and men were in high spirits and motivated to meet the enemy.

Those conditions grew increasingly nearer. "Appearances indicate a design on this place, but it may be a feint, to mask a real design on Baltimore," Navy Secretary Jones had written to Barney on August 1 from his post at the Navy Yard in Washington City. His words had reflected the reality of rational confusion. "If however their force is strong in troops, they may make a vigorous push for this place [Washington]. In that case they probably would not waste much time with the flotilla."

On August 21, Barney knew that the British had advanced from Benedict to Nottingham, Maryland. They were coming in his direction. The enemy clearly held the advantage. Taking the bulk of his force, about 350 men, he left a unit of about one hundred others behind to prepare for implementing Jones's fatal order. What was that order? If the British approached, fire!

Van Ness couldn't get a straight answer. The process was maddening. Was he in charge of the Washington militia? Or was General Winder? He approached Winder, who hedged. Van Ness next asked Armstrong, who said that this embarrassing question was for the president to answer.

The major general took the issue to Madison, who responded as unclearly as the others. He didn't know. The decision belonged to Armstrong.

What was Van Ness supposed to do? He sent a messenger to Armstrong. After two hours, the messenger returned. The command belonged to Winder.

What was he to do now? He'd spent months knocking on Armstrong's door and begging for more resources. Where Armstrong was cool and indifferent, Winder was indecisive and disorganized. Though wide-eyed and aware that things weren't going well, Van Ness knew that accepting Armstrong's decision was the right thing to do. As he explained, "I determined not to attempt to create any discordance or schism at a moment of imminent peril and when the cordial co-operation of all was so important; and, at the same time, whilst I held my commission of major general, not being able to serve under General Winder, I instantly sent my resignation to the secretary."

Cockburn did indeed intend to attack Barney's fleet stuck at the top of the Patuxent, but in his mind, this was only a mask for his greatest desire of attacking the nation's capital. With Lieutenant James Scott at his side, the admiral and his men boarded small boats and approached the American flotilla on August 22. "I plainly discovered Commodore Barney's broad pendant in the headmost vessel (a large sloop) and the remainder of the flotilla extending in a long line astern of her," Cockburn reported.

Barney's flagship was the *Scorpion*, which headed the rest of the gunboats.

"Here, then, was the boasted flotilla; we had brought them to bay, and in a few minutes we should see what they were made of," Scott boasted along with Cockburn. "The admiral, dashing on in his gig, led the attack."

As Cockburn, Scott, and their men closed in on Barney's fleet, they noticed smoke billowing from the *Scorpion*. Cockburn explained: "…we observed the sloop bearing broad pendant to be on fire, and she very soon afterwards blew up."

Scott put it more colorfully. "And in a few minutes the *Scorpion*, like the venomous insect she was named after, unable to wound her enemies, turned the sting of death upon herself, and exploding, blew stars, stripes, broad pendant and herself, into a thousand atoms."

Cockburn and Scott could hardly believe their eyes as sixteen of seventeen boats in rapid succession blew up. Scott reported that the sound "almost cracked the drums of our ears."

Barney had bested them. In orders from Jones, he had arranged for the remnant of his men to blow up their fleet and prevent capture.

Did Cockburn mind that he'd lost the opportunity to capture the ships? Hardly. No matter that Barney did his work for him, he'd met his objective nonetheless. With the flotilla unable to harass them, surely now Ross would agree to attack Washington.

As his men escaped, Barney knew exactly where he wanted to go. They had provisions for only two days. Only one place made sense.

This navy commandant was ready to act like an army soldier if need be to defend his nation's capitol. What he failed to do on water, perhaps he could accomplish on land. He would put aside Poseidon and become Zeus on earth to defeat the pirate Cockburn.

Though he'd wear his leather and silk belt, whose metal thread was embroidered with anchors, acorns, oak leaves, and the U.S. Navy insignia, he would battle like an Army man. Oak leaves were a Navy symbol because oak wood was used to build ships. Now he would stand among oak trees with cannon if need be. It was time to return to Washington City and defend it with his blood.

———

"The enemy are in full march for Washington," Monroe wrote the president on August 22. A detachment of the British military was six miles from the Woodyard in Maryland. Because the closest American unit was too small to engage them, they retreated back to the Woodyard.

Replying to Monroe at ten o'clock a.m. on August 22, 1814, Madison expressed comfort over Monroe's order to his State Department employees: "The papers of all the officers are under way to retired places."

Purchasing coarse linen bags, State Department clerks were packing away critical documents, including the original Declaration of Independence, the Articles of Confederation, the U.S. Constitution, treaties, laws, and some papers of George Washington. They were hanging these packed bags around the room in the clerk's office to be ready in case they needed to quickly load them into a wagon and evacuate to the countryside.

Knowing that the force of 10,000 he'd hoped for had not materialized, Madison also told Monroe: "I fear not much can be done more than has been done to strengthen the hands of General W[inder]."

He took comfort that the British wouldn't want to venture too far from their escape plan—their ships. Madison added: "But the crisis I presume will be of such short duration, that but few even from the neighboring country will be on the ground before it is over."

Now it was time for him to leave and join Winder to discover how many troops they had at Long Old Fields. But first, Madison needed to say good-bye to Dolley.

Though he lacked the passion to devise multiple plans and strategy options, as he'd done for Canada operations, Armstrong hadn't completely ignored the president's orders. On July 4, 1814, he had issued a requisition for 9,600 men. The notices were intended for the executives of each state: 2,000 from Virginia, 5,000 from Pennsylvania, 6,000 from Maryland, and 2,000 from District of Columbia, making the aggregate number 15,000. This excluded the regular troops, the 36th Regiment and 38th Battalion. Winder was tasked with implementing and in some cases forwarding or sending these requests to the states.

But he delayed some of the president's orders. Ten days after receiving instructions from Madison, Armstrong issued a circular on July 12 to the governor of Maryland, and another circular to the governors of Virginia and Pennsylvania on July 17. Because Winder was traveling around Virginia and Maryland in July, he often didn't receive Armstrong's correspondence in a timely manner. As a result, Winder didn't follow up or write the governor of Pennsylvania until August 3.

The problem in Pennsylvania was that an 1807 law authorizing the governor to call up the militia had expired on August 1, 1814. The governor didn't receive Winder's letter until August 6. He would not be able to reauthorize the militia law until October, when lawmakers reconvened. The problem was different in Virginia, where the governor had already called up 15,000 militiamen on June 22 to defend the commonwealth's shores. These men would not be available to comply with the July 4 requisition of the federal government. Armstrong responded to the Virginia governor that only 2,000 of the 15,000 should be put under Winder's leadership.

Though the war secretary had technically complied with Madison's instructions, he had sabotaged the ability of these militiamen to be trained and ready. Winder understood that Armstrong intended to draw up and designate these forces but "that no part of it should be called into the field until...it probable that a serious attack be contemplated."

They'd failed to listen to Van Ness's suggestion to have a continuous on-duty militia, watching and waiting twenty-four hours day. Such a precaution was just too costly in Armstrong's view. What would the cost to the country be for his failure?

CHAPTER TWENTY

The British Are Coming

heirs was a romantic relationship. "All my affection embraces you," Madison had once written to Dolley.

A few days later, he was even bolder when he offered a simple social kiss for her sister Anna and a romantic onslaught for his wife. "Give Miss (Anna) a kiss for me and accept a thousand for yourself."

Though rarely apart, they were separated for a while in 1805 when Dolley recovered from a knee problem in Philadelphia. She warmly expressed her love to James: "To find that you love me, have my child safe...seems to comprise all my happiness."

The most famous letter that Dolley ever wrote was dated August 23, 1814. Though a copy of it didn't surface publicly for twenty years, it describes what had happened on August 22 and what took place on August 24. Regardless of when she wrote it or if she later edited it, this letter is how she wanted to be remembered.

The correspondence begins a tad generically with "Dear Sister." Because her sister Anna lived in town, most likely she intended it for her other sister, Lucy Todd, who was back home in Kentucky.

Before leaving her at the White House on August 22, James had held an emotional conversation with Dolley. He was deeply concerned about her safety. Yet, he wanted her to stay.

Dolley wrote, "He inquired anxiously whether I had courage, or firmness to remain in the President's House until his return, on the morrow, or succeeding day, and on my assurance that I had no fear but for him and the success of our army, he left me."

As worried as he was about leaving her, James needed her to finish an important job at the White House: "To take care of myself, and of the cabinet papers, public and private."

Thus, she spent her time packing memorandums, correspondence, and, possibly, her husband's unpublished documentation of the proceedings of the Constitutional Convention. Though they were still unknown to the public, Madison's notes on the Constitution were the best records of the secret debate that created the U.S. Constitution. One day, those letters would become very well known.

Such papers were too precious to leave behind. Dolley had an important task that would have drawn her into her husband's office and the cabinet area of the adjacent East Room. There she made sure the papers of her husband's administration were packed and ready for an evacuation should the need arise.

———

Francis Scott Key was born in Frederick County, Maryland. He attended preparatory school starting at age ten at St. John's College in Annapolis, where his grandmother lived. He continued through college and studied law after contemplating becoming a preacher. Advocating for others proved as natural for him as breathing.

After graduation he became an attorney and set up shop in Georgetown, Maryland, just outside of Washington City. He was also destined to be a family man. Marrying Mary Tayloe Lloyd, he became the father of eleven children.

Local residents in both Georgetown and Washington had read Key's name in the newspaper many times, but not for heroics or politics. Instead he took out classified advertisements. As a trustee overseeing real estate, he often advertised lots for sale in the growing housing and business market of the nation's capital.

He also had some business dealings with President and Mrs. Madison. In June 1810 he notified Mrs. Madison that their servant Joe "has been anxious to purchase the freedom of his wife." Millie, Joe's wife, belonged to the Key family. Francis's parents owned a plantation in rural Maryland. Joe had asked the Madisons to take in Joe's wife and child. Appreciative of Millie's excellent service, Key was agreeable to give her freedom. "I have therefore at his request drawn up the enclosed deed of manumission." Key would later become an advocate for creating a freemen's colony in Africa.

Patriotic to the core, Key was also part of the Georgetown militia. On August 19, 1814, General Smith mustered the militia of Georgetown and Washington. At age thirty-five, Key was not the youngest but neither was he the oldest to answer the call of his country that day. The militia convened only to discover that they did not have enough weapons to do any good. They dismissed and rallied again the next day with a few more resources. Though still inadequately supplied, they marched toward Benedict, Maryland. Combined with the Washington militia, their numbers totaled 1,800.

They were not alone when they arrived on August 22 at Battalion Old Fields, which was eight miles from Marlborough and eight miles from Washington. Joining them were Commodore Barney, his flotilla, marines, and regular soldiers from the 36th and 38th Regiments, for a total of 2,700 men. Though far from the 10,000 that President Madison had hoped to convene, they were not a force of nothing. Under the circumstances, every hand that could help was welcome. At the same time, General Stanbury's 1,400 men from Baltimore arrived in Bladensburg, Maryland.

On August 23, those camping at the old fields formed lines to show their readiness to march and fight. Hoping to motivate his soldiers, President Madison reviewed them.

General Smith knew of Key's ability to advocate for others. In the crisis ahead, he would look to him for counsel and allow him to speak for him. Such as was the skill that Key brought with him wherever he went.

━━━

Joseph Gales had received so many reports from so many different sources that it was impossible to sort fact from fiction. Devoted to freedom of the press, Gales told his readers the truth as he saw it on August 23: "Nearly all the rumors that reach us from the scene of action below are evidently so exaggerated and so contradictory that it is impossible to form from them anything like a correct and satisfactory opinion either of the strength or operations of the enemy."

Observation is an important skill for a newspaperman. Gales had figured out that the contrasting fever and coolness of the reports he had received were based as much on the individual's temperament as the truth itself. "Each man brings the tidings dictated by his own fears and impressions; consequently we are inundated by numerous reports that bear no likeness to the truth."

With such confusion in the newspaper, the residents of Washington didn't know what to think. Should they flee? Should they stay? Should they be afraid?

━━━

The morning of August 23, Cockburn and Scott along with their marines marched to Upper Marlborough, Maryland, where Cockburn conferred with General Ross.

With Barney's flotilla burned and no longer in their way, Cockburn had a strong argument for convincing Ross to attack Washington. Hadn't they agreed to take this one step at a time? Yes. Hadn't they agreed that if they defeated Barney's flotilla, then there would be no force to oppose them from the water? Yes, they had.

Ross was practical and concerned about the size of their force. Cockburn was prepared for such oppositional thinking. Though the admiral was disappointed that only about 4,500 men, less than a fourth of the 20,000 he had hoped for, were at their disposal, given the apathy of the Americans, it should be more than enough.

Ross responded by agreeing, in spite of Cochrane's wavering and the admiralty's conservative request to stay close to the ships.

A good judge of personality, Cockburn detected that Ross was more prone to follow than lead. The admiral realized that to get his way, he needed to be Ross's best confidante, frequently deferring to his leadership while also offering, genteelly, his opinion.

Thrilled with Ross's decision to attack Washington, Cockburn immediately sent Scott to convey the decision to Cochrane, who remained aboard one of the ships miles away at the Patuxent River. Though he knew it would take Scott most of the day to reach Cochrane, Cockburn understood the need to notify the admiral of their plan. Promotions wouldn't come without Cochrane's pleasure. Surely Cochrane would trust their decision, especially with Barney's flotilla out of the way. Surely.

Meanwhile, Dolley was receiving messages from James. She wrote her sister about the events of August 23: "I have since received two dispatches from him, written with a pencil."

Madison had spent the previous night in camp. Noting that the troops were in high spirits, he wrote Dolley that "the reports as to the enemy have varied every hour. The last and probably truest information is that they are not very strong, and are without cavalry or artillery; and of course that they are not in a condition to strike at Washington."

What relief he offered. Without cavalry or cannons, James didn't believe the enemy would move from their position in Marlborough, about twenty miles away "unless it be from an apprehension of our gathering force, and on a retreat to their ships."

Though he expressed some optimism, she detected that he was trying to weigh the balance with caution. He wrote, "They may have a greater force or expect one, than has been represented or that their temerity may be greater than their strength."

Madison added an important detail for his beloved. He hoped to return to her at the White House that evening, August 23.

Later that day she received another note from him. This second dispatch was "alarming, because he desires I should be ready at a moment's warning to enter my carriage and leave the city."

What a shock that was! Contradicting his earlier message, he boldly proclaimed, "That the enemy seemed stronger than had been reported and that it might happen that they would reach the city, with intention to destroy it."

How did she respond to the alarm? She wanted to communicate courage, expressing a sentiment similar to that which she had written to her cousin Edward about rumors that Cockburn was planning to take a bow in her drawing room in 1813. "I am accordingly ready; I have pressed as many cabinet papers into trunks as to fill one carriage; our private property must be sacrificed, as it is impossible to procure wagons for its transportation."

With the determination of an eagle, she was ready to leave her perch and fly from her nest, taking eagle ornaments and the red curtains but leaving behind her beautiful gowns and turbans. Material items were nothing compared to the danger facing her beloved husband.

━━━━━━━

Scott arrived at Cochrane's flagship late in the day on August 23 to convey Cockburn and Ross's decision to invade Washington. When he arrived, he found several advisors surrounding commanding Admiral Cochrane.

"The captain of the fleet was with him in the cabin when I delivered the information and message with which I was charged," Scott later wrote. "A long discussion ensued: the junior officer, appearing to think the attempt was too rash, stated his opinion to that effect."

The response worried Scott, who knew Cockburn better than anyone else. What would happen if Cochrane didn't approve of General Ross's decision?

Scott listened as Cochrane assessed the information. Wasn't the Chesapeake Bay notorious in the summer for diseases? Wasn't the heat oppressive? Why hadn't the admiralty sent more reinforcements? Wouldn't October be a better time to attack Washington City, after summer diseases had passed? New Hampshire was ideal this time of year, wasn't it? Many factors weighed on the British officers and Cochrane. In Scott's words, "And finally an order was penned for the rear admiral, (intended of course as a guidance to General Ross also) and handed over to me with directions to proceed without a moment's loss of time to headquarters."

Cochrane also instructed Scott to read and memorize the instructions. If he was caught by the Americans, he must eat the paper.

"The orders contained in that letter were to the following effect: That under all circumstances the rear admiral had already effected more than England could have expected with the small force under his orders; that he was on no account to proceed one mile farther," Scott reflected.

Not only was Cockburn ordered to stand down, but he was also required to turn around. "But, upon the receipt of that order, the army was immediately to return to Benedict to re-embark; that the ulterior and principal objects of the expedition would be risked by an attempt upon the capital with such inadequate means."

Scott now returned under the darkness of night. Worry guided him as much as his horse. Because attacking Washington had been Cockburn's goal all along, how would he respond to Cochrane's decision to abandon the plan?

"I am determined not to go myself until I see Mr. Madison safe, and he can accompany me, as I hear of much hostility towards him, disaffection stalks around us," Dolley wrote protectively to her sister.

Though she planned to wait for James's return, those who had guarded her had already fled, including those encamped near the White House. "My friends and acquaintances are all gone; Even Col. C— with his 100 men, who were stationed as a guard in the enclosure."

Dolley's sister Anna was just as alarmed. She had scribbled a quick note to Dolley, writing, "My Sister, tell me for God's sake where you are and what [you are] going to do?"

Also experiencing a shortage of carriages, Anna had asked her husband to pack their piano or anything he could get "in a wagon if the British are coming—We can hear nothing but what is horrible here." With so many people fleeing town, Dolley debated with French John, one of her most reliable servants, about what to do.

Born in Paris, Jean Pierre Sioussat, or French John, was thirty-three years old in 1814. After deserting from the French Navy, he came to America and later joined the service of Mr. Anthony Merry, the British diplomat to the United States during Jefferson's tenure. When the Merrys departed Washington in a huff after President Jefferson insulted them, Sioussat joined the household of Mr. Erskine, the British diplomat who replaced Mr. Merry. After the British fired Erskine and ordered his return to England, French John joined the Madison staff as a porter. By 1814, he was married and had two children, a four-year-old son and a one-year-old daughter.

"French John (a faithful domestic,) with his usual activity and resolution, offers to spike the cannon at the gate, and to lay a train of powder which would blow up the British, should they enter the house," Dolley wrote.

Unable to bear being responsible for the destruction at the White House, she added, "To the last proposition I positively object, without being able, however, to make him understand why all advantages in war may not be taken."

Believing that his intentions were noble, Dolley knew she could rely upon him in an emergency.

―――

"Have they artillery? No. Have they cavalry? No. Then don't tell an old soldier that any regular army will or can come," Armstrong told Winder the night of August 23.

Concerned and confused, Winder had returned to Washington with his men that night so they could go home for a quick change of clothes and a meal before convening again at Washington headquarters near the Naval Yard.

An exhausted Winder then knocked on the door of Secretary Armstrong's quarters, known as the Seven Buildings. Winder expressed worry over the possibility of an imminent invasion by the British only to listen with great alarm to Armstrong's rant.

"We are more frightened than hurt, or like to be. What do they want, what can they get in this sheep walk," Armstrong continued. "If they want to do anything they must go to Baltimore, not come to this barren wilderness."

Winder left, hoping that Armstrong was right but fearing that he was wrong.

What Armstrong failed to understand is that Cockburn didn't need artillery. The admiral wore brashness more than practicality on his shoulders. He didn't care that Washington was no better than a sheep pasture. This was the place of Madison's seat of power and America's symbolic monumental buildings. This was the place to strike before all others because it was the heart of a government built on representation of the people. What could possibly stop him?

―――

Scott reached Cockburn's and Ross's "shepherd's quarters" at two o'clock in the morning of August 24. He gave the message to Cockburn, who read it. Keeping his composure, Cockburn waited for Ross's opinion. Soon blind obedience would combat justified rebellion.

Ross expressed diffidence, acknowledging the small force and their uncomfortable distance from their ships.

"Having perused it, he [Ross] remarked that there was now no other alternative than to return. 'No,' replied the admiral, 'we cannot do that; we are too far advanced to think of a retreat: let us take a turn outside, and talk the matter over,'" Scott later recounted.

As Ross and Cockburn took a walk about camp, Scott heard some of the conversation, which he later recorded. "'If we proceed,' said our energetic commander, 'I'll pledge every thing that is dear to me as an officer that we shall succeed. If we return without striking a blow, it will be worse than a defeat—it will bring a stain upon our arms.'"

Cockburn did not let up easily. How could he? This is what he had been working toward for fifteen months.

"'I know their force—the militia, however great their numbers, will not—cannot stand against your disciplined troops. It is too late,' continued the admiral. 'we ought not to have advanced—there is now no choice left us. We must go on.'"

Hearing this, General Ross struck his hand against his forehead and agreed. "Well, be it so, we will proceed."

Because some of the soldiers and marines had heard they were to retreat, the men could not have been happier at the change. "A low murmuring burst of enthusiasm involuntarily escaped from the lips of the officers and men, sufficiently indicative of the spirit that animated the hearts of the gallant band. In less than five minutes the whole army were in full march for the capital of the United States."

How did Cockburn justify their decision to his superior? As if pretending that he never received the communication, Cockburn coyly wrote Cochrane that he had joined Ross and conferred with him about further operations against the enemy, "and we were not long in agreeing on the propriety of making an immediate attempt on the city of Washington."

Ross asked Cockburn to relocate his naval forces and join him. "In conformity therefore with the wishes of the general, I instantly sent orders for our marine and naval forces."

Cockburn was thrilled. "I also most readily agreed to accompany."

Finally, the British would launch an attack on the U.S. capital city, and Cockburn would help lead it. No matter that he was an admiral and that this was a land assault, he had what he wanted. Sure, he would defer to Ross, who had top authority while on land. But Cockburn secretly knew that he had Ross in the palm of his hand.

Leaving a company at Upper Marlborough, the rest broke camp "and bivouacked before dark about five miles nearer Washington."

They were heading toward a town called Bladensburg, a village on the left bank of the Potomac's Eastern Branch in Maryland. This hamlet was seven miles from the White House. Filled with so much delight, Cockburn could almost taste one of Dolley Madison's cakes.

CHAPTER TWENTY-ONE

Spyglasses

"We feel assured that the number and bravery of our men will afford complete protection of the city," wrote Joseph Gales.

A spirit of optimism guided Gales as he set the type on the August 24 edition of the *National Intelligencer*. His confidence was in the patriotism of the men who had arrived from Baltimore and camped near Bladensburg.

He noted that the influx of the men at Bladensburg was separate from General Winder's troops. "The Baltimore troops, about 2500, completely equipped, have arrived in our vicinity, and last night 700 men reached the city from Virginia. These, and reinforcements every moment expected, added to our other forces, will secure the safety of the metropolis."

Soon the destination of the British would be clear, as Gales shared with his readers. "In a few hours we believe the enemy's object will be developed and the issue perhaps determined."

What he didn't anticipate was just how much his business would soon be in the line of fire.

———

Around sunrise on August 24, 1814, President Madison, who had returned to the White House the night before, received a pressing message addressed to Secretary Armstrong from General Winder. Madison opened it and, seeing the message's urgency, immediately sent it to Armstrong's residence a few blocks away.

Because Winder had requested a meeting and speedy counsel, Madison quickly dressed and left the White House. Accompanied by a free African, James Smith, the president rushed on horseback to Winder's current camp at the Navy Yard along the Potomac River's eastern branch.

As one of Washington City's original residents, Madison knew the history of the Navy Yard first hand. In 1799, the government designated Washington City to become one of six new shipbuilding sites in the United States. The federal government established the yard along 7th, 8th, 9th, and M streets.

Soon it became a robust manufacturing site. The Navy Yard featured a commandant's house, brick guard buildings, wooden wharves, a canal, and timber sheds. Commandant Thomas Tingey often purchased barrels of whisky for breaks of refreshments. Second only to such grog for construction workers was the use of derrick cranes, the latest in building technology employed in London but not in the United States until the creation of the Washington Navy Yard. Workers used derrick cranes soon to erect the tall masts on seventy-four-gun ships.

As Madison well knew, what stood out the most at the Navy Yard was its gate, a work of art and architecture. No one who visited the site could miss this distinguished double gate, which included northern and southern ends separated by forty feet, covered by a hipped roof, and connected by double rows of columns. Benjamin Latrobe designed the gate, which was completed in 1806.

The north end featured two columns topped by a sculpture featuring an eagle holding an anchor in his talon as well as a Greek-style frieze. The south end was a Greek arch that rose from ground level. Once again, Latrobe drew on Greek symbolism for the new republic.

Madison was well aware of Latrobe's gate critics. William Thornton, the capitol's original architect and a rival to Latrobe, called it a "monument to bad taste and design" and called the eagle "more like a fat goose." He said the anchors were "fitter for a cock boat than a gun boat." He also made a prediction that "not until the extinction of time will such an arch ever be made again." Thornton was wrong. Latrobe had started a trend that became known as Greek Revival style architecture. His was the first design in the United States in that style. Hence, even a manufacturing site sought to symbolize, through its architecture, the ideals of the United States.

Madison's cabinet needed all the inspiration they could get that day from the Navy Yard's gate. Soon Monroe, Navy Secretary Jones, and Attorney General Rush arrived at their meeting point. Debating what to do, they had been deliberating for an hour when Treasury Secretary Campbell, who was ill, joined them. Conspicuously missing was Armstrong. What could be keeping him? They all suspected the answer. Indifference.

By 10 a.m. a messenger arrived with news. The British were coming, advancing to Bladensburg. With great urgency, Winder immediately left for Bladensburg and ordered his troops, some of whom were still straggling in from their nearby homes, to follow him.

About this time, Secretary Armstrong arrived. Unhappy with his tardiness, Madison didn't hide his displeasure, as he later reflected. "The latter [Armstrong] had been impatiently expected, and surprise at his delay manifested."

Madison and his cabinet told Armstrong of the enemy's march to Bladensburg. The president described the scene matter-of-factly. "He was asked whether he had any arrangement or advice to offer in the emergency. He said he had not; adding, that as the battle would be between militia and regular troops, the former would be beaten."

What should they do? To Madison there was no other choice for him and his cabinet. They must all go to Bladensburg and by their presence show support for the fighting men. As they left the building to mount their horses, Secretary Campbell pulled Madison aside. Because Campbell resided in the same boardinghouse as Armstrong, he had had several opportunities to observe the war secretary's behavior and demeanor. He was greatly concerned about Armstrong's aloofness. Madison later wrote that Campbell "was grieved to see the great reserve of the secretary of war...who was taking no part on so critical an occasion."

Campbell identified Armstrong's reserve as rooted in the selection of General Winder to corral the troops. He recommended that the president encourage Armstrong to offer his military knowledge and experience to the crisis at hand as a way to engage the indifferent and dour war secretary.

Madison, while keeping his outward demeanor cool, was inwardly hot. He couldn't believe that Armstrong had mistaken his duties, especially after he had put them in writing just weeks earlier in that August 13 memo. "I could scarcely conceive it possible that General Armstrong could have so misconstrued his functions and duty as secretary of war."

With urgency guiding him as much as anger, Madison approached Armstrong and expressed his concern and surprise at his reserve over the situation at Bladensburg. "I hoped he had not construed the paper of instructions given him some time before, so as to restrain him in any respect from the exercise of functions belonging to his office."

Armstrong replied that he had no such construction from those paper instructions. Pressing his point with teacher-like orders, Madison said, "At such a juncture it was to be expected that he should omit nothing within the proper agency of secretary of war towards the public defense."

He suggested that Armstrong ride ahead to join Winder and offer him advice. Agreeing, the war secretary mounted his horse and rode toward Winder on the road to Bladensburg from Washington.

Ill and unable to go to the battlefield, Campbell handed Madison his dueling pistols and holder. The president at first resisted and then, recognizing the practicality and wisdom of the gesture, accepted them. Madison and Rush, along with Jim, decided to ride over to the marine barracks before heading to Bladensburg.

When Madison arrived at the barracks, he discovered Commodore Barney, who, unlike Madison, was unable to conceal his anger. Chafing and cursing at being relegated to doing something a lower-ranking corporal could do, Barney explained his dilemma. Instead of going to Bladensburg to fight, he had been ordered to stay put and blow up a bridge.

Recognizing that Barney could be more useful in battle than staying behind, the president made an immediate decision. Overruling the ridiculous orders, he ordered the patriot and his flotilla men to the battlefield.

Then the president and his entourage headed to Bladensburg.

With a population of fewer than 200 according to the 1810 census, Bladensburg, Maryland, was not known for much before 1814, except for the infamous dueling grounds on the town's western edge along the road to Washington. Another road nearby on the western side was the path to Georgetown. Both roads converged at a wooden bridge, which spanned a few yards over a narrow segment of the Anacostia, the eastern branch of the Potomac River. The village of Bladensburg was immediately to the east of the bridge.

Blazing blood heat blanketed Bladensburg the morning of August 24. One British officer described it this way: "The sun beat on us in full force; the dust, without a breath of air to disperse it, occasioned the greatest inconvenience both to eyes and respiration. Never did I suffer more from heat and fatigue."

The temperature was so oppressive that Ross ordered his men to stop and refresh themselves at a creek halfway to Bladensburg. The break wasn't quite enough. A few of them, including one of Ross's aides, collapsed from sun stroke before they arrived near noon on the east side of Bladensburg.

The 85th Regiment led the way, followed by the 44th and 4th infantry plus Cockburn's marines. Cockburn and Ross rode on horseback and concealed their position behind the redbrick houses dotting the streets of Bladensburg. Both pulled out their spyglasses and surveyed the Americans across the creek. What they saw was far more impressive than they had expected. The ground west of the bridge was a hill dotted with fences and bushes. Lines of Americans filled the terrain.

"On reaching which the place, with the advanced brigade, the enemy was discovered drawn up in force on a rising ground beyond the town," Cockburn described of the American position.

They saw General Stansbury's brigade of 1,400, who had marched from Baltimore. Stansbury had arranged his men in arc-shaped lines about a quarter of a mile west of the town's bridge. Their defenses featured cannons, including two eighteen-pounders. Attached to Stansbury's brigade were Colonel Pinckney's riflemen, who had taken positions among bushes. Joining them were the Baltimore 5th, a unit of 800, and another battalion of 800 from Annapolis.

Though their spyglasses gave them a good view, what Ross and Cockburn couldn't yet see was just how disorganized the Americans were behind those arc-shaped lines. They didn't know that General Winder had given his men an instruction. When they retreated, they were to use the road to Georgetown, not Washington. The mistake was on the word *when*, not *if*.

━━━━━━━

Francis Scott Key accompanied General Smith to Bladensburg. They were part of the advance group of militias, the rest of whom had gone back to Washington the night before and were now hurrying to the battlefield under the orders of General Winder.

Smith and Key discussed where to form the militia. Ever the advocate, Key offered to represent General Smith to the commanding general. When General Winder arrived on the road near noon, Key approached him and offered Smith's opinion that "several troops coming from the city could be most advantageously posted on the right and left of the road near that point."

But Winder lacked a battle plan. Though he had spent the past two months surveying the different locales within the tenth military district of Washington, he had failed to war game or draft contingency plans. He didn't have any preplanned instructions of how to form battle lines if the British came to Bladensburg. Now all was haste with no time to waste.

Winder told Key that he would defer to Smith's judgment on where to locate the militia. But the disorganization was so great and communication in such disarray that General Stansbury on the front line didn't even know that Smith's militia had formed lines behind him near the road to Washington.

Monroe also weighed in on the arrangements. He relocated Sterrett's regiment, the Baltimore 5th, to an orchard, which was nearly a quarter of a mile from where the regiment originally formed. At the orchard they were too far away to cover the lines more exposed to the enemy. Colonel Beall's 800 men from Annapolis also arrived so hastily that they were unable to identify a strategic position for aiding the main line.

———————————

Despite his frailties and sickly tendencies, James Madison was a master horseman. On the road to Bladensburg, he quickly recognized that his horse was going lame. He had no choice but to dismount while someone brought him another horse. The delay didn't cost them much time.

Soon Madison, Jim, and Rush arrived on the western side of Bladensburg. Their immediate goal was to find General Winder. Cheers rang out as his party rode past the troops and militia that had formed their lines and taken their positions on the hill.

What Madison didn't realize at that moment was the location of the British Army and Navy. He began riding toward the town's bridge with an intention to cross it. On the other side, General Ross and his men were making plans and forming their lines.

"Mr. Madison! The enemy are now in Bladensburg," an observant American sentry shouted and watched in horror as the president sped toward the bridge with an obvious determination to cross.

Stunned, Madison stopped his horse. Then he called out, repeating the words to his party with Paul Revere–like urgency. "The British are now in Bladensburg. The British are now in Bladensburg." And with that, this skilled horseman turned his horse around and headed for the hill with Rush and Jim following him.

Finding both General Winder and General Armstrong, Madison quickly discovered that the secretary of war hadn't followed his command of offering advice to Winder. Hot from the blatant disobedience and sweating from the heat, Madison ordered Armstrong to immediately advise Winder. The president watched as Armstrong approached Winder.

Before he could overhear their conversation as he intended, however, his horse became unruly. By the time he had soothed the animal, he missed listening to Armstrong's and Winder's conversation. Instead, Madison approached Armstrong and asked if he had offered any suggestions to improve the military arrangements on the field.

"He said that he had not; that from his view of them they appeared to be as good as circumstances admitted."

If Madison's unruly horse was any indication, the circumstances were chaotic at best.

━━━━━━━━

One way that Madison had shown his love for Dolley when they were apart from one another in the past was to indulge her with tidbits of the social world. For example, while she was in Philadelphia recovering from her knee problem in 1805, he wrote to her, "I have no news for you; unless you wish to know...that the Tunisian Ambassador is expected soon from Norfolk."

Sometimes he was not as successful, as when he wrote, "I can give you no city news. The wedding of Mr. Simmons' has produced a round of parties; but I have not attended one of them."

Why didn't he go? Though business matters provided an excuse, he likely didn't want to attend without Dolley. She was everything to him. A reserved, introverted man, he was married to the most popular extrovert in town. Life was certainly not the same without his wife, especially when he met a memorable foreign visitor.

"We are to have as a guest an ambassador from Tunis who is on board one of the frigates arrived from the Mediterranean," he once wrote.

The North African diplomat's name was Sidi Suleiman Melli Melli. He most likely gave Madison a Tunisian saber as a gift. In the seventh century, the Bedouin, a nomadic desert tribe of Arabia, migrated to North Africa. Bedouin women in Tunisia performed sword dances at weddings. The ability to balance the sword symbolized carrying their husband's honor. Likewise, Middle Eastern men often danced with swords to show strength and military power. If Melli Melli gave Madison a sword or saber, he understandably might have conveyed some of its symbolic meaning within his culture.

When Dolley first heard in 1813 that Cockburn wanted to take his bow in her drawing room, she vowed to protect herself with the Tunisian saber. That day had come. Staying at the White House was a way to protect her husband's honor, as well as the nation's symbolic architectural masterpieces. Now the possibility of Cockburn visiting grew with each passing minute.

About the time Madison arrived in Bladensburg on August 24, Dolley's letter continued with a timestamp for her sister. She shared her increasing concerns about James.

"Wednesday morning, twelve o'clock. Since sunrise I have been turning my spyglass in every direction and watching with unwearied anxiety, hoping to discern the approach of my dear husband and his friends."

Directing her glass through the upper windows of the White House had given her expansive views of the small city and the sprawling lawns. She saw no sign of James's return. What she did see disturbed her.

"But, alas, I can descry only groups of military wandering in all directions, as if there was a lack of arms, or of spirit to fight for their own firesides!"

Even the mayor of Washington City had called on her twice. Though he asked her to leave the White House, and while even the men guarding her home had left, she refused to abandon her post. Why leave when she had the spirit of the Tunisian saber and her husband's honor to inspire her?

There was one thing that she needed to do, however. After all it was Wednesday, the day of the week frequently devoted to her weekly open-house parties. The president and his officers were sure to be hungry once they returned victorious from the battlefield. It was time to fire up the spits.

━━━━━━

To Cockburn's dismay, Ross began to hesitate after seeing the lines of Americans because he couldn't determine the depth of the American front.

"On the opposite side of the river," Ross reported, "the enemy were posted on very commanding heights. Artillery covered the bridge over which the British army had to pass."

The general held a quick conference with his officers. Detecting hesitation in Ross's assessment, one asked: "What will be said of us in England if we stop now?"

Cockburn could not have agreed more. Would the general waver? The admiral knew the truth. Except for defending Norfolk, this was the biggest display of boldness he had yet seen from the Americans.

He and the other officers waited for Ross's decision. Yes, many American troops lined the hill. Yes, they had artillery. But how strong was their will to fight? If Cockburn was right, the U.S. forces were most likely to flee in a panic rather than stand their ground. Ross agreed.

"If it rain militia, then," Ross allegedly replied of his decision, "we will go on."

A relieved Cockburn relished in the proposition as Ross ordered the vanguard of the 85th Regiment to advance. Led by Colonel Thornton, the guard left their covered position in the town of Bladensburg and marched onto the bridge.

―――――

While standing by her post and planning a victory dinner for her husband's officers, Dolley received this frantic but polite note from her friend Eleanor Jones, the wife of the navy secretary.

"In the present state of alarm and bustle of preparation, for the worst that may happen, I imagine it will be mutually convenient, to dispense with the enjoyment of your hospitality today," Eleanor wrote on August 24, 1814. She asked Dolley to excuse her absence along with that of her family members.

"Mr. Jones is deeply engaged in dispatching the marines and attending to other public duties."

Eleanor's situation was difficult. Their carriage horse was sick and their coachman had abandoned them. She explained that she was "busy packing up ready for flight, but in the event of necessity we know not where to go, nor have we any means yet prepared for the conveyance of our effects."

Despite receiving regrets, Dolley's dinner preparations continued. Oh, how she hoped to see James sitting at the State Dining Room table under the watchful eye of the portrait of George Washington. How comforting and exciting it would be if his cabinet and the military's officers enjoyed a meal that night to celebrate a victory! Hope and optimism were her best companions under the circumstances. What would happen if the battlefield turned out differently?

CHAPTER TWENTY-TWO

Bladensburg Races

Leading a group of marines behind the British infantry, Cockburn and Scott waited for the battle to begin.

The U.S. artillerists were ready. As soon as they saw the British front line fill the bridge, they fired their great guns. Soon Lieutenant Scott observed "roars of musketry; round, grape, and small shot came like a hail-storm" and swept out the redcoats in the advance.

Forced to step over their dead and wounded comrades, the next wave of British soldiers marched onto the bridge. They successfully crossed. As the infantry advanced, their leader, Colonel Thornton, came within a few feet of the U.S. artillery. Suddenly his horse fell from under him. Thornton got up and led his men to the crest of the hill on foot. The American fire didn't let up, wounding Thornton and others.

Following the British advance were the 44th and 4th Regiments along with the admiral's marines. Now it was their turn.

Mounted on a charging horse, Cockburn couldn't have appeared more brazen had he held a pirate's flag. His uniform stood out the most, with his "conspicuous gold-laced hat and epaulettes fully exposed within 100 and 30 or 40 yards of his foes."

Together Cockburn and Scott directed their marines to prepare and launch their rockets into the American lines. *Ready. Aim. Fire!* Their rockets soared through the sky, leaving red glares and startling many. But they weren't the only ones rattled.

A round shot soon threw Scott from his horse. Realizing that the incoming fire was heavy and highly worried about the eye-catching appearance of his brazen commander, the lieutenant encouraged Cockburn to take cover.

"I trust, Sir, you will not unnecessarily expose yourself, for, however much the enemy may suffer, they will regard your death as ample compensation."

How did Cockburn respond? Failing to heed Scott's suggestion to take cover by a stone barrier, the admiral didn't move.

"Poh! Poh! Nonsense!" Cockburn replied, as he watched two marines prepare their rockets.

The rockets soared into the sky and hit the American ranks, causing panic.

"Capital! Excellent," he replied. The precision of the rockets gave him great pleasure. At the same time, one of his marines standing next to him fell wounded.

Then as the admiral spoke to another nearby marine, "a musket shot passed between the admiral's leg and the flap of his saddle, cutting the stirrup leather in two, without doing any injury to him or the horse."

Dismounting his horse, Cockburn allowed Scott and another marine to hurriedly fix his broken stirrup with twine. Suddenly another shot soared over the saddle and hit the other marine aiding Scott. The shot "dismissed my assistant to the other world," as Scott described.

Despite these close calls, Cockburn felt the adrenaline that comes with being on the front lines. British soldiers and marines infiltrated the road to Washington like a pack of wolves chasing cats. While the marines fired their rockets, the infantry threw off their knapsacks and charged at the American front line with bayonets. They broke to the right and left to engage in hand-to-hand combat if necessary.

Yet they soon had fewer and fewer hands to combat. American artillerymen abandoned their guns and retreated in a great panic. The effect was as contagious as yellow fever, but with no incubation. The retreat was instant.

━━━━━━━━━━

Military meteors from the redcoats streamed through the air. Because Congreve rocket technology was new to the Americans, few had seen the effect of the red glare. Saying they scared more than they harmed, General Winder tried to encourage his men to disregard them. But when a rocket soared over the president's position, Winder knew he couldn't ignore the weapons, either. Fearing for the president's life and safety, he took action and advised Madison to fall back to the rear of the line. The president complied.

Soon, the message of the battlefield's reality spoke louder than any rocket. It was no use, as Madison reflected: "When it became manifest that the battle was lost; Mr. Rush accompanying me, I fell down into the road leading to the city and returned to it."

They took the road to Georgetown instead of the road to Washington. Not long after they left, a rush of men flew past them as if they were horses on a race track. The Americans were in full retreat and disarray.

Concerned more than ever about his wife, he sent a messenger ahead to warn her. Oh, how he hoped she was safe. How he longed to embrace his beloved Dolley.

━━━━━━━━━━

While James and the army retreated, Dolley learned the news. Madison had sent James Smith with a message.

"Three o'clock. Will you believe it, my Sister? We have had a battle or skirmish near Bladensburg, and I am still here within sound of the cannon!"

Though he had sent her the news through messengers, she initially responded with shock and denial. "Mr. Madison comes not; may God protect him! Two messengers covered with dust, come to bid me fly; but I wait for him."

Focusing on the good, Dolley reflected on completing the job that James had given her earlier to pack his papers and other valuables, including the silver plate. "At this late hour a wagon has been procured, I have had it filled with the plate and most valuable portable articles belonging to the house; whether it will reach its destination; the Bank of Maryland, or fall into the hands of British soldiery, events must determine."

One treasure, however, required special attention. "Our kind friend, Mr. Carroll, has come to hasten my departure, and is in a very bad humor with me because I insist on waiting until the large picture of General Washington is secured, and it requires to be unscrewed from the wall."

Charles Carroll, who owned a house called Bellevue on the heights of Georgetown, was a friend. He was well intentioned, but he failed to see the significance of the portrait in that moment.

Perhaps she was walking through the state floor, going from window to window with her spyglass when she thought of it. Maybe she checked on the forty place settings dotting the table in the State Dining Room when she glanced up and saw the portrait. Maybe she had sat down at the piano in her music room and glanced through the doorway when the idea came to her. Regardless of how it came about, Dolley realized that she couldn't leave the President's House without making sure the portrait would be safe too.

After all, this painting was larger than life. A gift to the White House from Congress in 1800, it was a national treasure. Sure, it was replaceable. Copies of the painting existed. But Dolley saw the symbolism behind it. If Cockburn captured the painting, he would have his men parade it through the streets of London and plop it in front of the prince regent's feet as a symbol of their capture of Washington City. Such a dishonorable thing wasn't going to happen on her watch.

But removing it from the wall required more than a quick tug. French John and the Irish gardener Thomas McGraw tried to figure out how to detach it from the wall. According to Dolley, however, "This process was found too tedious for these perilous moments. I have ordered the frame to be broken, and the canvas taken out, it is done."

Though she ordered the frame to be broken, the painting shows no sign of being cut. Observing that the task required a ladder, fifteen-year-old Paul Jennings reflected that French John and McGraw came to the rescue. Very likely they were able to remove it from the wall without breaking the frame. They may have broken or removed the outer frame while keeping the canvas attached to its inner frame and preventing it from being cut.

During this time, Mr. Jacob Barker and Mr. DePeyster of New York stopped by. They had come to check on their friend Dolley. As good fortune would have it, Barker had brought a wagon. "And the precious portrait placed in the hands of two gentlemen of New York, for safe keeping."

With this business concluded, it was time to say good-bye.

"And now, dear sister, I must leave this house, or the retreating army will make me a prisoner in it, by filling up the road I am directed to take. When I shall again write you, or where I shall be tomorrow, I cannot tell!!"

While Barker and DePeyster drove the wagon carrying the painting through Georgetown and found a house in Maryland to hide it, State Department clerks placed the nation's archival documents in a wagon and took them to a mill three miles above Georgetown. Fearful that the enemy would seize a nearby cannon foundry, they drove the documents even further, to Leesburg, Virginia, three dozen miles away from Washington. There they found an abandoned house. And from this hiding place, the clerks protected the Declaration of Independence, the U.S. Constitution, and other irreplaceable historical treasures.

———

Determined to do his part, Commodore Barney hurried to the Bladensburg dueling grounds on the road from Washington. "When I arrived at the line, which separates the district from Maryland, the battle began."

He wasted no time. He posted his men on the road to the east of General Smith's men but not as far west as General Stansbury's. "I sent an officer back to hurry on my men; they came up in a trot; we took our position on the rising ground."

Decisive and controlled, Barney arranged his cannon in a battery and posted his flotilla men to his right. "During this period the engagement continued, and the enemy advancing, our own army retreating before them, apparently in much disorder."

Then they waited for the enemy's approach. "At length the enemy made his appearance on the main road, in force, and in front of my battery, and on seeing us, made a halt. I reserved our fire."

Barney's hesitation proved to be wise. "In a few minutes the enemy again advanced, when I ordered an eighteen pounder to be fired, which completely cleared the road; shortly after, a second and third attempt was made by the enemy, to come forward, but all were destroyed."

Then the British crossed into an open field and tried to flank Barney's right side. His men, including former slave Charles Ball, fired back, but they were on their own. "By this time, not a vestige of the American army remained, except a body of five or six hundred, posted on a height, upon my right, from whom I expected much support, from their fine situation."

The British fired muskets, "one of which shot my horse under me; who fell dead between two of my guns. The enemy, who had been kept in check by our fire, for nearly half an hour, now began to out-flank us on the right."

About 200 redcoats pushed up the hill toward the corps of Americans who were stationed there and "to my great mortification, made no resistance, giving a fire or two, and retired."

Likewise Barney's ammunition drivers had fled in a panic. With two killed, his remaining men were now alone to fend off the enemy without ammunition.

"At this time, I received a severe wound in my thigh...but to the honor of my officers and men, as fast as their companions and messmates fell at the guns, they were instantly replaced from the infantry."

Realizing that the British were now completely in their rear and he had nothing left to defend himself with, Barney ordered his men to retire, though he was too wounded to join them. "Three of my officers assisted me to get off a short distance, but the great loss of blood occasioned such a weakness that I was compelled to lie down. I requested my officers to leave me, which obstinately refused; but, upon, being ordered, they obeyed; one only remained."

Soon he saw a British soldier and called out to him. The soldier agreed to send Barney a British officer.

———

Though he had resigned his position, Van Ness couldn't sit around and do nothing. No matter that he was no longer major general of the Washington militia, he would fight as a volunteer.

Astonishment greeted Van Ness as he arrived in Bladensburg after the battle began. He couldn't see any distinct lines or detect any sort of battle plan. Worst of all, the retreat was chaotic.

"In that part of the field on which I moved, and afterwards, during the retreat, I could discover or learn nothing like a system or an order of battle, of retreat, or of rallying, or reforming," he later reflected.

He also discovered that he wasn't alone in his confusion. "Several of the officers of the militia of the city and Georgetown, (General W. Smith's brigade) whom I met with in the course of the affair, (and who, with their men, were generally in good order, and deeply regretted the want of opportunity to act efficiently) appeared, in this respect, to be in the same predicament with myself."

And so they retreated to Georgetown into "inglorious circumstances." He began to ask questions. Mingling among those who had retreated, he gathered important facts about the battle, its failures, and its many errors, especially cardinal ones. Like a catalogue, he documented them into his mind. When the time was right, he would put them on paper. Maybe someone could learn from their mistakes—that is, if America survived as an independent nation.

───

A British officer helped the wounded Joshua Barney. Which one was it? The accounts differ. According to Barney, the officer who came to him was Captain Wainwright. Lieutenant Scott, however, also claimed credit for rescuing the dashing American hero.

As Barney relayed: "In a few minutes an officer came, and, on learning who I was brought General Ross and Admiral Cockburn to me."

Regardless of which officer was his escort, Cockburn suddenly had the chance to meet the man his men had chased earlier in the summer. For all his policies of rewarding average Americans when they failed to fight back, he admired the fire in Barney's belly. So did Ross.

Barney, who was acquainted with Admiral Cochrane, reportedly looked up and said, "That is not Admiral Cochrane?"

"It is Admiral Cockburn," the admiral replied, using the British pronunciation of Co-burn.

"Oh, Cock-burn is what you are called hereabouts," Barney answered in the American pronunciation. "Well, Admiral, you have got hold of me at last."

"Do not let us speak on that subject, Commodore; I regret to see you in this state. I hope you are not seriously hurt."

"Quite enough to prevent my giving you any trouble for some time."

Humor relaxed the tensions. General Ross announced that he was giving Barney parole and offered him refuge in Washington or Bladensburg. Barney chose Bladensburg.

"Those officers behaved to me with the most marked attention, respect, and politeness, had a surgeon brought, and my wound dressed immediately," he reflected.

"Barney was a brave officer," Ross later said, noting that they wouldn't have been successful if half of the American forces had shown his bravery.

According to Scott, Cockburn later claimed: "If I had had five hundred such brave fellows as yours in this position, I could have defied 10,000 of the best troops in the world."

━━━━━━━

After the battle of Bladensburg, bravado and boasting dominated Cockburn's official, but technically inaccurate, report to Admiral Cochrane: "That the enemy, 8,000 strong, on ground he had chosen as best adapted for him to defend, where he had had time to erect his batteries and concert all his measures, was dislodged as soon as reached."

While his numbers were off—many historians note that only 6,000 men had attempted to get to Bladensburg—the outcome was not. "And a victory gained over him by a division of the British Army not amounting to more than 1,500 men headed by our gallant general whose brilliant achievement of this day it is beyond my power to do justice to, and indeed no possible comment could enhance."

Though he knew that he had influenced Ross, he was careful not to take the credit. No matter his heart, bragging too much for one's own personal gain wouldn't give him a promotion. He had to let others do the boasting for him. That was the Royal Navy way.

"The contest being completely ended and the enemy having retired from the field, the general gave the army about two hours rest."

Little did Cockburn know the decision to take a break would cost them precious time for capturing the prey they desired most.

After evacuating the White House, Dolley fled to Charles Carroll's residence, Bellevue, in Georgetown. Eleanor Jones, the wife of the navy secretary, and their family also joined her. The people of Washington were fleeing in all directions, taking refuge wherever they could in Virginia and Maryland.

James was Dolley's top concern. Where was he? Was he safe? Had the British captured him? What had happened at Bladensburg? She soon found out.

Though James had arrived at the White House not long after her departure, they did not reunite there. He rested briefly and decided to evacuate town. Dolley and her entourage left Mr. Carroll's house and met James near the Potomac River. Relief swept over both of them to behold each other. But they didn't have time for a long embrace.

He gave her a plan. Believing it wasn't safe for them to stay together, he suggested they separate. Under the protection of a cavalry unit, she should find a place of shelter wherever she could. Then they would meet at an inn about sixteen miles beyond Georgetown the next day. Though she would have preferred to stay with him, under the circumstances, she trusted his plan.

No one knew when the redcoats would arrive in Washington. The only certainty was that the British were coming.

Normally many boats were available to ferry eager passengers across the Potomac into Virginia. The loss at Bladensburg, however, had led to a panic. With most of the boats sunk, only one was left, and it was small.

Hence, transporting Madison's party across the river would take several trips. The president, Monroe, Rush, Mr. Carroll, and another officer ferried over to the other side. By this time, night was settling over the horizon. Knowing that the British had burned forty of sixty buildings in Havre de Grace the previous year, they could easily imagine the horror that might rise on that horizon by midnight.

CHAPTER TWENTY-THREE

Capitol Conflagration

Once again, Cockburn couldn't have been happier. He had finally gotten what he wanted: the chance to invade Washington City. If he was lucky, he would capture Mr. and Mrs. Madison, too.

After a rest, the dutiful general and pirate admiral rode from Bladensburg to Washington. The 200 or so men following them were mostly those who hadn't fought at Bladensburg, including many slaves turned into British fighters in hopes of becoming free, and Cockburn's Royal Marines and sailors. Ever by his side was Lieutenant Scott.

"In the land of liberty, a clear open road led to the capitol, which now rose before us in the twilight," Scott recalled.

The two-winged U.S. Capitol building welcomed them with an eerie silence. No hustle. No bustle. This castle that usually housed congressmen, not monarchs, seemed as lifeless as a cemetery. Deciding to lead the advance with an offer of parley, Ross ordered a soldier to carry a white flag of truce. The general hoped to negotiate with the U.S.

government over monetary or other capitulation terms. Cockburn had made similar agreements with several Chesapeake communities. If the towns agreed not to fight, the British soldiers and marines would spare houses and private property. Would Washington City do the same?

They waited for an answer while stopping near a red-bricked mansion at the corner of Constitution Avenue, Maryland Avenue, and Second Street Southeast.

An American or perhaps a group of patriots had an answer for their flag of truce: gunfire.

"And on the general, myself, and some officers advancing a short way past the first houses of the town without being accompanied by the troops, the enemy opened upon us a heavy fire of musketry from the capitol and two other houses," Cockburn reported of the houses on his right and left.

Sniper fire shot and killed Ross's horse. Though Cockburn hadn't voyaged with Ross across the Atlantic, he knew how important the animal was to the general. Everyone knew. This wasn't just any ordinary horse. Ross had relied on the beast time and time again while fighting Napoleon's military forces in Europe. Now his most reliable horse was gone.

Also gone was the flag of truce. Replacing it was a determination to silence the snipers. Though the defenders got away, Cockburn sent Scott to search the mansion, which was unoccupied but owned by Robert Sewall of Maryland. The British burned it and another one.

As Cockburn later reported, "These were therefore almost immediately stormed by our people, taken possession of, and set on fire, after which the town submitted without further resistance."

Ah, Cockburn and Scott later boasted their version of facts by boosting the numbers. Scott claimed that sniper fire had come from hundreds of Americans hiding in several houses and the Capitol to create a crossfire effect. "Common sense should have led the authorities to sue for favorable terms for the city, instead of ensconcing a few hundred militiamen behind walls to impede our progress," Scott reflected.

While the admiral and his officers considered their choice to burn private property as justified casualties of warfare, Americans viewed their actions as barbaric.

"All of this is even more absurd than false. The other houses set on fire were not near Sewall's house. One of them was General Washington's house," Congressman Charles Ingersoll later wrote about a house belonging to the late first president's estate.

Americans later insisted that the source of the gunfire was a lone gunman positioned at the empty Sewall house, which Albert Gallatin had rented for twelve years before leaving for Europe to negotiate peace with England. The man who fired the shot was thought to be a local Irish barber who was drunk.

Regardless, Cockburn knew that their decision to burn the properties had the desired effect. No one dared resist them again on their next stop, a tour of the U.S. Capitol.

━━━━━━━━━

Meanwhile, U.S. Commodore Thomas Tingey made a decision about the Navy Yard. Like Barney before him, he was prepared to implement Navy Secretary Jones's orders should the fateful hour come.

Jones had earlier given Tingey the responsibility of preparing the Navy Yard to burn it if necessary. If the British marched to Washington, Tingey was to set fire to the stores, provisions, and ships at the Navy Yard to deny the enemy the pleasure of plundering such valuable military items and using them against Americans later. Tingey complied, prepared the yard, and sprinkled a trail of powder throughout.

At half past three o'clock in the afternoon on August 24, Jones learned that the U.S. forces were retreating from Bladensburg. Leaving Tingey in charge at the Navy Yard, he rode over to Mr. Carroll's house in Georgetown, where he found his family with Dolley Madison. Soon he received word from the president to join him and other cabinet members at Foxhall works, an iron foundry near Georgetown.

Tingey's problems increased when he received a flurry of objections from residents who lived near the Navy Yard. They rightfully feared that their houses would go up in flames if he set fire to the gunpowder trail. Though he promised to take "every possible precaution for the safety of their property and families," he soon discovered that his words weren't enough.

"A deputation also of the most respectable women came on the same errand," he reported. With the pleas of the ladies tugging on his heart, he responded compassionately. "I would delay the execution of the orders, as long as I could feel the least shadow of justification."

Tingey, however, received a dispatch from Secretary Armstrong that "he could protect me no longer."

Burning the Navy Yard now seemed inevitable. Increasing his worry over collateral damage was the change of the winds, which began blowing south, southwest around five o'clock p.m. By 8:20 p.m., he knew he could no longer delay. General Ross was sending a unit of British soldiers to the Navy Yard. He had no choice but to implement Secretary Jones's order. "The matches were applied, and in a few moments the whole was in a state of irretrievable conflagration."

With the Navy Yard ablaze by his own hand, Tingey escaped by boat to nearby Alexandria. Hence, not long after the British arrived in Washington, an American set the first fire to U.S. government property.

———

With the business of removing the portrait complete, French John and Paul Jennings, a teenage slave, had stayed behind for a while after the Madisons left the White House. French John or Paul likely contained the fires in the kitchen to avoid accidentally catching the house on fire—an irony under the circumstances.

French John shut doors and windows and transported the Madisons' pet parrot, a macaw, to the Octagon House, where the French minister to America resided. Because the Octagon housed a diplomat, it was guaranteed immunity from an invading British force and could provide protection for the Madisons' pet.

Departing around twilight to cross the Potomac River, as the British were entering the city, Paul Jennings was the last to leave. Earlier in the day, he had arranged the damask napkins on the State Dining Room table and followed other urgent instructions. Dolley's brother-in-law, Mr. Cutts, had "sent me to a stable on 14th street, for his carriage," as Jennings recalled.

He also noted that some vandals entered the White House before the British arrived. "In the mean time, a rabble, taking advantage of the confusion, ran all over the White House, and stole lots of silver and whatever they could lay their hands on."

Then he left the abandoned White House.

━━━━━━━━━

As the British formed a line facing the U.S. Capitol, they couldn't help but notice the unusual combination of rustic magnificence. The three-storied Capitol consisted of two independent wings. The Senate wing was on the north; the House, on the south. Connecting them in the middle was a covered wooden walkway. Though seeing it for the first time, these British observers could tell that something was missing. That something was a dome.

"It was an unfinished but beautifully arranged building," as Lieutenant Scott described it.

Cockburn couldn't have been more excited as he and his men entered through the east door of the north wing. Before him was the most symbolic building of America's representative government. This was where America's laws were made by leaders elected by the people. This was the place where men had declared war against his country and king. This was to be the first of his glorious attack.

With increasing adrenaline, the admiral watched with gleeful mischief as his force fired volleys into the Capitol.

No one fired back, giving them the all clear to storm it.

Then with the awe of tourists, the enemy brigade marched into the magnificent stone vestibule. Inside they found a wonderland of architecture and art. They saw marbled columns carved to look like corn stalks at the top. Italian artists had chiseled these columns, as well as arched entrances, domed foyers, and vaulted ceilings. If Scott's recollection mirrored his boss's, such beauty impressed them both: "The interior accommodations were upon a scale of grandeur and magnificence little suited to pure republican simplicity."

Why was the U.S. Capitol so regal? Hadn't the Americans traded royalty for representation? The British couldn't believe that the people who so hated kings and castles had built a capitol "infected with an unseemly bias for monarchical splendor."

Cockburn soon found a treasure trove. On the west side of the Senate wing, one of his men discovered Congress's library, which was a two-story room with a wooden floor and flat ceiling housing 3,000 books on shelves. Because it was filled with so much paper and wood, it was the most flammable room in the building. The admiral took at least one as a souvenir to prove his unmistakable presence, a book titled *An Account of the Receipts and Expenditure of the United States for the Year 1810*. After all, he couldn't very well pose for hours while an artist painted his portrait to capture the moment.

The admiral signed the book and intended to give it to his brother, Sir James Cockburn, the governor of Bermuda. His inscription read, "Taken in the President's room in the Capitol at the destruction of that building by the British on the capture of Washington, Aug. 24, 1814, by Admiral Cockburn."

Next to the Senate chamber, Cockburn's and Ross's redcoats found portraits of the king and queen of France, Louis XVI and Marie Antoinette. How perfectly perfect this was. These gems gave them an opportunity to vandalize and perhaps make some money in the process. Because Louis XVI had supported America's revolution against England, the British military gleefully cut the pictures from the frames and stole them. What price they would bring at another port, no one knew. Yet they were ideal items for trading or selling.

When the British military entered the House of Representatives chamber in the south wing, they saw one hundred skylights that hung like paneled ribbons along the grand domed-painted ceiling. In addition to seeing Corinthian columns joined by curtain swags along the perimeter, they also viewed handsome desks for each member of Congress arranged in semicircles surrounding the speaker's chair. Nearby was a beautiful clock. Hanging above that was a magnificent gilded, sculpted eagle whose wingspan stretched twelve feet. Carved by an Italian sculptor, the eagle was one of Benjamin Latrobe's favorite contributions to his renovation of the Capitol.

Scott also saw the symbolism. The speaker's chair was "surmounted by a gilt eagle, with extended wings and ruffled crest, looking towards the skies, emblematical, it is to be presumed, of the rising greatness of the young nation."

With such a site, what was a pirate admiral to do? Why, have some fun, of course. Why not? He had dreamed of this moment for months. Without the poetry of Shakespeare but with the humor of a court jester, Cockburn plopped into the House Speaker's chair while his men filled the House chamber and sat in the seats belonging to congressmen.

"Shall this harbor of Yankee democracy be burned?" Cockburn called out in his mock trial. "All for it will say aye."

With the rowdiness of pirates drinking ale after capturing another ship, his men cheered and cried out in the affirmative.

Any nays?

No. The vote was unanimous.

Ah. Time for orders. Hence, his men complied. They piled desks, chairs, books, and anything else they could find into mounds in the center of the chamber. Using gunpowder, they sprinkled the piles to prepare for an instant conflagration after their fiery rockets struck them.

"Its funeral pile was lighted up as the clock under it told the hour of ten," according to Scott.

As they thrust their rockets into the doomed dome-less Capitol, the place became an instant inferno. The worst in man joined forces with the worst in nature to create despicable destruction. Arson. "The position of the Capitol was elevated; the fiery beacon must have shed a sadly brilliant light upon the American habitations for miles around."

Indeed. The flames were massive, floating high into the sky. From their covered post in an abandoned house in Leesburg thirty miles away, the clerks guarding the Declaration of Independence and other national archival papers grieved in horror as they saw the flames of the Capitol and Navy Yard in the great distance.

━━━━━━━━

Years earlier George Washington, who had been a land surveyor as a young man, made a critical decision about the location of the President's House. The city's first master planner, Pierre L'Enfant, had envisioned a palace about five times larger than the mansion eventually built. L'Enfant had already placed the stakes documenting the perimeter, which was in direct view of the U.S. Capitol, a mile and a quarter away along Pennsylvania Avenue.

Washington disagreed. Tapping his land surveyor skills, he recalculated the stakes of the President's House to make the house smaller. He also relocated the north entrance, which moved the house out of the direct line of sight with the U.S. Capitol. Thus, Pennsylvania Avenue bent to accommodate the change. As a result, the grand boulevard extended from the Capitol several blocks before making a turn northward at Fifteenth Street.

Mrs. Suter ran a tavern and boardinghouse near this elbow. Though the Capitol didn't have a direct view of the White House, Mrs. Suter's property did. Boarders at her tavern could enjoy the architectural glory of the White House and the adjacent Treasury Building while savoring a great meal. Such was her spot's reputation. Little did she know how far knowledge of her tavern extended.

A few days before the British advanced on Bladensburg, Mrs. Suter had heard a knock on her door. When she opened it, she discovered a British deserter, a straggler begging for food. With her sons called up to the militia, the widow was nervous to allow an English stranger into her tavern. One of her boarders, the postmaster general, had advised her against feeding the lad.

Yet, she also had compassion for a youth so abused by the likes of Admiral Cockburn and other British serpents. Could she really turn away someone who was hungry? Didn't he seem sincere and look a mess? Wasn't he like her sons, and wouldn't she want someone else to feed them if they were in a similar situation? What was this tavern keeper to do?

She remained true to her job and her business and fed him, though he ate outside.

With the Capitol burning behind him, Cockburn mounted his horse. His uniform typically featured erect gold epaulettes glistening on the shoulders of his blue jacket distinguished by a red diagonal sash and gold buttons. With such plumage adorning his fierce instincts, he rode through the streets of Washington with a combination of a proud peacock, ferocious lion, and a slippery snake not to be trusted.

Cockburn, along with Ross and Scott and a line of redcoats, traveled on horseback down Pennsylvania Avenue, which was a wide boulevard lined with beautiful green trees.

Along the way, several British officers stopped by the houses of frightened women and the few remaining men in town. They gave instructions to the residents. Stay inside. Keep quiet. If you do, all will be well.

Following the officers on foot were one hundred men who walked in a double-file line. The leader of this unit carried a knife and wore a *chapeau de bras*, or a bicorne hat typical of the Napoleonic era.

In the middle of the redcoats' line were two men who carried lanterns to light their way, though by this point with the Capitol on fire, the need for light was hardly great.

The men marched quickly, and mostly quietly, except for a handful of ruffians who began to talk.

"Silence! If any man speaks in the ranks I'll put him to death!" their leader called out.

While his men were forced to walk in silence, Cockburn was anything but quiet. When the admiral saw an American man peering out of the window of a house on Pennsylvania Avenue, he decided to have some fun. He and Ross rode up to the house, which provoked a question from the nervous resident.

"Gentlemen, I presume you are officers with the British army?" the American called out. "I hope, Sir, that individuals and private property will be respected."

Cockburn's response bore the tone expected of an admiral. He even pulled off his hat and wished him a good evening in a polite and sociable manner.

"Yes, Sir, we pledge our sacred honor, that the citizens and private property shall be respected," the admiral promised, overlooking the fact that they had burned private houses on Capitol Hill.

Perhaps he detected a doubtful look on the man's face because he added: "Be under no apprehension. Our advice to you is to remain at home. Do not quit your houses."

Pleased at the agreement in the man's eyes, Admiral Cockburn revealed the question most plaguing him as he prepared to capture the White House. "Where is your President, Mr. Madison?"

The man said he didn't know and couldn't tell. But he supposed the president was a considerable distance away by now.

Pity. Tasty cakes would have to wait. Cockburn's hopes of capturing the Madisons now faded with each step of his horse down Pennsylvania Avenue. Though having the pleasure of Mrs. Madison's company now eluded him, what awaited him at the White House was something more dazzling than he ever expected to find.

CHAPTER TWENTY-FOUR

White House Inferno

When Cockburn and Ross arrived at the elbow of Pennsylvania and 15th Street, they decided to engage in more mischief. Why not? With all they'd accomplished, they were hungry. Besides, who would dare deny them food when they carried weapons of war? Cockburn was pleased because Ross had followed his lead and taken on a teasing but terrorizing tone. They stopped by Mrs. Suter's tavern.

Finding her alone with only servants for company, Ross announced that they had "come, Madam, to sup with you."

They could tell by her relaxed demeanor that she mistook them for American officers. Her tone quickly switched as she realized who they were. Replying that she didn't have any vittles to eat, she suggested they try a tavern on another street.

Explaining that he "preferred her house, because he had some acquaintance with her," Ross referred to the incident of the U.S. postmaster who had recently discouraged her from feeding a British deserter, "a poor British soldier in distress." A more accurate term would be spy.

Then they insisted that she prepare a meal for them and several of their officers. Ross said they "should return after visiting the treasury."

Seeing fear in her eyes, they were confident that she would comply. Indeed, after they left, she killed some chickens from her yard and warmed some bread to await the return of the men who were burning her neighbor's house and her nation's seat of government.

———

Wonder what little Jemmy thinks of his war now? Such was the contemptuous attitude of George Cockburn as he beheld his pearly white treasure the night of August 24. Though disappointed to find the Madisons weren't at home, he was still as happy as he could possibly be. Here was his opportunity to bring glory to England.

Cockburn and Ross gave orders. Some of their men invaded the President's House, while others stayed outside and prepared to launch their rockets or fiery poles.

Many, especially the officers, strode the steps and boldly placed their boots onto the floor of the entry hall. They quickly scattered throughout the rooms. Cockburn couldn't have been more delighted to tour this mansion and see the beautiful rooms decorated by Mrs. Madison.

Soon his nose overtook his bulging eyes. While many valuables surrounded him, including small engraved drawings of Dolley and Madison, his fine dress sword, her gowns, and others, what attracted the most attention that night was the dining room. That's because it was full of something that Cockburn and his men hadn't seen much of all day long—food and wine. Though abandoned, the White House was set and ready to entertain the admiral as if he had received an invitation.

Lieutenant Scott described the feast that awaited them: "A large store of super excellent Madeira and other costly wines stood cooling in ice in one corner of the spacious dining-room."

While Dolley was physically absent, her hospitable presence was very much felt. The optimistic effort she had made to prepare a victory celebration for her husband and his officers took the form of a table set for a party of forty, complete with silver bowls covering the plates. To Cockburn's and Scott's delight, the $500 china set along with silver knives, forks, and spoons glistened while fully cooked food rested on the hearth.

"We found the cloth laid for the expected victorious generals, and all the appliances and meals to form a feast worthy the resolute champions of republican freedom," Scott recorded.

Cockburn did what any leader would do. He put the primal needs of his officers ahead of their mission. They could wait to finish the job. Hence he ordered them to partake of the providential feast. After all, they'd had a very long day, from marching from camp at daybreak and marching again at sunset. Setting fire to buildings was hard work.

Scott was very pleased by his boss's decision to enjoy the moment. "Never was nectar more grateful to the palates of the gods, than the crystal goblet of Madeira and water I quaffed off at Mr. Madison's expense."

A feast like this wouldn't be complete without one key thing: a toast. And Cockburn knew exactly who should join him: an American who owed his paycheck to the happenings of Capitol Hill.

━━━━━━━

While in Washington, Cockburn had acquired a traveling companion of sorts. He had picked up, or, more accurately, temporarily kidnapped, a young man. Roger Weightman was a bookseller who owed his livelihood to the happenings of Congress. A U.S. government contractor, he frequently printed reports for the House of Representatives. Somehow Cockburn got ahold of him. He wanted an American witness, someone who could relay the story of how the pirate-like admiral achieved his finest conquest.

On entering the dining room, Cockburn insisted that young Weightman sit down and join them. Not only that, but he also required Weightman to make a toast and drink to Jemmy's health. As a victim of kidnapping, Weightman felt the force of the cutlass in his back and the coercion to do just that. Hence, he gave a toast.

Under Cockburn's leadership, the toasting took on a life of its own. One officer toasted to the health of the prince regent of Great Britain. Another lifted his glass to His Majesty's success on land and sea. Still another exhorted: "To peace with America and down with Madison."

Such toasts wouldn't be complete without taking a souvenir, something to remember the moment. Cockburn looked around and told Weightman to take an item. The young American spotted a valuable ornament. Cockburn protested. No, no, that was too costly and he "must give [it] to the flames." Then he handed Weightman a trinket from the mantle piece to serve as his souvenir.

Now it was Cockburn's turn to take a memento. He grabbed a cushion from what he concluded was Mrs. Madison's chair. He hoped Jemmy wouldn't mind, because "this will remind me of Mrs. Madison's seat."

Someone else found one of Madison's hats, an old *chapeau de bras*, and gave it to the admiral. Using the tip of his bayonet, he declared that if they couldn't capture "the little president" they would parade his hat in England.

Scott also joined in the looting fun. He and others swiftly passed through the mansion's second floor, which served as the Madisons' private quarters. The mahogany furniture flanked walls that may have been decorated with pink, green, and yellow floral wallpaper. Dolley had given a scrap of the wallpaper to her friend Mary Latrobe by lining it in a box as a memento of Mr. Latrobe's design work on the interior. Where exactly the wallpaper was placed is a mystery.

When Scott entered the president's private quarters, many of the drawers were already opened, creating a mess of disarray. Scott thought that this was the result of the Madisons' quick departure. Very likely, some of the sloppiness was left by looters who had visited the White House in between Mrs. Madison's escape and the British arrival, as Paul Jennings later recorded.

Though the dresses Dolley Madison left behind were as lovely as they were valuable, Mr. Madison's wardrobe had an immediate, practical application, particularly for Scott, whose own clothes were highly spoiled. Madison's "snowy clean linen tempted me to take the liberty of making a very fair exchange.... I accordingly doffed my inner garment, and thrust my unworthy person into a shirt belonging to no less a personage than the chief magistrate of the United States."

Scott had also noticed something else of value. "On the walls hung a small portrait of the President's lady." He was not alone. One of the British marines or soldiers took this miniature of Dolley and another one or two of Madison, as Dolley later claimed.

Still another officer stole Madison's fine dress sword while another took a small walnut medicine chest. The most innovative theft was the British lad who hung around after dinner. This pirate captured a whole bounty of booty by taking a tablecloth from the dining room and tying plates, knives, and forks into it.

With the looting complete, Cockburn knew it was time for the real fun to begin. This was better than any other raid he had ever conducted. Here he was, fulfilling his dream. What would they say back in England? He wouldn't be just an admiral. He would be the hero who burned the White House of the rebellious Englishmen who called themselves Americans. Fame would come with such a glorious victory.

Hence, it was time to prepare the kindling for the long-awaited moment. British sailors and marines piled up the furniture, such as the dozen Grecian cane chairs in the red oval room and the beds in the bedrooms. Using whatever they could find, they created stacks and piles throughout the house.

The president's mahogany bed with its elegant linens was particularly attractive. The Brits took lamp oil and poured it on bed linens and curtains topping the furniture piles. One captain claimed: "Our sailors were artists at the work."

Once they had piled the furniture, poured the lamp oil, and smashed the windows, they were ready for the final act. So was Cockburn.

Making sure everyone had left the house, the admiral likely smiled with a buccaneer's glee. He watched triumphantly as fifty sailors and marines surrounded the house. Each man carried a long pole that held a ball of oily rags about the size of a plate at the end of it and stood in front of a broken window or door. After each of the men had lit the end of his pole, the pyrotechnic commander gave the order: *Fire!*

In unison, they thrust their fire poles and hurled them like javelins through the windows and doors. Flames instantly engulfed the White House, destroying in one moment the house that George Washington had chosen for his successors.

The sky was reddened by the double blazes of the White House inferno and the Capitol conflagration. They were President Madison's greatest humiliation and Cockburn's finest triumph. The admiral would now be the man forever linked with destroying the symbols and monuments of American power and strength.

―――――

While James crossed the river, Dolley returned to Georgetown and led a party of ladies to find shelter in Virginia.

What slowed their progress? Nothing less than nineteenth-century traffic. The road was filled with so many wagons carrying passengers and precious belongings that progress was incredibly slow. At times the women left the coach and walked just to keep their sanity. They made it only two and half miles beyond Georgetown when they decided to stop for the evening.

Finding their friend Matilda Love at home in her house, they took shelter on the Virginia side of the Potomac River for the night. Dolley, the woman known for her hospitality, suddenly found herself playing the role of an imposing guest with Mrs. Love as her host.

The women had no way to know for sure what was happening in Washington. But as the British began to burn the city, they could see flames lighting up the sky.

In front of a window, Dolley gazed at the flickering light on the horizon. All she could do was pray, cry, and hope that a better day would come for her country and her husband. A war that once seemed distant in faraway Canada had arrived on their doorstep. Where it would lead and how it would end was anyone's guess.

"Washington was, by such conduct, as completely at our mercy, as any city taken by storm," Scott later recalled.

Meanwhile, Ross and Cockburn had not forgotten Mrs. Suter. They, along with a party of ten officers, returned to the frightened woman's table.

As they ate, Cockburn blew out the candles. He teased and tortured Mrs. Suter by saying that he "preferred the light of the burning palace and treasury" to the pale moonlight.

Though he doubted the Madisons were close by, he didn't give up trying to discover their hiding place. He also announced to Mrs. Suter that he wanted to show President Madison the streets of London. Did she know the whereabouts of the Madisons?

Ever the patriot and showing more wisdom than she had before, she replied simply. No, she did not.

"It was near midnight, when, in passing a handsome row of houses, we observed one standing a little aback and apart from the rest," Scott relayed.

After dining at Mrs. Suter's, they advanced down Pennsylvania Avenue toward the burning Capitol when "some good friend of the editor of the *National Intelligencer* pointed it out to the admiral, as the office of the American government paper."

Had the man truly been a friend to the Irish American editor, Joseph Gales, he wouldn't have revealed the brick building's location. Nor would he have suggested that Mr. Gales's paper was a government entity. Very possibly, the person responsible for revealing the location was a

Federalist who opposed the Republican-leaning editor. Scott, who knew that Admiral Cockburn devoured American newspapers as often as he took afternoon tea, understood the *National Intelligencer*'s significance.

"It had ever taken the lead, and given the keynote to the republican press, in vilifying England and the English. The editor was reported to be an Irish renegade."

America had no such literal thing. Yes, the tone and content of newspapers often leaned one political direction or the other. Such had long been the case. But Gales didn't operate a newspaper funded by the U.S. government. He was friendly and favorable to Madison; nonetheless, freedom of the press was taken seriously. Gales operated a private business in a public town.

Cockburn decided to set fire to Gales's newspaper building. If he couldn't capture Madison, he could at least destroy his best press.

"Its fate was decreed, and a few minutes would have seen it a prey to the devouring element—when a party of ladies, inhabitants of the adjoining houses, came forward to meet the admiral," Scott said.

The ladies didn't know who Cockburn was, only that he was an officer. They asked him to spare the building from fire because it was in such close proximity to their homes, which would burn right along with it.

"Well, good people I do not wish to injure you, but I am really afraid my friend Josey will be affronted with me, if after burning Jemmy's palace, I do not pay him the same compliment."

Josey was Cockburn's nickname for Joseph Gales. As he had done in Havre de Grace after hearing the pleas of women, Cockburn recalled his order to torch the place. Then he left a guard there overnight. "Never fear. You shall be much safer under my administration than Madison's," he promised.

Scott recalled the ladies' reaction: "The success of the fair petitioners emboldened others to advance, and in a few minutes the admiral was surrounded by a host of lovely women, who certainly outshone their countrymen in generalship on the capture of their metropolis."

The admiral easily charmed the ladies with his courtesy and manners. Then when one of the ladies invited him into her house to partake of refreshments, he accepted. Just as Scott was about to enter the house, one woman asked the name of the gallant officer.

"Why, that is the vile monster, Cock-burn," Scott replied, emphasizing the American pronunciation. "A half-uttered shriek of terror escaped from the lips of some of them, as the dreaded name tingled on their ears. The announcement was electrifying."

The ladies were shocked and disgusted. This amused Scott, who remembered Mr. Boyle's advertisement from the summer of 1813. "My plighted word at last convinced them of the astounding fact that they had absolutely stood in the presence of, and amicably conversed with, that most venomous of all 'British serpents,' and for whose head a reward of one thousand dollars had been publicly offered."

When it came to Cockburn's last name, Scott noted that "the Americans always pronounced the name as two long distinct syllables."

They enjoyed some refreshments and returned to headquarters on Capitol Hill. Congressman Charles Ingersoll later accused Cockburn of spending the night at a brothel. He called him the "harlequin of havoc."

"I make no war on letters or ladies," Ross confessed that night.

Unlike his counterpart, Ross's conscience bothered him. On Capitol Hill, General Ross had taken the house of Dr. James Ewell for his headquarters. When he discovered that the building housed a private family and the bedroom he was to use was the wife's chamber, he resisted Dr. Ewell's hospitality.

"I cannot think of trespassing on the repose of a private family, and will order my baggage out of the house immediately."

Dr. Ewell insisted that he stay, and promised to cooperate if the British spared his house. Ross agreed.

"I am a married man myself with several sweet children, and venerate the sanctities of the conjugal and domestic relations," Ross explained.

The general shared of his regrets with Ewell, claiming that he didn't know that the Library of Congress was housed inside the Capitol until after the burning. He also didn't know how revered Mrs. Madison was until it was too late.

"I have heard so much praise of Mrs. Madison, that I would rather protect than burn a house which sheltered so excellent a lady," he said.

Say what he might, he did just that. Ross went along with Cockburn. He may have been a commanding general, but he played the role of foal to Cockburn's leading mare.

They had to wonder, too, what had happened to Dolley.

CHAPTER TWENTY-FIVE

Displaced or Conquered?

The next morning, before the sun rose on August 25, Dolley took the lead. Committed to meeting the president at the inn sixteen miles from Washington, she departed with the ladies toward their countryside destination. The citizens they would meet along the way would reveal more about her husband's reputation and fall from grace than she ever wanted to know.

Panic-filled people became pedestrians on the paths of Virginia. No one felt safe anywhere. Rumors followed Dolley as she traveled to the inn. Without instant communication and reliable sources, all they had were nuggets of news. Yet falsehoods were so prevalent that the truth was elusive. One rumor rose to the surface: that Cockburn's atrocities were worse than they had been at Hampton, where British soldiers had stolen women's honor.

Though this wasn't true, they carried the fears of possibility with them. If the British had burned the White House and Capitol, what would they do next? Would they declare America conquered? Did they

255

plan to advance up the coast and demand the capitulation of other major cities like Baltimore, Philadelphia, New York, and Boston? Or were people overreacting?

Hence, Dolley and her group headed onward, not knowing if they would have a dwelling to return to or if they would be able to return.

———

Also on the morning of August 25, while rain covered the sunrise, Cockburn returned to the *National Intelligencer* building. "Make sure all the C's are destroyed, so the rascals can't abuse my name anymore."

Instead of burning the building, Cockburn ordered some of the officers and marines to use ropes to pull the building down. They picked out the letter Cs from the printing press and stole them.

"I'll punish Madison's man, Joe," the admiral said, "as I have his master, Jim."

Scott reported: "The reams of paper, files of gazettes foreign and domestic, and all the inflammable materials, had been previously conveyed to some distance in the rear, and a bonfire made of them."

The admiral and Scott considered the destruction of the *National Intelligencer* as a just purification against "the instruments of corruption and falsehood emanating from a traitorous proprietor."

That same day, Ross and Cockburn received a group of residents from nearby Alexandria. They offered to surrender their city in exchange for sparing the buildings. Certainly. Cockburn and Ross agreed. The officers' only disappointment was that the British ships assigned to invade Alexandria hadn't yet arrived.

———

What was the extent of Cockburn's destruction? The U.S. Capitol. The White House. The Treasury. The War Office. The British burned every government building except the one housing the post office and patent office.

The British force also burned two ropewalks, which were private businesses. They knocked over barrels of tar and spread out hemp and cords in a train. Because of this pyrotechnic arrangement, the ropewalk fire ran rapidly along the building's six hundred yards.

Cockburn described the destruction as complete in a letter to Cochrane: "In short, Sir, I do not believe a vestige of public property, or a store of any kind which could be converted to the use of the government, escaped destruction; the bridges across the Eastern Branch and the Potomac were likewise destroyed."

———

Meanwhile, Mrs. Madison and her entourage reached the tavern chosen by the president. A black sky hovered over the building's roof and apple orchard. Forked lightning lit up the sky. Winds whipped through the orchard, tossing apples as if they were as light as snow flakes.

The worst in nature manifested itself in the form of a storm, matching the whims of the British. Dolley was grateful that she had outrun and outpaced both—at least so far. She needed Providence's promise to be with her wherever she went.

———

The luck of the British behind its Irish commander vanished with the sun. Acts of nature and accidents of man changed the fortunes of the British arsonists in the afternoon of August 25.

"About noon, one of the severest squalls, or more properly speaking tornadoes, which I ever witnessed, passed over Washington," Scott recalled.

The storm uprooted trees and tore off roofs. Debris flew threw the air. One British officer died when winds from the storm threw him from his horse.

Around two o'clock, Ross sent a unit to Greenleaf's Point, the place where the Potomac River meets its eastern branch. Though the Americans had burned the fort located there, the British had heard that stores of valuable gunpowder remained.

However, someone had thrown a large quantity of gunpowder into a well that wasn't full of water. Some of the powder remained dry above the water line. It soon exploded, killing at least twelve British soldiers and severely injuring thirty. Scott reported that "many of the latter were so dreadfully mutilated that instant death would have been a blessing to them."

Ross had had enough. It was time to evacuate and return to their ships. As night enveloped the destroyed city, he ordered his men to quietly slip away and retreat toward Bladensburg: "The object of the expedition being accomplished, I determined, before any greater force of the enemy could be assembled, to withdraw the troops and accordingly commenced retiring on the night of the 25th."

———

Filling the tavern were others seeking shelter. Many were ladies who had attended Dolley's open-house levees and whose husbands and sons had been at the battle in Bladensburg. When they discovered that Dolley was among them, some of them became angry at her. Why should they be under the same roof as the woman whose husband had caused such a calamity to befall their city and country?

Paul Jennings, one of Madison's slaves who eventually bought his freedom, later recalled more details of the threat Dolley encountered at that inn. As Dolley's African servant, Sukey, described it, "The lady of the house learning who she was, became furious, and went to the stairs and screamed out, 'Miss Madison! If that's you, come down and go out! Your husband has got mine out fighting, and d__n you, you shan't stay in my house; so get out!'"

Shocked but composed, Mrs. Madison complied. She traveled to Mrs. Minor's house, a few miles further.

The storm also delayed the president's arrival. By this time, Colonel Monroe had left his party to join General Winder, who led what militia he could still keep together. General Armstrong and Treasury Secretary Campbell had gone to Fredericktown, Maryland. Madison and Mr. Rush along with their escorts slipped into the shelter that evening, where his party rested and ate.

———

Giddy-up replaced gloating in Cockburn's demeanor.

Though sad that his fun had come to an end, even the admiral knew that they didn't have enough men to occupy Washington. They could destroy but not take over without reinforcements. He agreed with Ross's method for retreating. Their men created campfires and gave the appearance that they planned to spend the night. Then they departed after dark.

Not every American was fooled by the maneuver, as one patriot reported.

"Hearing the tramp of the retreating foe, one of the ladies of our household stepped to the door and there encountered a group of British officers asking a last drink from the old pump."

"Great God, Madam!" Cockburn said. "Is this the kind of storm to which you are accustomed in this infernal country?"

"No, Sir. This is a special interposition of Providence to drive our enemies from our city," she replied.

Not even Cockburn could argue with that.

———

At midnight the fortunes of the Madisons changed again. A rumor that the British were coming awoke them. Once again, the president had to make a quick decision. Worried for her safety if she stayed with him, James determined to depart immediately and travel farther into the woods to avoid capture.

While James left under the cover of darkness, Dolley left at daylight. Deciding to leave her companions behind, Dolley disguised herself, used another carriage, and flew further into the countryside. A single escort, a Mr. Duvall, accompanied her. All she could do was wait for word from her husband on what to do next.

After hovering in a hovel during that night, Madison also traveled further, going to the Montgomery Courthouse, where he had planned to meet up with a segment of Winder's militia. When he arrived, he discovered that the army had already moved on. Madison then traveled to a Quaker settlement known as Brookville. The Quakers there took good care of him, giving him supper and lodging. They spread beds for guards throughout the house and placed guards around the house.

"All the villagers, gentlemen and ladies, young and old, throng'd to see the President. He was tranquil as usual, and tho' much distressed by the dreadful event, which had taken place not dispirited," one of the Quakers later reflected. While many community members stopped by to see him, Madison had time to think and contemplate his next move. Here among the peacemakers, he knew more than ever he had to find a path to peace.

He could not possibly emerge as the same leader that he had been. The British may have won this battle, but this scholarly president lacking extensive military service couldn't let them win. He would return to Washington as soon as possible and lead like never before.

━━━━━

"My Dearest," he began in a letter to Dolley. He wrote from Brookville on August 27 at ten o'clock a.m. "I have just received a line from Colonel Monroe saying that the enemy were out of Washington and on the retreat to their ships, and advising our immediate return to Washington. You will all of course take the same resolution."

He added, "I know not where we are in the first instance, to hide our heads." Though Mr. Rush had offered his house, Madison decided that he needed to consult with a former member of Congress, his brother-in-law, the husband of Dolley's sister Anna. "I may fall in with Mr. Cutts and have the aid of his advice."

James returned to the city quickly, by five that evening, and stayed at the Cutts's home on F Street, about a block from the destroyed Treasury Building.

Now it was Dolley's turn to find her way back to James.

PART III

Phoenix by the Dawn's Early Light

The smoldering fires of the Capitol were spices of the phoenix bed,
from which arose offspring more vigorous, beautiful and long lived.
—U.S. Congressman Charles Ingersoll, 1814

President James Monroe (1817–1825) moved into the rebuilt White
House. This drawing depicts a crowded event a few years later in
1829. *Courtesy Library of Congress*

CHAPTER TWENTY-SIX

Phoenix Spices

When the news of the burning of the Capitol and President's House reached London, adulation and hurrahs broke out.

"War America would have, and war she has got.... Washington is no more," the editors of the state-controlled newspaper *London Courier* published.

England's *Evening Star* continued the joy: "The reign of Madison, like of Bonaparte, may be considered as at an end."

The *National Register* of London printed that Madison had shot himself. A downright lie, that was.

Back in America, Congressman Ingersoll later reflected: "It was an attack, not against the strength or the resources of a state, but against the national honor and public affections of a people."

He went on to note that though invading armies often captured capital cities, they didn't burn them. The respect of nations for each other, except for accidents, usually led armies to spare monuments, records of history, halls of legislation, and art when capturing a capital.

Ingersoll was particularly outraged that the British had violated this code, especially after battling Napoleon. "After twenty-five years, of the fiercest warfare, in which every great capital of Europe had been spared, almost respected by enemies, it was reserved for England to violate all that decent courtesy towards the seats of national dignity."

Ingersoll saw the issue as one of fairness, for, as he pointed out, "the object of the expedition, both General Ross and Admiral Cochrane officially reported to their government, was the complete destruction of the public buildings: barbarism which Vienna, Lisbon, Berlin, Amsterdam, Madrid, Munich, Moscow, and Paris, were not subjected to when captured in this century."

He wasn't the only American who felt that way. In Ghent, John Quincy Adams had a similar reaction after he learned of the burning of the U.S. Capitol and President's House. The news had set back the peace negotiations with the British.

"There is scarcely a metropolis in Europe that has not been taken in the course of the last twenty years. There is not a single instance in all that time of public buildings like those being destroyed," he wrote in a letter to his wife, Louisa, shortly after he learned of the burning.

He deplored a recent instance of an invading military force setting fire to a major city. "The army of Napoleon did indeed blow up the Kremlin at Moscow, but that was a fortified castle, and even this act has ever been and ever will be stigmatized as one of the most infamous of his deeds."

━━━━━━━━

As soon as she received her husband's letter dated August 27, Dolley departed for Washington. By this time she was no longer the Quaker queen costumed in her best silks. She had camouflaged her appearance, wearing the shawl of a simple farmer's wife. Her journey progressed well until she reached the Potomac River and its Long Bridge, which was burned at both ends.

Posted there was Colonel Fenwick, whose assignment was to ferry war ammunition and the needs of the military across the river. When she arrived, he didn't recognize her and refused to escort her across the river. Only military people were allowed on his ferryboat. Orders were orders.

Disfigured at the battle of Queenstown, Fenwick's body was riddled with the marks of musket fire. He had also lost an eye and his ability to use a hand. Ever the patriot, he was unbending and refused to let this farmer's wife cross the river on his ferryboat.

Dolley didn't give up. She sent her escort to Fenwick again and asked him to come to her carriage in person. Please. No. Please, again. No and no. What should she do?

With no other option, she revealed her identity. As soon as he realized he was facing Mrs. Madison, he agreed to whisk her along with her borrowed carriage across the river in his boat.

Destruction greeted her path as she traveled the debris-filled roads to her sister's house. Adding to the devastation was anger. Americans had scribbled on the Capitol's charred walls "The capital and the union lost by cowardice." Other graffiti proclaimed: "John Armstrong is a traitor" … "Fruits of war without preparation" … "This is the city of Madison" … "George Washington founded this city after a seven years' war with England—James Madison lost it after a two-years' war."

Dolley knew her husband's heart was broken. Seeing that broke her heart, as did the sight of the White House as a blackened shell. They rode over and surveyed the ashes together. Tears no doubt unraveled her. Exterior walls showing the shape of a large rectangle were all that remained. The inside was gone. Their piano, clothes, chairs, curtains— all were blackened. The muddy pit was an ash heap of history. They'd lived in the capital city since it began. Now, after a mere fourteen years, Washington appeared at an end.

Had the father of the U.S. Constitution been the one to lose the country? Would they now be severed into two countries, with the Federalists in New England leading a return to England? The weight of such responsibility was heavy on Madison's heart, and on Dolley's.

What would they do? Where would they go? What would happen to their country and this capital city? Would it become ancient ruins, uncovered in future centuries by archeologists as the failed city? Or would it rise like a phoenix?

Just as Madison had played a role in the birth of Washington City, so its destiny was tied to him, his wife, and the unsung average Americans who would rally for their capital city, their country, and the U.S. Constitution.

———

Many Americans had to ask, were they ready for the American experiment to end this way? Were they willing to be conquered and subjected again to the king? Yes, they were angry and blamed Armstrong and Madison. Yes, they wondered how the general government could have let such an awful thing happen. But this land was their land. This was America's turf and it was time to fight with all they had.

"The immediate and enthusiastic effect of the fall of Washington, was electrical revival of national spirit and universal energy," Congressman Ingersoll reflected.

Mr. Madison's war had been unpopular among many Americans. The embargoes had cut off the livelihoods of individuals, sinking people into poverty. The government was borrowing money to fund the war and would soon default. Though the regular military didn't have enough men, Congress didn't have the legal power to draft regular soldiers, and the militia proved ineffective at Bladensburg. America was often strong where it should have been the weakest: at sea. Conversely, generals and officers frequently mismanaged battles on land, weakening Madison's hand in treating for peace.

After the burning of the U.S. Capitol and White House, something changed. People awakened to the higher calling of patriotism, the call that many of their parents had heard a generation earlier during the American Revolution. Ingersoll had witnessed this resurrection first hand.

"The smoldering fires of the Capitol were spices of the phoenix bed, from which arose offspring more vigorous, beautiful and long lived," he wrote, tapping the image of a phoenix to explain this phenomenon.

A phoenix is a mythological bird that lived for hundreds of years before dying on a funeral pyre. After being dusted with embalming spices and ignited by the sun, the red- and gold-feathered bird resembling an eagle rose from its ashes with renewed vigor to live another epoch.

Literature is rife with phoenix symbols and references. "And glory, like the phoenix 'midst her fires, exhales her odors, blazes, and expires," wrote English poet Lord Byron in 1809. Thomas Watson proclaimed in a sonnet in 1582: "O golden bird and phoenix of our age." Theologian John Wesley wrote in 1775: "He seems to think himself a mere phoenix." Early Christians used the story of the phoenix as a culturally understandable image to help Romans accept the resurrection of Christ.

Many in America would soon rise—not just one, not two, but a phoenix multitude.

Madison was the first to rise up with renewed vigor. He started by doing something he should have done months earlier. On August 29 the president mounted a horse and rode with all due speed to the living quarters of General John Armstrong. This weak-looking president arrived with an unmistakably robust spirit. They held a frank face-to-face conversation "on the state of things in the district, then under apprehensions of an immediate visit from the force of the enemy at Alexandria."

When the British arrived on ships at Alexandria, the people agreed to capitulate in exchange for a promise that the enemy wouldn't burn their houses. The result was mostly a ravenous display of looting. The British wiped out warehouses of supplies and other goods. With Alexandria under the enemy's mercy, the residents of Washington City rightfully feared a return visit.

After discussing these threats, Madison got right to the point with Armstrong: the fallout over the destruction of Washington City. "I observed to him that he could not be unaware of the great excitement in the district produced by the unfortunate event which had taken place in the city," Madison wrote of the conversation.

Indeed. Madison then explained that the excitement was now personal. "That violent prejudices were known to exist against the administration, as having failed in its duty to protect it [the city], particularly against me and himself as head of the war department."

Threats of personal violence toward the president were strong, but not nearly as strong as the threats coming from the troops against the war secretary. Madison had just "received a message from the commanding general of the militia informing me that every officer would tear off his epaulettes if General Armstrong was to have anything to do with them."

The president noted that Mr. Monroe was an acceptable alternative and had filled in for Armstrong during his previous absences from Washington City, including when Armstrong went to Canada in the fall of 1813.

Madison wanted to know Armstrong's thinking on his future, of "what was best to be done. Any convulsion at so critical a moment could not but have the worst consequences."

Armstrong responded that he was "aware of the excitement against him; that it was altogether artificial, and that he knew the sources of it...that the excitement was founded on the most palpable falsehoods."

Yet, the disgraced war secretary knew he could no longer stay in Washington and was willing to resign.

Concerned with the timing and wanting to give Armstrong an honorable exit instead of strong boot, Madison suggested "that a temporary retirement...was on the whole less objectionable, and would avoid the existing embarrassment."

The war secretary wasn't finished, however. Believing the charges against him were groundless, Armstrong defended himself. He claimed that "in relation to the defense of the city...there had been no deficiency on his part."

Madison agreed that some of the specific charges against Armstrong were unfounded. Yes, Armstrong had issued orders to Winder and others. The problem was the secretary's aloofness. His attitude indicated that "he had not taken a sufficient interest in the defense of the city, nor promoted the measures for it."

The president also rebuked Armstrong by agreeing with the war secretary's critics: "I could not in candour say that all that ought to have been done had been done and in proper time."

Once again Armstrong defended himself, arguing "that he had omitted no preparations or steps whatever for the safety of the place which had been enjoined on him."

Madison disagreed strongly: "That it was the duty of the secretary of war not only to execute plans, or orders committed to him, but to devise and propose such as would in his opinion be necessary and proper; that it was an obvious and essential part of his charge."

The president was puzzled, too, because he knew from personal experience that Armstrong had not only responded to military suggestions for other war fronts, such as Canada, but had also frequently initiated and recommended his own. In fact, he'd presented so many plans to his generals that he'd sometimes confused them on what the final plan was.

Madison was frank, saying that he "had never appeared to enter into a just view either of the danger to the city...or of the consequences of its falling into the hands of the enemy."

The president accused Armstrong of never proposing or suggesting "a single precaution or arrangement for its safety, everything done on that subject having been brought forward by myself." In fact, their differences seemed to lead Armstrong to make minimal arrangements. Not even the precautions discussed in cabinet meetings had been fully implemented, especially acquiring weapons.

Madison took no pleasure in speaking this way, but the urgency of the situation drove him to it. As he later wrote, "I had selected him for the office he filled from a respect to his talents, and a confidence that he would exert them for the public good; that I had always treated him with friendliness and confidence."

Aware that his presidency would end in two years, Madison proclaimed that his greatest desire now was "leaving my country in a state of peace and prosperity." His second wish was to preserve harmony among his cabinet.

Armstrong agreed that he would leave town the next morning and return to his family in New York, where he could think about his future. The war secretary didn't need that long. By the time he reached Baltimore, he had made his decision and sent Madison his resignation letter. The president accepted it.

Suddenly the president who had once been too deferential to his wayward cabinet member was now the most decisive man in Washington.

━━━━━━

At the same time that Madison and Armstrong held their frank conversation, the British force reached Benedict, Maryland, and boarded their ships. There, Admiral Cochrane contemplated their next move. The question was simple: Which American city should they attack next?

The answer soon became a secret, hidden even from Cockburn.

━━━━━━

Commodore John Rodgers took up his pen at ten p.m. the night of August 29, 1814. With the news of Washington weighing on him like a dozen anchors, he wrote a letter from his post in Baltimore to Navy Secretary Jones, who had returned to Washington.

It began, "I have received your letters of yesterday's date, and would to God it had been in my power to have reached Washington in time to have aided in its protection." This heavy-hearted man lifted his spirits by looking at the positive and observing the spices of the phoenix. "The people now begin to show something like a patriotic spirit: they are fortifying the town by all the means in their power, and those who direct their exertions, are pledged to me to defend the place to the last extremity, otherwise I should have been at Washington before this could reach you."

Not to be outdone, he was willing to send a detachment of his men to Washington "more with a view to guard the executive, than anything else." Why? A seasoned military man, he knew that looting and other uncivilized acts often tormented a town after it had been sacked.

But Rodgers's heart was heavier for his native state. This was understandable because his mother's home had been partially burned by Cockburn's men at Havre de Grace. He, along with General Samuel Smith and General Armistead, knew that Baltimore was a desired prey of the British lion.

The buzz in Baltimore had whipped up a frenzy of fear. "It is believed here that, after a short pause, the enemy will attack this place." If the British took Baltimore, they could easily find success in Philadelphia, which was up the road.

As such, Rodgers preferred to stay in Baltimore to prepare defenses: "Consequently I could wish to remain, until the place is better fortified and there is more certainty of my being able to render essential service elsewhere at any rate."

But always a patriot, he offered his brawn and brain anywhere Jones wanted him to go. "I shall be ready to march with all my strength at a moment, wherever you may think our services can be of more benefit, for believe me, that I would cheerfully spill the last drop of my blood to revenge my injured country."

Rodgers couldn't let the British win. He would do whatever it took and go wherever Jones ordered. "I repeat again, that I am ready at a moment's warning, to direct my course to any other point, where you may deem our services of more importance."

He wasn't the only one determined to go home.

CHAPTER TWENTY-SEVEN

Phoenix Multitude

With his property now a pile of bricks, his typeset stolen, and his collection of international newspapers burned, what was Joseph Gales to do?

He tapped his resourcefulness. Though a southerner by adoption, Gales turned to Yankee ingenuity. Gales borrowed a set of type from another source. Sure, it wasn't enough to print a two-to-three-page newspaper each day, but it was a start, enough for one page a day. He began publishing the *National Intelligencer* again on August 30, six days after the destruction of his business by Admiral Cockburn.

He explained his paper's absence. "After an intermission of several days owing to the unfortunate events hereinafter noticed, we have it in our power to issue a paper in the present reduced form, which we hope in a day or two to change to its usual shape and condition."

He published copies of letters from General Winder chronicling the events of the past few days and notices about the president's actions. By doing so, Joseph Gales become one of the first in Washington to show a patriotic, phoenix-like spirit. He wasn't going to let the British destroy freedom of speech or press—the reasons his family had come to America in the first place.

━━━━━

Another phoenix to rise from the ashes of Washington lived in neighboring Georgetown. The news that Richard West brought Francis Scott Key, on September 1, 1814, was distressing.

West lived in Upper Marlborough, where the British force had camped on its march to Bladensburg. His friend and neighbor Dr. William Beanes had allowed Ross and Cockburn to use his house as their headquarters. In exchange for preserving his home, Beanes, a noncombatant, pledged to be peaceful.

When the British army marched back to Marlborough en route to their ships after destroying Washington, several of them became disorderly. Fearing theft and arson, Beanes arrested a straggler. Furious that Beanes had broken their agreement, Ross ordered him arrested. Under the cover of night and without allowing him to change from his bedclothes into proper attire, British soldiers seized Beanes from his home.

West had recently taken a letter from Maryland's governor on Beanes's behalf to British headquarters. Ross was unbending. Realizing that he needed an attorney's skill for advocacy, West then rushed to Georgetown to see Key, his brother-in-law.

What should they do? General John Mason, who was responsible for prisoner-of-war exchanges, was aware of Beanes's plight, as was Secretary Monroe. Beanes needed an advocate, one skilled in fighting for others using the weapons of logic, persuasion, and diplomacy.

Perhaps Georgetown's *Federal Republican* newspaper rested on a table that day as West and Key talked in Key's Federal-style multistory house. That morning, editors for the *Federal Republican* gave their readers a surprise. Instead of bashing Madison and his war as they'd done numerous times—this same newspaper in Baltimore was so against the war that its editorials had played a role in the Baltimore riots that broke out after the war started—the editors printed an editorial called "Peace."

Though still desiring a quick end to the war, they acknowledged that Americans now faced a new plight. Previous objections to the war and party preferences needed to be set aside. "The country must be defended, the invaders must be repelled. Infinite distress and misery, still deeper disgrace, will befall us, if the force sent to our shores, is not overpowered."

Like the *Federal Republican*, Key wasn't pro-war. He had recently written his mother and bemoaned the fact that the war wasn't going well publicly and was also hitting him personally in the pocketbook. "The expenses of living here are enormous and the practice much lessened," he explained to his mother.

He had been thinking of joining his parents, who farmed and sold wool, in rural Maryland. "I really think I shall try to purchase a small flock of sheep in the spring, and if the war last on, I shall be obliged to leave this. I can come up to Pipe Creek and turn shepherd," he'd suggested.

For the time being, however, he would remain a lawyer, not a herder: "I have not determined upon anything but to stay here and mind my business as long as I can."

With this mindset, he had stayed in Georgetown throughout 1814. Now, after the fall of Washington, what good was his law practice or farming if the British continued to burn and pillage American cities? Maybe he could do something by finding a way to help Dr. Beanes.

As the *Federal Republican* newspaper had printed that day, the time had come to take up the mantle of the American Revolution. "It is absolutely necessary, unless the country is to be abandoned by the people...that every man should awake, arouse, and prepare for action," the editors wrote.

Sorting out what led to the burning of Washington could come later. Now was the time for action.

In case any of their readers were shocked at their sudden change, the *Federal Republican* editors reassured them of their principles. Political discussion and a free exchange of ideas and opinions were essential rights. Those were now at stake as long as the British occupied the East Coast in any form. They'd received, from a reliable source, news that Admiral Cockburn and other officers were planning to attack again.

"The admiral has said distinctly 'we must prepare for another severe struggle' not meaning a single battle, but a series of hard contested fights. He says, that every assailable point on our sea coast will share the fate of Washington, and that there is no other place which will experience the same moderation and clemency."

Instead of capitulating like Alexandria, each sea coast city needed to prepare to defend its citizens. It was time to "omit no sacrifice, spare no expense, to save the country. It is seriously threatened, and can only be saved by extraordinary exertions, such as our fathers made before us."

The editors' words reflected West's and Key's attitudes and concerns. "No man who is mindful of what he owes his country and his own character, can advocate submission, where resistance is practicable. The fight will now be for our country, not for a party."

Key and West came up with a plan. Key would answer the call of his country. He wouldn't directly take up arms, but would hold a flag of truce to advocate for Dr. Beanes. He knew where to start. Fortunately, the man he most needed to talk to was now living with one of Key's friends, former Congressman Cutts.

———

That same day, September 1, 1814, Madison's pen continued to flow with vigor. He issued a proclamation to the American people. "Whereas the enemy by a sudden incursion have succeeded in invading the capital of the nation," he began, noting the lack of militia to defend it, "they wantonly destroyed the public edifices...some of these edifices being also costly monuments of taste and of the arts, and others depositories of the public archives."

He observed that all nations create memorials and monuments of historic value that should be respected. Madison let the American people know that Fort Washington, which guarded Alexandria, had been destroyed. His administration had also received a letter from Admiral Cochrane that he'd written before the burning but Monroe didn't receive until afterward.

"Whereas it now appears by a direct communication from the British commander...to be his avowed purpose to employ the force...'in destroying and laying waste such towns and districts upon the coast as may be found assailable,'" he continued, observing that the British claimed they burned Washington in retaliation for alleged destruction in Upper Canada by the U.S. Army. To Madison, this was merely a pretense, an excuse.

Perhaps more than anything, Madison was angry that the British had violated "principles of humanity and the rules of civilized warfare" during a crucial time, "at the very moment of negotiations for peace, invited by the enemy himself." The president was determined more than ever "to chastise and expel the invader."

Showing leadership, Madison continued by "exhorting all the good people thereof to unite their hearts and hands in giving effect to the ample means possessed for that purpose." He asked all civil and military members to execute their duties and "be vigilant and alert in providing for the defense."

He appealed to Americans' patriotic devotion, so that "none will forget what they owe to themselves, what they owe to their country and the high destinies which await it."

He also reminded them of "the glory acquired by their fathers in establishing the independence which is now to be maintained by their sons with the augmented strength and resources with which time and Heaven had blessed them."

Sometime that day, either before, after, or during the writing of this proclamation, the knock at the door came. Madison welcomed Mr. Key. He was well acquainted with him. Seven years earlier, he had received a letter from Key and another attorney requesting his help. They had been defense attorneys for a prisoner held in Washington's marine barracks. The marine commandant and the navy secretary had prohibited them from meeting with their client. They needed Madison, who was then secretary of state, to intervene. "We are constrained to trouble you on a subject which we have in vain endeavored to effect without your intervention," Key had written back then in a letter to Madison. He could have used the same words to describe Beanes's plight.

Key tapped Madison's sense of justice. Both shared a passion for advocacy and the rule of law. Presenting a plan, Key proposed that he visit the British fleet under a flag of truce. Then he would try to secure Beanes's release. The case was tricky to be certain, but it was something he had to do.

Swift and sure was Madison's response. He agreed with Key and asked General Mason to intervene. Mason immediately wrote a letter on behalf of Beanes. He also gathered letters from wounded British soldiers, including a key officer, who were still recovering in Washington. These men wrote letters to General Ross proclaiming the good treatment that the Americans had given them. Mason then authorized Key to travel to Baltimore to join John Skinner, who was the U.S. prisoner-of-war exchange agent. Procuring a ship, together they would find the British fleet and do their best to secure Beanes's release.

It was in this way that Madison played a quiet, behind-the-scenes role in the circumstances that led to crafting the national anthem.

———

"The disgraceful loss of the capital and the agitation it has excited brought me to town; where the effect upon the populace is such as might be expected," Senator King wrote his friend, Senator Gore, on August 30, 1814.

As soon as he heard about the fall of the nation's capital, Senator King feared for his hometown, New York City. Hurrying from his Long Island home into the city, King called upon the governor, the defense committee, and the military general assigned to protect New York—a post previously held by General Armstrong. All were alarmed, but they were also undecided on what to do.

"My object was to induce the government to call forth and bring to NY 20,000 militia, and as the U.S. have no funds, and have deserted our, as well as their own, protection, to stimulate the city corporation to pledge themselves to provide the means of subsistence for these troops," King explained, believing that local resources should now be used to prevent an attack on New York.

This was a huge switch for King. Earlier he'd expressed the idea that the federal government, not local militias, should be called upon to protect local communities. The reality now was different. The credit of the U.S. government was so weak and unstable that New York banks would not loan bills without better security.

King concluded that if New York's governor, Daniel Tompkins, signed Treasury notes, each bank would provide $500 for building defenses to protect New York's port from attack.

When the senator broached the subject with Tompkins and asked him to sign the Treasury notes, he found the governor resistant. King responded with such patriotic pro-defense fervor that he might as well have been James Madison, not a war-opposing senator.

King proclaimed that "the time had arrived when it was the duty of every man to put his all at the requisition of the government, and that he himself was ready to do this."

Tompkins replied tersely that "he should be obliged to act on his own responsibility, and should be ruined."

"Then," King replied, "ruin yourself if it becomes necessary to save the country, and I pledge you my honor that I will support you in whatever you do."

Governor Tompkins signed the notes, and New York residents organized into voluntary military corps.

King also spoke to a group of New York bankers. Because the war had drained banks of hard money, these bankers had stopped issuing payment in specie, or money in the form of coins. King knew, however, that they needed to take a risk in the form of credit.

"We are in a critical situation, and it is therefore our duty to get out of it the best way we can," King told them. "The enemy is at our doors and it is now useless to enquire how he came there: he must be driven away and every man join hand and heart, and place shoulder to shoulder to meet him."

The bankers were so moved by his speech that they gave him a rousing applause and shouted cheers of agreement. Understanding the nation's financial needs, they decided to limit their debt to a total sum and issue notes or credit as if it were exchangeable for hard coins.

Something was changing in Rufus King. No matter his past opposition to the war and Madison, his home city was now in danger. During this time of peril, he believed that it was the duty of all citizens to defend each other and their country. Though his opinion of President Madison hadn't changed, he was taking action like never before to work together for the common good. He, too, was rising like a phoenix.

———————

Washington Irving had not forgotten his fond memories of Dolley Madison from his visit to the White House in January 1811. Writing biographies of naval heroes like James Lawrence and Oliver Perry had changed him. Hence, something stirred within him when he heard about the destruction of that fine white house in Washington. Something deep. Something patriotic. Something passionate that led him to do something no one expected this satirist turned journalist to do.

Irving learned the news of the burning of the U.S. Capitol and White House while aboard a steamboat in Albany, New York. A fellow passenger sneered, wondering what "Jimmie Madison" would say now.

This passenger's contempt sounded very much like Admiral Cockburn's "Jemmy."

Irving gave a quick retort. "Sir, do you seize on such a disaster only for a sneer?"

Steam suddenly sprung from Irving's lips.

"Let me tell you. Sir, it is not now a question about Jimmie Madison or Johnny Armstrong. The pride and honor of the nation are wounded."

He may have started as a writer of comedic fiction, but he was very grounded in reality. "The country is insulted and disgraced by this barbarous success, and every loyal citizen would feel the ignominy and be earnest to avenge it."

Indeed. Irving's local paper, which had opposed Madison on many occasions, now echoed the need for unity. "Believe us fellow citizens. This is no moment for crimination and recrimination, which necessarily follows.... Let one voice and one spirit animate us all—the voice of our bleeding country and the spirit of our immortal ancestors."

With a firm grasp of what to do, Irving joined the militia led by the New York governor Daniel Tompkins. He became Colonel Washington Irving, an aide-de-camp to Tompkins, who sent him to Sackett's Harbor in October 1814. Arriving on horseback, Irving issued Tompkins's orders to send militia reinforcement to Commodore Isaac Chauncey's fleet to fight the British.

Chauncey was surprised to meet Irving, alias Dietrich Knickerbocker, the satirist turned soldier. "'You here?' Chauncey exclaimed, in extending his hand; 'I should as soon have thought of seeing my wife.'"

Irving stayed with Chauncey for two days. "During which time he took me round the little fleet, and I had a fine opportunity of witnessing their admirable order and equipment. It is a gallant little squadron," Irving wrote.

During this time he most likely met a man whose name he would never forget. Ichabod Crane, who had earlier served as a marine for Stephen Decatur aboard the USS *United States*, served in Sackett's Harbor.

Meeting Crane and hearing stories of other patriots inspired Irving to add summaries of the naval war, including ones about hero Stephen Decatur, to his *Analectic Magazine*. After the war, Irving returned to satire and short stories. Within five years, he published his most famous work, *The Sketch Book of Geoffrey Crayon*, which featured short stories such as *Rip Van Winkle* and *The Legend of Sleepy Hallow*, whose main character was named Ichabod Crane.

Immediately after burning Washington and returning to his ship, Cockburn got what he wanted out of Cochrane: praise to the admiralty. On September 2, 1814, Cochrane wrote a letter to his superior about Cockburn's bravery.

"I have before had occasion to speak of the unremitting zeal and exertions of Rear Admiral Cockburn during the time he commanded in the Chesapeake under my orders—the interest and ability which he has manifested throughout this late arduous service justly entitle him to my best thanks, and to the acknowledgements of my Lords Commissioners of the admiralty."

The glory was unabashed. The man who burned Washington couldn't have been a better servant to the king.

"To Rear Admiral Cockburn, who suggested the attack on Washington, and accompanied the army, I confess the greatest obligation for his cordial co-operation and advice," Ross wrote in his official report, giving credit to the admiral for their success in Washington.

Whatever Cochrane's earlier reluctance to invade Washington, he showed a united front to his superiors. Glory and promotions should be their reward.

With Washington in ruins, the issue of where Congress should convene had crossed Senator King's mind several times. Wouldn't Congress be better off meeting in another city, at least temporarily? What about permanently? Yes, if they were lucky.

"Whether Madison will issue a new proclamation founded upon the destruction of the public buildings at Washington (which was contrary to the usage of modern war) and recommending to Congress to meet at Lancaster [Pennsylvania] or elsewhere, we can only conjecture," he wrote to Senator Gore.

He also complained about the failure of Bladensburg. "So far as regards the common defense, the general government has deserted its duties. Without money, without soldiers and without courage, the president and his cabinet are the objects of very general execration," he observed.

Though he knew that Madison's unpopularity was justification for relocating the capital, he doubted the president would do it.

"I shall not be surprised if he [Madison] suffers the members to assemble at Washington and adjourn to some other place; this will save him from deciding; if he had any character he would convene Congress at Philadelphia, but this he will be afraid to do," he added.

Before the burning of the Capitol, King had planned to arrive in Washington in early October, not by September 19, when Congress planned to resume business. Now he was so worried about his country that he didn't want to be late.

He shared his sentiments with Congressman Mason in a letter on September 2. "Where Congress will meet next no one knows, some believe that the president will recommend Lancaster, more that he will do nothing."

Though he loved New York, King was practical. "Philadelphia should be the place, but lest its accommodation should prove too agreeable, and so operate against the rebuilding of Washington, it is likely that a majority will be found in favor of some inconvenient temporary residence."

He decided that he would wait as long as he could before departing for Washington in case news arrived from the president announcing that Congress would reconvene somewhere else. "In the present alarm I feel unwilling to be absent when the session opens, and if I could contribute anything to bringing Congress to Philadelphia I should be anxious to do it."

King was most worried about the peace negotiations. "We have no tidings from the envoys, nor have I better means, than when we separated, to predict the issue of their mission."

Indeed. Newspapers had also recently updated Americans on the status of the peace talks at Ghent. The most up-to-date information was from July 20. Though most of the American peace negotiators were already in Ghent, the British delegation had yet to arrive. The news was "nothing favorable to peace."

"Your letter of this date reached me at 6 PM—Would to God it was in my power to return to Baltimore immediately as I am well assured that our seamen would be of more service there than they are likely to be here," Rodgers wrote from Washington to General Samuel Smith on September 1.

Following Navy Secretary Jones's orders, Rodgers had sent a detachment of his men to the Potomac River to chase British Captain Arthur Gordon's squadron away from Alexandria. As he had promised, Rodgers had joined his men.

While he made preparations at Washington's charred Naval Yard, Rodgers listened to Secretary Jones, who was conflicted about calling him to Washington and Alexandria when the threat against Baltimore was so strong. Jones was convinced that the British had been reinforced with additional troops. The thought worried him so much that he gave Rodgers permission to return to Baltimore if an emergency arose.

Calculating that he could arrive in Baltimore within twelve hours, Rodgers had procured a stagecoach to transport his sailors by land if the British made an advance there. He needed to inform Smith in Baltimore.

"I can assure you that I feel deep interest in the welfare of Baltimore and am satisfied that I shall be with you with 7/8ths of my force should the enemy attack you; and this is an object on which I have set my heart."

Rodgers was determined that Admiral Cockburn and General Ross would curse the day they undertook their expedition against America.

CHAPTER TWENTY-EIGHT

White House Phoenix

Baltimore was the nation's third-largest city in 1814, boasting a population of more than 46,000 in 1810. Its pride and joy was its harbor, where sailmakers, shipwrights, and merchants earned their living on the oasis of blue ocean.

An international seaport resting forty miles from Washington, Baltimore had bred its fair share of honorable men and rascals. The British military hated Baltimore because privateers who operated out of the harbor had attacked them. The U.S. government had given these ship owners permission to use their private vessels to capture British ships. Indeed. These privateers had captured more than 500 British ships.

Burning and looting Baltimore would be a valuable, pocket-enriching venture, as Cockburn well knew. The city was a treasure chest waiting to be opened. Marylanders everywhere knew it, too, including John Rodgers and Francis Scott Key.

Fearing that General Winder would try to lead Baltimore's defense, a group of Maryland military officers approached the city's committee of vigilance and safety. They wholeheartedly threw their support behind Smith. It didn't matter that President Madison had appointed Winder to lead the 10th military district, which included Baltimore. Nor did it matter that Winder was the nephew of Maryland's new governor. This wasn't going to be a conflict between federal and state authority. What mattered most right now was success.

Winder had failed at Bladensburg. By selecting Smith, the town leaders believed that they had a better shot at successfully fending off the enemy. Though protesting to Monroe, who had become secretary of war after Armstrong's resignation, Winder gave in. Agreeing to command a regiment from Virginia, he took a demoted position and became a team player. Like Van Ness before Bladensburg, he put aside his pride and served in whatever capacity he could.

Smith took charge of Baltimore's defense like no one else could. He, along with Fort McHenry Commander Major George Armistead, Commodore Oliver Hazard Perry, and Lieutenant Robert Spence, would do his part. Smith would command the forces and tap the likes of John Rodgers and many others to bring brawn and might to the effort. Local newspaper editors agreed.

"The spirit of the nation is roused," the *Niles Register* of Baltimore reported. "War is a new business to us, but we must 'teach our fingers to fight'—and Wellington's invincibles shall be beaten by the sons of those who fought at Saratoga and Yorktown."

They would become American phoenixes in Baltimore.

━━━━━━━

Cockburn seethed at the news. On September 4, Cochrane sent him new orders for a new destination. Was it Baltimore? No. Philadelphia? No. New York? Not even close. Instead, Cochrane had ordered Cockburn to take his flagship, the *Albion*, and lead a convoy of vessels loaded with prizes from Washington to Bermuda. Then he was to rejoin Cochrane at a more northern location along America's east coast.

Although Cochrane had praised Cockburn on paper to the admiralty, he had also cut him out and cut him short. He seemed to be seething that Cockburn had turned a blind eye to his final order not to invade Washington. Cockburn was fortunate that the mission had succeeded. Because he had disobeyed orders, if he had failed in Washington, his career would have been in jeopardy.

Tangible proof of Cochrane's displeasure came through a Royal Navy custom. Instead of allowing Cockburn to choose an officer, promote him, and allow him the honor of taking the victorious news to London, Cochrane deferred to Ross to choose the messenger instead. The person who felt the sting the most was Scott. Cockburn would have chosen him, no doubt. Scott longed to return home and receive a promotion. Instead he was denied the glory because of his boss's defiance.

Cochrane also prevented Cockburn from conferring easily with Ross about their next move. He did this by having Ross quartered as a special guest on his own flagship, the *Tonnant*, instead of Cockburn's ship, the *Albion*. In this way, Cockburn lost the ability to quietly convince Ross of the merits of a quick and immediate attack on nearby Baltimore, the most obvious choice for their next target. Failing to hit it quickly could have dire consequences by giving the Americans time to regroup, should they be so inclined.

Though he intently disagreed, Cockburn was aware of Cochrane's reasons for retiring instead of attacking Baltimore. He knew that Cochrane despised the hot climate of America's southern states. He was right. Just the day before, on September 3, Cochrane had written the First Lord of the admiralty.

"As soon as the army is all re-embarked I mean to proceed to the Northward and if possible try to surprise Rhode Island, where we will quarter upon the enemy and the troops as well as the ships meet with every refreshment." September was a sickly month for the locals in Virginia, much less Cochrane's army, which lacked immunity from regional diseases, so he thought. Rhode Island offered the cooler temperatures that Cochrane craved. He figured that he could return to Baltimore with reinforcements in October, when the weather was less warm.

It wasn't that Cochrane failed to recognize Baltimore's value. In fact, he considered it "the most democratic town and I believe the richest in the country" and added that "this town ought to be laid in ashes."

He also had another reason for delaying besides the weather. Cochrane had detected reluctance in General Ross's heart. Indeed. Ross had told the officer that he sent a messenger to London to tell the admiralty he wouldn't attack Baltimore.

As he read his new orders, Cockburn may have wondered if Cochrane now regretted isolating Ross from his influence. Ross didn't seem inclined to punish the sins of the Americans. Neither Cochrane nor Cockburn doubted Ross's loyalty and zeal to England, but they saw a lack of passion for warfare in the general. The man seemed to long for home, for his wife and children, more than fighting. He'd had enough of that in Europe against Napoleon.

Cochrane put Ross's reluctance to attack the U.S.A. crassly: "When he is better acquainted with the American character he will possibly see, as I do, that like spaniels they must be treated with great severity before you ever make them tractable."

Hence, as Cockburn came to grips with his superior officer's decision to leave the Chesapeake and send him to Bermuda, all he could do was obey and hope that something would change Cochrane's mind and change it quickly. Because of his earlier disobedience, he had to tread lightly.

———

No matter the era, grief is a natural process, a cycling and recycling of shock, anger, depression, and acceptance. One of Madison's friends reported that "he looks shaken and woe-bygone. In short, he looked as if his heart was broken." Yes, his heart was broken for his country, but he wasn't the only one. Dolley, too, was dispirited and longing for a multitude to defend America's shores.

"Mrs. M. seem'd much depress'd, she could scarcely speak without tears.... Mrs. M. lost all her own property," wrote a friend who visited Dolley not long after her return to Washington.

Indeed, Dolley revealed to another friend, "In short, it would fatigue you to read the list of my losses, or an account of the general dismay, or particular distresses of your acquaintance.... but I cannot tell you what I felt on re-entering it [Washington City]—such destruction—such confusion!!"

Anna Marie Thornton, wife of the Capitol's architect, also visited Dolley shortly after her return. She saw her grief first hand. "We stepped in to see Mrs. Madison, she was very violent against the English—wished we had 10,000 such men as were passing (a few troopers) to sink our enemy to the bottomless pit."

Mrs. Thornton also showed her Federalist leanings. After all, her husband William was possibly the one who revealed the location of Gales's newspaper to Admiral Cockburn. "She had better attribute the loss of her palace to the right cause, viz want of proper defense in time.... The Secretary of State said they were all d___'d Rascals from highest to lowest."

Grief was a frequent companion for Dolley that autumn. What would bring her out of it? She would have to find a new purpose in life.

The dinner aboard the admiral's ship on the afternoon of September 7, 1814, was the most surreal that Francis Key had ever experienced. He had expected to meet with an officer or two, perhaps the captain of the ship, but not with the supreme commander. Now he was here with his American counterpart, Mr. Skinner. Together they dined with Admiral Cochrane and General Ross aboard the admiral's flagship, the *Tonnant*.

The day before, in a small boat carrying a flag of truce, Key and Skinner had swept alongside a smaller British vessel, the *Royal Oak*. From there they had followed the *Royal Oak* to find the admiral's flagship further south in the Chesapeake Bay. Cochrane learned of their intentions right before his dinner on September 7. Not wanting to delay and in a hospitable mood, Cochrane invited them to join him and General Ross.

At first all was pleasantries. They engaged in small talk while they ate. And given the circumstances, what else could they discuss? Finally, the captain of the fleet hurled an insult at America. Skinner fired back. Key was unimpressed, as he later wrote: "Never was a man more disappointed in his expectations than I have been as to the character of British officers. With some exceptions they appeared to be illiberal, ignorant, and vulgar, and seem filled with a spirit of malignity against everything American. Perhaps, however, I saw them in unfavorable circumstances." Indeed he did.

With insults flowing faster than the wine at that dinner, General Ross intervened and offered to speak privately with Mr. Skinner about Mr. Beanes. This disappointment left Key out of a key conversation. All he could do was wait and hope that Skinner could prevail upon Ross to release Beanes.

He knew, however, that Mason had given them a good strategy. If Ross argued that Beanes had violated his pledge to refrain from hostile acts, then Skinner would respond that Ross's first withdrawal from Marlborough had relieved him of that pledge. The next strategy was to present letters from wounded British officers and soldiers testifying to the humane treatment they were receiving from the Americans. In this way, Ross could release Beanes in the name of good will.

If those strategies failed, then Skinner and Key were authorized to give Ross a receipt for Beanes as if he were a prisoner of war and release a British war prisoner in return. This approach, however, could open a Pandora's box by giving the British permission or justification to start hauling off other unarmed citizens for the sole purpose of releasing genuine British prisoners.

Key later learned what happened during Skinner's and Ross's meeting. Skinner presented the case for releasing Dr. Beanes. Ross silently read the letters from General Mason and the British wounded.

"Dr. Beanes...shall be released to return with you," Ross replied, pleased with the treatment the British wounded were receiving from the Americans.

Ross wrote a letter to Mason. "Dr. Beanes having acted hostilely towards certain soldiers under my command, by making them prisoners when proceeding to join the army, and having attempted to justify his conduct when I spoke to him on the subject, I conceived myself authorized and called upon to cause his being detained as a prisoner," he explained, not backing down from his original claims.

Then he acknowledged civility. "The friendly treatment, however, experienced by the wounded officers and men of the British army left at Bladensburg enables me to meet your wishes regarding that gentleman."

Ross promised to release him, though he believed he was justified in retaining him. "I shall accordingly give directions for his being released... but purely in proof of the obligation which I feel for the attention with which the wounded have been treated."

Skinner's and Key's joy at securing the release of Dr. Beanes lasted only a second or two. Earlier that morning, Cochrane had made a decision. He was going to attack Baltimore. Why the change? The promise of plunder and intelligence made the difference. After the attack on Washington, he'd sent out another British raiding party to rural Maryland. Though the commander, Sir Peter Parker, had been killed, his men brought back valuable plunder and supplies. They also brought intelligence that attacking Baltimore would be easy. The American will to fight was weak.

Hence, while Mr. Beanes would be released to them, Key and Skinner couldn't leave until after the attack on Baltimore. Cochrane said to them, "Ah, Mr. Skinner, after discussing so freely our preparation and plans, you could hardly expect us to let you go on shore in advance of us."

With no room left on the crowded *Tonnant*, Cochrane put Key and Skinner aboard the vessel *Surprise*, which tugged their truce boat. For now they were stuck, held hostage in a British convoy and witnesses to the next attack.

As one who didn't support the war, Key felt conflicted. Baltimore was not his favorite place. He despised the pro-war riot that took place there at the start of the war and led to the deaths of Revolutionary War veterans who opposed the war.

"Sometimes when I remembered it was there the declaration of this abominable war was received with public rejoicings, I could not feel a hope that they would escape," Key later recalled.

But Baltimore was a family place, too. He knew it was filled with innocent women and children and Americans seeking to live quiet lives.

What worried him was Cochrane's pledge to give Baltimore the Havre de Grace and Washington treatment. "To make my feelings still more acute, the admiral had intimated his fears that the town [Baltimore] must be burned, and I was sure that if taken it would have been given up to plunder. I have reason to believe that such a promise was given to their soldiers. It was filled with women and children."

All he could do was wait, watch, and pray.

———

Commodore John Rodgers arrived in Baltimore on September 9, 1814. As he wrote to another commodore, "I reached here the evening before last direct from Washington. There are now upwards of 15,000 regulars and militia exclusive of about 1,000 seamen and marines, which I have formed into a brigade consisting of two regiments, and now encamped in the environs of this town."

Rodgers witnessed the fruits of the labor of the phoenix multitude. Newspapers had called on the scattered militia to reconvene. Residents near and far had given supplies, such as pickaxes, hay, and wagons, to the cause. Bankers had contributed more than $660,000, and individuals had given smaller amounts. Young and old, free and slave, all had mustered to build a line of earthen works to protect the city's most vulnerable places on land.

"Forts, redoubts, and entrenchments are thrown up all round the town and the place now has nothing to fear, even should the enemy make his appearance tomorrow," Rodgers reported of Hampstead Hill.

The defensive barriers stretched more than a mile from the harbor to the road on the East leading to Philadelphia. Rodgers and his men held the center of the barriers. Located on a hill, they built a redoubt called Rodgers's bastion. The fortification held sixteen cannon, including twelve and six pounders.

Then suddenly, their efforts seemed all for naught. Word of the British leaving the vicinity spread like wildfire through the ranks.

"It is understood however that he has descended the bay and whatever might have been his intentions that he will not now attempt an attack on this place with any such force as he can command at present," Rodgers wrote.

His hasty departure from Washington City and all of Smith's preparations now seemed anticlimactic. According to the latest reports, Cochrane and his fleet were sailing away from Baltimore, not toward it. Fatigued, Rodgers began to wonder where he should go next: "I hope to leave here in two or three days for Philadelphia, as I begin to feel tired of playing soldier, and more particularly as there will not be any occasion for our services."

How wrong he was.

———

Finally. He was here, on his way to attack Baltimore. What was Cockburn to do? Nothing but smile from ear to ear.

Early in the morning, around three o'clock a.m. on September 12, the British landed their force of more than 4,000 at North Point just outside of Baltimore. Cockburn and Ross led the advance guard of fifty men. Behind them was Colonel Arthur Brooke, who led the rest. Among them were 600 of Cockburn's marines.

After starting his journey down the Chesapeake toward Bermuda a few days earlier, Cockburn had learned that Cochrane had changed his mind. Fortunately, he had gone only eight miles. He'd turned around his ship and joined Cochrane's convoy as they headed for the Potomac River.

Cochrane had one more thing he needed to do before attacking Baltimore. He had to learn the outcome of Captain James Alexander Gordon's expedition to Alexandria, where he'd destroyed all of the town's military installations after taking Fort Washington. Soon Gordon met them with twenty-one ships loaded with prizes, including more than 13,000 barrels of flour.

Meanwhile Cockburn and Cochrane continued to disagree on strategy. They specifically differed on whether the main assault should come by land or sea. Cockburn favored having marines and sailors lead a water assault against Fort McHenry. A land assault should support the water bombardment. Cochrane disagreed. He favored placing more men in the land assault aided by ships in the water.

As the superior officer, Admiral Cochrane won the debate and set up the troops to go ashore at North Point and attack Baltimore by land. Bomb ships and frigates would get as close as they could to the fort to support the land assault.

Despite their strategic differences, Cockburn came out smiling like a pirate. If they captured Baltimore, they would have dozens, if not hundreds, of ships filled with valuable goods to take back to Bermuda. Best of all, if Baltimore fell, Philadelphia would soon follow. What started out as an attempt to harass America's east coast could turn into capturing it.

Once again under overwhelming heat, they marched the morning of September 12 toward the city of Baltimore. Cockburn continued to relish riding on a charger horse and wearing his gold-laced hat, which made him an obvious target. He rode along the line and often trotted from left to right at a foot pace, which increased his odds for being hit. He and Scott marveled at how often enemy fire came at him but missed.

Soon they came across a house. They burned it and carved a Union Jack in the mantel of another dwelling.

Something was different, however. Cockburn found his normally cautious friend General Ross in an unusually cocky mood. It was as if they were twin brothers. Whatever his previous reservations about attacking Baltimore, Ross was committed to their mission, driven by duty.

Together he and Cockburn came across the farm of Mr. Robert Gorsuch. Emboldened and hungry, they ordered this American farmer to serve them a meal. He complied.

A conversation ensued about their plans. Soon Ross allegedly boasted to Mr. Gorsuch: "I'll eat in Baltimore tonight—or in hell." How right he was, if these legendary words are true.

CHAPTER TWENTY-NINE

Dawn's Early Light

About the time that Ross and Cockburn enjoyed a leisurely breakfast, a member of their advance guard captured three Americans, who were part of General John Stricker's advance of 150 light troops. A British soldier escorted them to the general and admiral. When Ross asked them how many American forces were in Baltimore, they boasted: twenty thousand. Yet the number was closer to 16,000.

"They are mainly militia, I presume?" Ross supposedly inquired.

When the Americans confirmed the information, Ross may have repeated this mantra: "I don't care if it rains militia."

Cockburn couldn't have said it better himself, and perhaps he did say it instead of Ross. But what the Americans didn't say was far more important than what they did report. They didn't tell Ross and Cockburn that Stricker's brigade of more than 3,000 was only four miles away, camped near a Methodist meetinghouse.

After eating at Gorsuch's, Cockburn, Ross, and their officers rode along a road covered by a thick wood. By this point they were about five miles from the place where their ships had landed. Suddenly they came across Stricker's advance unit of American riflemen and artillerymen. Shots broke out immediately. The British returned it. Back and forth the firing went until the Americans fled into the woods and the British chased them.

A British officer estimated the number of Americans in this unit was about 400. Surprised at such strength from the enemy, Ross decided that his advance party needed more men for protection. He would go back and get them.

"I'll bring up the column," Ross offered to Cockburn.

Soon a ball passed through Ross's arm and entered his chest. He fell from his horse. Coming quickly to his friend's side, Cockburn made arrangements for Ross to be returned to a British ship. He died on the way.

"It is with the most heartfelt sorrow I have to add that in this short and desultory skirmish, my gallant and highly valued friend, the major general, received a musket ball through his arm into his breast, which proved fatal to him on his way to the water side for re-embarkation," Cockburn later wrote to Cochrane.

With Ross dead, who was in charge of the land forces? Cockburn couldn't officially lead on land because he was an admiral. Hence, Colonel Brooke was now in command. Cockburn joined Brooke as he advanced from their landing point at North Point.

Later they came across General Stricker's force of thousands divided into five regiments: the 5th, 6th, 27th, 39th, and 51st Regiments of Maryland. They were a portion of General Smith's army. Because these Americans wore uniforms, Brooke mistakenly assumed they were regular U.S. army soldiers, not militia.

Stricker's force occupied the woods and began firing against the British from the thicket. This was the very dastardly warfare that Cockburn had long despised and scorned at Havre de Grace. To him such tactics were cowardly, albeit effective.

Brooke responded by ordering an attack. They fired artillery. They fired Congreve rockets. The Americans returned the assault. But as the British attacked with an intention to surround them, the American line gave way and fled. The British casualties included fewer than fifty killed and nearly 300 wounded. The Americans lost two dozen killed and nearly 140 wounded.

To Cockburn and the Royal Military, the route was akin to the dispersion of the Americans at Bladensburg. To the Americans, the outcome of North Point was different. Yes, they had lost this battle. Yes, they had retreated. But unlike Bladensburg, they had regrouped immediately. A creek gave them a protected place to rally.

After the battle of North Point, Cockburn and many of the British forces stopped by a stream to fill their canteens and water their horses. As the admiral's horse drank from this clean pool of water, he heard a loud volley coming down from above. The fire killed several men and struck his horse in the shoulder. Once again, he was unhurt. Such was the charmed life of Admiral Cockburn.

As night approached, Brooke ordered his men to camp on the battlefield near the Methodist Meeting House, which had become a hospital for the wounded on both sides.

The next morning, September 13, brought the start of something new for Cockburn: American obstruction. The British cared for their wounded, broke camp, and marched toward Baltimore, only to find that the Americans had cut down trees and created other obstacles to slow their march. Stop. Start. Clear the road. The pattern persisted and delayed their arrival.

When they did arrive, they beheld earthen works and a line of redoubts stretching a mile in length. How did Cockburn respond? He chomped at the bit to attack. Surely, even with these obstacles and this sizable force of multiple thousands, the Americans would flee, wouldn't they? Why wouldn't they? Had they really changed?

Yet, he had quickly figured out that Colonel Brooke was cut from a similar cloth as General Ross. Caution guided him. But unlike Ross,

Cockburn had not yet earned Brooke's trust. He hadn't had time to court him or whisper in his ear.

What Cockburn didn't know in that moment was the fallout from his arson. By burning the U.S. Capitol and White House, he had ignited an uncontrollable fire of American patriotism. The redoubts were tangible evidence that the Americans had extinguished all doubt about this war. Fight they would. To the death. They were not about to let the Brits conquer them and force them into rule by a king once again.

Now all Cockburn could do was submit to a mere colonel's choices. The prospects for a British victory seemed to fade with each passing hour.

———

Fort McHenry was the defensive star in Baltimore's crown. Fearing an attack by the British in 1776, the people of Baltimore constructed an earthen fort in the shape of a star. They named it Fort Whetstone. The British smartly left Baltimore alone. Nearly two decades later, in 1794, Napoleon launched a war against England. Congress decided to construct a series of forts along the coast. French engineers began construction on the star-shaped fort protecting Baltimore's harbor in 1798. The fort was named for Fort McHenry after James McHenry, the nation's second war secretary. During the first year of Madison's administration, the U.S. Army organized its first light artillery unit at the fort.

Fort McHenry's location was ideal because it overlooked the Patapsco River at the place where it divided into two forks, the northwest branch leading to the city's harbor and the Ferry Branch. Thanks to the efforts of Commodore Rodgers and others, the Americans sealed off the northwest branch through a line of armed barges.

———

Twelve days had passed since he'd first approached President Madison about rescuing Beanes. By the morning of September 13, Key knew something was imminent. Cochrane had ordered him and Skinner off the *Surprise* and onto the truce boat they had taken to find the fleet. Then the admiral left the larger *Tonnant* and made the small *Surprise* his flagship.

Another sign that things were changing was Dr. Beanes, who had now joined them aboard the truce boat. A nearby armed ship kept them under surveillance, ready to fire if the truce boat tried to slip away. This, too, was another indication that the British were reading for an imminent attack.

At six o'clock a.m. Cochrane ordered five bomb ships—the *Aetna*, *Devastation*, *Meteor*, *Terror*, and *Volcano*—and other war vessels to move into a line less than three miles away but facing Fort McHenry.

Fire! The order came. The shots dispersed, but they were too far away to hit the fort. Move closer! The ships moved closer; two miles away. This distance would have to do. The fort's long guns prevented the British rockets from getting any closer without risk of cannonballs crushing their planks.

From his position eight miles away, Key could hear the shots. With a spyglass he could also see them. The blasts continued with a near rhythmic consistent pace. Each bomb ship hurled five bombs an hour. These bombs were spherical ten- and thirteen-inch shells that showered shrapnel upon exploding. Some fell short; some long. Others burst directly over the fort.

Key could see additional weapons besides the bombs. The British schooner *Cockchafer* and the rocket ship *Erebus* also fired rockets. At 8:40 a.m. U.S. artillery hurled cannonballs into the *Cockchafer*'s main sail and ripped it to pieces. What did Cochrane do? He wisely withdrew the *Cockchafer*.

What Key couldn't ascertain was how many men Major Armistead, Fort McHenry's commander, oversaw. Though the Americans clearly returned fire, their guns couldn't reach the ships. While he couldn't know what was going on in the fort or how many bombs were reaching the fort, he could discern that a white flag of surrender hadn't appeared above the fort. All he could see was a small U.S. flag, a speck in the distance.

From his position camped with the land troops two miles from the Baltimore defenses, Cockburn received a letter from Cochrane the night of September 13. The news disappointed him more than it surprised him. With Ross gone, he had lost his influence. Cochrane's letter proved it.

"It is impossible for the ships to render you any assistance—the town is so far retired within the forts," Cochrane wrote to Cockburn. The Americans had sunk so many ships that Cochrane couldn't get a bomb ship through the channel to attack the U.S. land trenches.

"It is for Colonel Brooke to consider under such circumstances whether he has force sufficient to defeat so large a number as it [is] said the enemy has collected; say 20,000 strong or even a less number and to take the town," he explained, clearly designating Brooke as the ultimate decision-maker, not Cockburn.

Cockburn realized that Cochrane opposed a further land attack for humane reasons: "Without this can be done it will be only throwing the men's lives away and prevent us from going upon other services."

He knew what other services meant. The admiralty had their eye on New Orleans, the lynchpin for controlling the Mississippi River.

Cockburn read practicality into Cochrane's assessment. "At any rate a very considerable loss must ensue and as the enemy is daily gaining strength his loss let it be ever so great cannot be equally felt."

How could that be? Cockburn had to wonder. These were the same Americans who had fled to the woods in Havre de Grace. They were the same bunch who had done nothing of substance to protect their capital city. They were the ones who'd fled like scared geese out of Bladensburg. Yet, he could see with his own eyes. They'd built impressive entrenchments. They'd taken out General Ross. They'd injured his own horse just the previous day. They had a will to fight after all.

Cockburn was powerless. Sure, Colonel Brooke had called a war council and had invited him to attend. But too many others supported caution. He was outnumbered. On land, he had to defer to the army commander, no matter rank or experience. All Cockburn could do was wait and watch as he listened to the bombs bursting at the fort nearby.

———————

After twenty-five hours of ear-piercing terror from bombs, the silence that followed after seven o'clock a.m. on September 14 was welcoming but hardly golden to Francis Scott Key's ears. What colors would he see as he placed his eye behind the spyglass and pointed it toward the fort? He didn't know which was worse, beholding the British Union Jack flag above Fort McHenry or the white flag of surrender. Both would mean victory for the British and capitulation once again from his countrymen.

Suddenly he noticed it. Gone was the American battle flag measuring seventeen by twenty-four feet that had flown over the fort. Instead, he saw the most beautiful colors cast against a canvas of a multi-hue sunrise. The stars and stripes, fifteen of them to represent that nation's fifteen states that had grown to eighteen by this time, flapped briskly from the fort that morning. The sight could mean only one thing. The Americans still held Fort McHenry.

The flag that Key saw that morning measured forty-two feet by thirty feet. It was the largest flag ever flown at a U.S. fort. Months earlier General Armistead had requested that Fort McHenry "have a flag so large that the British will have no difficulty in seeing it from a distance." Commodore Barney and another officer had enlisted the talents of flag maker Mary Pickersgill. She made two flags, the smaller storm flag and the giant ceremonial flag. On that morning Key saw the larger flag, whose bright stars measured twenty-four inches from point to point. What he couldn't have heard that morning was the music at the fort. Because America lacked an official national anthem, the band played the popular *Yankee Doodle*.

What came next, Key didn't know. He was still hostage to the British fleet. The word eventually came. Anchors away. Finally, they were free. And as he sailed, his emotion gave way to words, poetic words that fit a familiar pattern. "O say, can you see, by the dawn's early light, what so proudly we hailed at the twilight's last gleaming...." Then the flag took center stage:

> Whose broad stripes and bright stars, through the perilous fight,
> O'er the ramparts we watched, were so gallantly streaming!
> And the rockets' red glare, the bombs bursting in air,
> Gave proof through the night that our flag was still there.

Suddenly Fort McHenry didn't just represent Baltimore. It symbolized America, as did the 1,000 men who defended it. And the flag didn't just soar over Baltimore, it unfurled over the entire United States. "O say, does that star-spangled banner yet wave, O'er the land of the free and the home of the brave?"

Four verses poured from Key's pen, including lesser-known flourishes that reflected faith: "O thus be it ever, when freemen shall stand, between their loved homes and the war's desolation! Blest with victory and peace, may the heaven-rescued land. Praise the Power that hath made and preserved us a nation." Some were surprising for a man who seemed to oppose the war: "Then conquer we must when our cause it is just, and this be our motto: 'In God is our trust.'" Each verse ended with the refrain, "And the star-spangled banner in triumph shall wave o'er the land of the free and the home of the brave!"

Key enlisted the tune "To Anacreon in Heaven." The melody was familiar to him. After all, he had written lyrics for it years earlier in 1806 in another song called "When the Warrior Returns." It was the tune for the well-known "Boston Patriotic Song," which was also called the "Adams and Liberty Song." Years earlier when John Adams became president, his friend Robert Treat Paine had written lyrics celebrating America and his presidency. Paine chose "To Anacreon in Heaven" as the tune. The song was the theme for a gentlemen's club in London, the Anacreontic Society, named after Anacreon, a lyric poet from Greece.

Whether the words flowed easily for Key that day or came to him in bits and pieces to organize into a poetic pattern, one thing is for sure. The result spoke of the emotion that he and so many other Americans felt upon learning that they had once again defeated the British.

Hope was brighter than ever. Maybe, just maybe, the Royal Navy would soon abandon America's shores permanently.

After a sleepless night under the sound of constant fire bombarding the fort, Rodgers could see the British campfires near the Methodist meeting house. But he knew it could be a trick. After all, George Washington had ordered his men to build campfires to cover their retreat at Long Island during the American Revolution in 1776. Ross had ordered his soldiers to build campfires in Washington City to fool the few Washingtonians left in town so his forces could slip away in a night retreat. Was the same thing happening now in Baltimore?

Rodgers knew the bombing had stopped. He could see that the British bomb ships were departing. Was the full force all retreating? It sure looked like it.

What Rodgers didn't know was that Colonel Brooke didn't want to live with the burden of throwing away the lives of men. He had ordered a retreat. They could not win in Baltimore, not without a larger force. The loss of Ross had dispirited them. They couldn't get their rockets close enough to Fort McHenry to make a difference. Cochrane's overnight attempt at victory had also failed. He'd sent a captain and twenty-two vessels to try to land near the fort and distract the Americans defending the land redoubts. One of the Americans saw them coming and opened fire, stopping their attempts.

While the silence continued, intelligence brought Rodgers clarity. From his position behind his bastion, he fired off a letter to Navy Secretary Jones on Wednesday, September 14. "The enemy has been severely drubbed as well his army as his navy and is now retiring down the river after expending many rounds of shot from 1,800 to 2,000 shells and at least seven or eight hundred rockets," he wrote.

Only 400 actually landed in the fort, damaging the walls, killing four, and wounding twenty-four.

Rodgers added a postscript. "I shall give you a more particular account as soon as I get a little rest. General Ross of the British Army is said to be mortally wounded."

Fatigued but no longer heavy hearted, Rodgers couldn't have been prouder. They had rallied at Baltimore and defeated the British. Washington had been avenged. The destiny of the nation seemed bright once again. The question was this: What would happen to Washington City? Would it remain the nation's capital?

CHAPTER THIRTY

Relocating the Capital City

"The destruction of the President's House cannot be said to be a great loss in one point of view, as we hope, it will put an end to drawing rooms and levees; the resort of the idle and the encouragers of spies and traitors." So printed the *New York Evening Post* on September 19.

They'd forgotten one thing: the patriotic determination of a Quaker socialite and her scholarly husband. Perhaps by proving the *Post* wrong, Dolley could find her purpose in the aftermath.

———

Cockburn knew it was true. They'd let too much time pass between burning Washington and attacking Baltimore. Foolish it was. Scott later put their defeat at Fort McHenry into perspective this way: "Unfortunately the lapse of eighteen days gave the enemy an opportunity of perfecting their defenses and collecting a large body of troops from the surrounding country.... The advantages this unfortunate delay gave to the enemy were incalculable."

Cockburn was careful to measure his assessment, knowing that it was presumptuous for a junior officer to "arraign the conduct of a respected commander-in-chief," but he blamed Cochrane without naming him. "It is easy to pronounce judgment at the conclusion of a game of chess, when the moves of the opponents have passed in review before you; the bystanders can then with facility point out the erroneous move that led to the defeat of one of the parties."

Four days after their defeat at Baltimore, Cockburn and Scott headed to Bermuda while Cochrane took a convoy to Halifax, in Nova Scotia in Canada. They would regroup, with Cockburn heading back to the east coast to harass and keep an eye on America's southern states, such as Georgia. The bulk of the British would go even further south and west, sweeping into the Gulf Coast and New Orleans.

Until a peace treaty received Madison's signature, the war was not over, and the political war would soon take center stage.

———

As a congressman, Madison had initially opposed having a permanent capital at all.

In 1783, while a member of the Continental Congress, Madison had objected to establishing a permanent capital at that time because "our acts are not those of the Medes and Persians, unalterable."

Southern members thought they had Pennsylvania delegates on their side. Instead, eastern members convinced Pennsylvania members to agree to let New York become the temporary seat by agreeing to vote for the Susquehanna as the permanent one.

The issue became part of the discussions of the first Congress under the U.S. Constitution in 1789. Madison was a congressman in that first Congress. In fact, he'd beaten his distant neighbor, James Monroe, for the seat.

Madison called the issue "the puzzling question as to the precise jurisdiction of Congress over the permanent seat."

Because communication methods were slow, Madison concluded that the seat of government would be an advantage to those who were geographically closest to it. The telegraph had yet to be invented, and he foresaw the need for instant communication to broadcast the laws of the new federal government to the states.

"If it were possible to promulgate laws, by some instantaneous operation, it would be of less consequence in that point of view where the government might be placed," he'd observed, knowing that without better technology, news would travel by days and weeks through newspapers carried by passengers on stage carriages or messengers on horseback to different parts of the nation. Madison also knew the Virginia-Maryland border along the Potomac was ideal because it was the geographic center of the thirteen original states. Madison had possibly written anonymous newspaper editorials on the issue.

He also knew that President George Washington played no documented role in the debate over the capital. Though his longtime preference for the Potomac River was widely known, Washington had allowed congressmen from Virginia, such as Madison, to fight for it for him. This allowed Washington to be a quiet force.

President Washington's first recorded mention of the issue in his diary didn't come until July 12, 1790, when he wrote about the bill that Congress had just sent to him. It was "an act for establishing the temporary and permanent seat of the government of the United States."

Twenty-four years later, in the fall of 1814, the question facing James Madison was this. Now that he was president, what would his role be? Would he follow the George Washington model and say nothing publicly? Would he take an active role? Or would he take a stealth one? What mattered most was the outcome, saving Washington as the nation's capital. He couldn't keep the British out, but could he keep the politicians in?

━━━━━━━━

Was the news true? With the destruction of the U.S. Capitol and President's House, would the nation's capital city be relocated to

Philadelphia? Temporarily? Permanently? Surely this was gossip. Surely it wasn't news. Surely it was the bluster of political winds taking advantage of precarious circumstances.

Joseph Gales couldn't believe his eyes on September 21, 1814, when he read the submission in front of him for the *National Intelligencer*. Congress had reconvened only two days prior. Yet here was an anonymous submission about removing the capital to another city.

"We hear some indistinct suggestions buzzed abroad of a design to endeavor, in consequence of recent events, to remove the seat of government temporarily or permanently from this place," as Gales described it.

Congress had reconvened September 19, squeezing into Washington City's Blodgett's Tavern. Paul Jennings, one of Madison's domestic slaves, described Blodgett's as "an old shell of a house on 7th Street." The three-story building had been a tavern, theater, and boarding house. "Both houses of Congress managed to get along in it very well, notwithstanding it had to accommodate the patent office, city and general post office, committee rooms, and what was left of the Congressional library, at the same time."

Gales knew that the House of Representatives, however, was particularly uncomfortable at Blodgett's. Though every spot in the tavern was occupied, not all members were there: only 157 of 176 members. What would happen when they all returned and they had a full house?

Though he may not have realized it, Gales held a powerful position in Washington. A Boston newspaper wrote that "Mr. Gales is not an inconsequential member of the political family in Washington."

What should he do? Should he print the editorial opposing relocation? He didn't want to alarm his readers. What if the writer of the letter was mistaken? Who was the author? Did he recognize the handwriting?

Embracing freedom of the press didn't mean publishing everything that came his way. He had to be sure before he printed the editorial. And so for now, Gales kept the letter quiet.

The news was true, as President Madison well knew. City councils and leading citizens in Philadelphia and Lancaster had sent petitions to U.S. government officials. They suggested relocating the nation's capital city to their town. Why? Because they had something Washington didn't have: buildings.

Both places knew that their halls of government could house the federal government—temporarily and permanently. They also knew that accommodations for members of Congress were far better in their towns than in Washington City, even before the fire.

While he didn't directly address this issue in his message to Congress, Madison made a bold declaration of his position on it nonetheless. On September 20, Edward Coles brought Madison's message to the Senate and House, where someone read it aloud. Years earlier Thomas Jefferson had broken with Washington's and Adams's tradition of delivering the president's message in person to Congress. Jefferson preferred to write it and have someone else read it. Keenly aware of his weak-sounding voice, Madison followed the Jefferson model. He was a far better writer than a public orator.

While his voice was absent, his message and declarations were clear. He was quick to highlight the crowning achievement of Fort McHenry. He also praised other victories, including U.S. successes on the Canadian side of the Niagara frontier, General Jackson's achievements in the South, and a crucial victory at Plattsburg.

Most important, the president announced that his top priority was to supply the Treasury, whether for "a return of peace or further and more effective provisions for prosecuting the war."

Though Madison hoped peace would come soon, the burning of Washington led him to "infer that a spirit of hostility is indulged more violent than ever against the rights and prosperity of this country."

The president knew that he had to show strength. As early as September 5, the editor of Georgetown's *Federal Republican* had praised

Madison for his decision to bring Congress back to Washington instead of arranging for them to meet in another city. "This is as it should be. If it be not intended to 'give up the ship' no consent should be granted to even a temporary removal of the seat of government."

Their position continued firmly, "and we trust that no representative of the people will hesitate for a moment in determining that a removal of the seat of government, under present circumstances, would bring dishonor on the country."

Their reasons reflected renewed patriotism. "The character of the nation is implicated in maintaining this as its capital, and it would be dastardly to abandon it." Madison couldn't have agreed more. He would not abandon Washington City. Aware of the whispers of relocation, the president made his boldest, strongest declaration in his message to Congress.

"However deeply to be regretted on our part, he [the enemy] will find in his transient success, which interrupted for a moment only the ordinary public business at the seat of government," Madison proclaimed. The British military had only temporarily, not permanently, stopped the federal government.

The president knew, however, that Congress would soon launch an investigation into why the nation's capital had been undefended. Every player, major and minor, would write his account of what happened.

He also knew that something had to be done quickly about the Capitol and the President's House. How bad was the damage? Could they rebuild using existing walls?

Hence, he made a decision. He asked Thomas Munroe for an assessment of clearing the debris from the sites. Munroe suggested it would cost $1,200 for the cleanup.

In his response to Madison, Munroe also forwarded a letter from an architect from Philadelphia, Robert Mills, the son-in-law of Samuel Smith, who had visited Washington to survey the damage. "I would take the liberty of suggesting to you, the propriety of recommending to the President to have the capital roofed in a temporary manner, for the purpose of preserving the work that still remains good internally."

Mills gave Madison the news he most wanted to hear about the remains. Some of the walls could be salvaged: "Without a precaution of this kind, the rain and frost of the winter will, if not entirely destroy, weaken the arches or vaults, that are now good...."

That meant rebuilding was possible. Decisiveness and determination flowed from Madison's words and actions more boldly than before. Hope for rebuilding was real, but time was also ticking. The forces for relocating were a foil.

After arriving in Baltimore and spending the night at the Indian Queen Hotel on September 16, Francis Scott Key shared his lyrics with one of his brothers-in-law, Judge Joseph Nicholson, who had led men under orders from General Smith. Nicholson arranged for anonymous publication of Key's poem. They used the title "Defense of Fort McHenry."

The poem was electric, popping up in newspapers across the nation. Washington Irving, who served as editor of a magazine, printed it as well. When Key returned to Georgetown, he had the pleasure of reading his poem in his hometown newspaper. Once again, Georgetown's *Federal Republican* continued its renewed patriotism. Not only did it publish all of the verses, but it also published Key's story, though without naming him.

"A gentleman had left Baltimore in a flag of truce for the purpose of getting released from the British fleet, a friend of his who had been captured at Marlborough.... and he was compelled to witness the bombardment of Fort McHenry, which the admiral had boasted that he would carry in a few hours, and that the city must fall."

That autumn, Key didn't experience the notoriety that would later come to him, though his Georgetown paper accurately relayed his emotions. "He watched the flag at the fort through the whole day with anxiety that can be better felt than described, until the night prevented him from seeing it. In the night he watched the bomb shells and at early dawn his eye was again greeted by the proudly waving flag of his country."

His poem would soon become known as "The Star-Spangled Banner."

━━━━━━

The debate of September 26, 1814, in Congress stunned residents of Washington City. Mr. Jonathan Fisk, a New York Republican, submitted a resolution to inquire into the expediency of removing the seat of government away from Washington.

"Resolved that a committee be appointed to inquire into . . . removing the seat of government . . . to a place of greater security and less inconvenience than the city of Washington," Fisk requested.

Mr. Joseph Lewis, a Federalist of Virginia, opposed the motion under any circumstances whatsoever. He didn't believe it was any more vulnerable than any other place east of the Alleghany Mountains, no more so than Philadelphia or Lancaster.

"If proper preparations for resistance had been made by those whose duty it was to have made them," Lewis complained, noting that the problem was not the location but a failure to protect it. "Let us not gratify the wishes of our enemy."

But the debate and fight was under way.

━━━━━━

Now that Congressman Fisk had submitted a motion to relocate the nation's capital city, Gales decided it was time. He had no choice but to publish the editorial opposing removal. As he explained to his readers in a note preceding the article: "The following communication was handed to us some days before the meeting of Congress, when the subject was first talked of."

Gales wanted his readers to know that he didn't believe it when he first saw it. "Want of room in our paper, and indeed, incredulity, on our part that it would ever be seriously discussed, made us lay it aside at the time, as rather premature."

He also knew that city leaders in neighboring Georgetown had suggested Georgetown College to Congress as a temporary meeting place. They'd also offered congressmen ten dollars a week instead of sixteen dollars for boarding at Washington hotels. This alone was proof enough that it was time to publish the article.

His commitment to freedom of the press was put to the test. Gales's own livelihood was at stake. And so he published the opinion of this editorialist, who was either an anonymous average Joe or perhaps even the prominent Jimmy Madison, who was aware earlier than most of the petitions to relocate.

"It is said that the city of Philadelphia hath very recently sent to this place a deputation of offering, under pretence of better accommodations for Congress, etcetera inducements for removing the government to that city."

Yes, it was true. Residents of Philadelphia, and also Lancaster, Pennsylvania, had sent a petition to Congress. To the anonymous editorialist, the offer was disrespectful.

"Can it be that any respectable portion of our fellow citizens of the United States should not only be destitute of sympathy in our recent misfortune but greedily seize the occasion to turn us quiet?"

The writer expected better of the people of Philadelphia. "They cannot be so devoid of justice, and though that place, like others, may have some selfish or discontented citizens, who would pursue their interests to the disregard of everything else."

Then the author, using the pseudonym Philo, presented his most logical arguments against abandoning Washington City. He tapped nostalgia for George Washington and the legal authorization of the U.S. Constitution. "Under a law of Congress passed in pursuance of the Constitution itself, the permanent seat of government hath been designed and fixed by the father of his country, in the most solemn and formal manner."

Abandoning the city of Washington would disgrace its namesake. It also would require the federal government to void contracts with the states of Maryland and Virginia, which had transferred land to establish the federal district. Local land owners had also sold property in good faith: "Contracts have been made with states and individuals the binding force of which, according to another provision of the U.S. Constitution, can neither be impaired or evaded."

It would also set a worrisome precedent. "If then the government begin to move, where will it stop?"

Perhaps the most powerful argument against moving the capital was the message it would send to the British government and the door it would open to future attacks. "Our disgrace would indeed be sealed, should our enemy or should the world be suffered to believe that with a handful of men they can drive our government from its seat."

Moving the government could also damage the current peace negotiations. "It would be considered as proof of its disorganization; and of the rapid progress made by the enemy towards our subjugation. It would be felt, in our pending negotiations, and lessen us in the estimation of all of Europe."

The author's concern about the peace negotiations perhaps suggests that Madison may have written this article or encouraged someone he trusted to do so. The need for unity, not a debate over location, was paramount in such a crisis. "Our national character and interests, therefore, unite with other important considerations, in favor of dispelling, without delay, all doubts on this subject."

As Gales published this anonymous article, all he could do was hope that it would persuade enough members of Congress to stay in Washington.

———

"It is laughable to see with what petulance and disrespect the *Intelligencer* notices the proposition lately made in the House of Representatives for the temporary removal of the seat of government," the editor of the *Massachusetts Spy* published on October 5.

He had harsh words, scathing even, for Gales. "The editor of that paper is one of the most debased and supple fools ever put into the hands of a wicked administration."

This editor saw Gales as merely an extension of Madison, claiming, "No drudgery is too low, no condescension too mean, no sacrifice of honor and conscience too great to be borne by him, if it will only conciliate the favor and forward the plans of his master."

Though Gales favored Madison, hadn't the British destroyed his property because of him? Perhaps it was time for Gales to be more cautious. Maybe he needed to show a more definitive separation.

———

Benjamin Latrobe's business partnership in Pittsburgh with Robert Fulton was in the pits, dying a death by a thousand cuts. Fulton's financial backers were suing him, and Latrobe was caught in a patent fight between Latrobe's son-in-law and Fulton. The war's financial devastation and the removal of hard money from New York banks to Canada was affecting everyone and business everywhere.

Knowing that the burning of the White House and Capitol had destroyed Latrobe's most tangible accomplishments in Washington City, a friend had written Latrobe a sympathy letter.

"I thank you for your remarks so flattering me to the Capitol. But I fear that it cannot be repaired. The frost will come on and destroy much," Latrobe replied on September 24, 1814.

His agony was matched by his architect's desire to fix things.

"I know exactly what it would be best to do, but I cannot intrude my advice and Mr. Madison will never employ me again, I am told," he concluded.

Would Madison dare hire Benjamin Latrobe again? Latrobe's wife, Mary, thought so, despite the past. She secretly wrote a letter to Dolley, and one to the president as well.

———

Madison wasn't following the Washington model of staying out of the removal question completely. Instead, he may have been creating his own model of stealth protesting. Perhaps he had made suggestions and whispered into the ears of men like Thomas Munroe, John Van Ness, and Congressman Lewis to use their words, expertise, and money in creative ways to keep Washington as the nation's capital city.

One of those men may have written an article that appeared in the Georgetown newspaper. Someone rose up and protested Congress in a letter addressed to the honorable men of the Senate and House of Representatives that was printed in the *Federal Republican* on October 1, 1814. The author identified himself simply as one of the people.

He noted the origins of establishing Washington City under the leadership of George Washington. The area's original residents had sold their property to the government with the promise that it would become the permanent seat of government. Not only did Virginia and Maryland hand over land, but they also provided money for the district to the federal government. Virginia gave $120,000 and Maryland gave $72,000 for buildings and ground improvements.

"President Washington, whose sense of justice always accompanied his public acts, thought it was reasonable, that the public buildings should be as equally distributed through the city, as public convenience."

Lots for government buildings were scattered throughout the city, not clustered in only one area. The author of this editorial knew that members of Congress had long been dissatisfied with this arrangement. The Capitol was a mile and a quarter from the President's House, which seemed a great distance with so few buildings in between.

"And thus the city is composed of villages and hamlets, so remote from each other, as to preclude the connected improvements of regularly built cities."

The author, however, understood the vision of George Washington. Those gaps would one day be filled: "But these inconveniences will daily decrease, and finally the city of Washington will be considered one of the most superb capitals of the world."

This prognosticator, noting that the U.S. Capitol and White House were repairable, was angry at suggestions to move the capital to

Philadelphia. "Because we have suffered many privations and have been invaded, are we therefore to be abandoned?"

He demanded more from Congress.

"No, from you we expect more magnanimous conduct; if every house had been laid desolate, we expected that you would have…called on your country to avenge the deed, until even the spirits of the dead had awoke and roused to a holy zeal."

The author didn't realize that Congress didn't need to avenge the deed. He and his fellow Washingtonians were rising like spirits from the dead with a patriotic zeal to fight for their city to remain the capital of the country.

CHAPTER THIRTY-ONE

Poor
Mrs. Madison

"Poor Mrs. Madison, it is said, shows the most sensibility on the subject," Congressman Jeremiah Mason of New Hampshire wrote from Washington to his wife, Mary, on October 6, 1814.

"In her flight from the enemy, she was not only without assistance or consolation from the inhabitants, but treated with abuse. The President left her to shift for herself," he wrote, noting that she endured abuses hurled at her husband. "The disgraceful and distressing stories told are innumerable." He appeared to be aware of the story of the woman cussing at her and kicking her out of her inn.

"The derangement occasioned by the visit of the enemy to this place is much greater than I had supposed. The destruction of the public buildings and papers produces serious inconvenience," he wrote.

Though he didn't explicitly say that Mrs. Madison was depressed, he took pity on her because many people had accused the administration of misconduct and condemned them for it. Mason also informed his wife of the political fallout on relocating the capital.

"The expectation of a removal to Philadelphia gains strength. It will be determined in a few days in the House of Representatives," he observed, though doubtful of the outcome.

"The discussion has created a most violent excitement among the people of this district and vicinity."

———

With all of the diplomats assigned to America relocating to Philadelphia, it was no wonder that people in Pennsylvania were confident of eventually becoming the state to hold the nation's capital once again. What better way to ensure it than to show how inept and undeserving the residents of Washington were to host the capital? What better way to do this than to highlight the many failures of the fiasco?

An observer for Philadelphia's *Democratic Press* went to Bladensburg and Washington City and reported his findings. He concluded that there were at least thirty commanding points along the road between Washington and Bladensburg that could have been used to defend the nation's capital. "How it has been permitted that this ground should be marched over in solid column by the British is now undergoing a serious investigation by a committee in the House of Representatives."

Indeed. He was correct. Congress's investigation was wide and far reaching. They asked every military commander, cabinet member, and even the president to submit letters and explanations of their actions to a special committee.

"There is a determination to probe to the bottom, and hold up to public exertion, if not public execution."

Some thought treason was behind Bladensburg and the invasion of Washington. But treasury, not treason, was the reason. A lack of funds and a failure of the War Department to prepare were among the reasons behind the fiasco.

This observer also told the people of Philadelphia the news they wanted to hear as a capital city in waiting.

"The removal of the seat of government is talked of by everybody."

Noting that the loss of public and private buildings was estimated at $2 million, he simply couldn't believe that anyone still believed that Washington City should be the nation's capital. The people there didn't deserve it. Indeed, "if you were to see the ground which was shamefully abandoned, and thus the capital left at the mercy of the enemy, and if you were to see the black and desolate ruins of the public buildings, which cost millions, you would stand astonished that any member not personally interested should hesitate to remove the seat of government."

Albeit tempered, he put forth his belief and hope for Philadelphia's return as the capital seat. "There is said to be a very large majority in the House of Representatives in favor of removal; the opinion in the Senate is more doubtful."

━━━━━

Three days later, on October 9, John Van Ness knew what he had to do. He rushed the report to Joseph Gales so it could be published the next day in the newspaper.

Van Ness absolutely could not let politics finish the job that the British military had started. Though Armstrong had failed the militia and military, he could not let Washington City die. And so he held a meeting with other concerned citizens. Together they nominated seven to form a committee to protest those in the House of Representatives who wanted to relocate the capital city. As chairman, he wrote a summary of their discussion and gave it to Gales.

"Resolved, that we view with deep concern the agitation of the question now under consideration in the House of Representatives to remove the seat of government from the city of Washington."

They considered the measure "repugnant to the Constitution and laws, subversive of public faith, injurious to the community at large, and ruinous to our private interest."

Mayor James Blake, Charles Carroll, and several other local leaders rallied with him. As a banker, Van Ness knew that Congress didn't have what Washington most needed to keep the seat of government. But he did. Money. How much would it cost to rebuild the U.S. Capitol and White House? Perhaps the answer to those questions mattered more than any of the others.

―――――――――

News about the peace negotiations came in October, and it wasn't good, nor was it what Senator King had long expected.

"Enclosed I send you the President's message of yesterday communicating the late dispatches from Ghent," King informed Senator Gore. "It would appear from the dispatch of the 19th of August that the negotiation has failed."

He couldn't have been more shocked or disappointed in Parliament. For so long he'd been certain that the British wanted peace. Yet, not only had they invaded and burned the capitol, but they had also put forward ridiculous terms for peace. It was as if they were trying to goad the American negotiators into calling off the peace talks. One major sticking point was a desire by the British to create a zone set aside for native tribes between British and U.S. territory.

King ranted two days later in a letter to his friend Mr. Morris, "The enemy now demand that the whole of this region should constitute an Indian reservation or barrier, between their and our territories."

Not even the pro-British King could reconcile this demand. He could see its implications, particularly if the neutral zone ran along the Mississippi River and affected the Missouri and Mississippi area tribes. Such barriers "would in effect deprive Congress of the power of admitting new states, since these territories alone remained out of which to form them!!!"

His frustration continued unabated. "Our rulers can neither make war, nor conclude peace. What are the minority to do?" he asked.

What King didn't know was that at about this same time, the U.S. peace commissioners learned of the destruction of Washington.

Horrified, John Quincy Adams soon suggested that they offer a plan to the British negotiators to return to the ways things were before the war—including the U.S.-Canadian border. The issue of impressment could be negotiated after a peace treaty in the form of a commerce treaty.

Because an antebellum position violated their current instructions from President Madison, the other commissioners were reluctant to agree to suggest it. But they decided it was worth the risk and tried it. The British accepted, and the two sides began a back-and-forth process to create a treaty. Fortunately, Madison had also come to the conclusion that antebellum was an option and had sent the commissioners permission. They received his new instructions a few weeks after they made the offer to the British.

Though King had no knowledge of these negotiations, he was awakening to the fact that Congress hadn't done enough to support the war. It was time to step up and do more until peace came. Instead of opposing Madison at every opportunity, King began to seek common ground.

He wrote, "The country is invaded; it is threatened with waste and destruction—must we not unite to defend it, must we not join in granting supplies; ought we not to hold a language firm and which cannot be misunderstood concerning the rights and honor of the nation?"

By this point King had concluded that England's refusal to make peace was vindictive animosity. The burning of the U.S. Capitol was all the evidence this lawyer needed to justify putting party politics aside and work together with the Republicans for the common good.

King was not the only Federalist in Congress who had awakened to the need to work together and take action. Both members of the House and Senate attended a meeting and agreed to an action plan. The character of the war had changed from futile attempts to invade Canada into a need to defend the east coast. In addition to deciding whether to relocate the capital city and conducting an investigation into why Washington wasn't better protected, they recognized the need to be proactive. King wrote of the meeting: "It has become the duty of all to unite in the adoption of vigorous measures to repel the invaders of the country and to protect its essential rights and honor."

They agreed to the following plan: "Congress should therefore grant supplies of both men and money, provided the same be done pursuant to the provisions of the Constitution, and according to an impartial estimate of the relative ability of the several states."

Because public credit was destroyed, they agreed on the need to raise taxes, especially indirect taxes, to pay for supplies and resources to fund the war. "The Federalists have at all times been ready and at every hazard to defend, and will be the last to consent to give up, the rights of soil and sovereignty belonging to the Nation. They will therefore concur in the grant of supplies upon equal and constitutional principles."

One more item of business attracted King's attention, and all of Washington City's, that October.

"The subject of removal will I hear be called up again on Monday," he wrote. "Whether an adjournment to Philadelphia will take place is uncertain. A majority is believed to exist in favor of removal, but they are not united in the place."

New York was out of the question. There wasn't enough support for it. "Unless we go to Philadelphia, we might as well remain where we are."

———

On October 14, 1814, Gales promptly published the latest debate in the House of Representatives over removing the seat of government. The day before, they had read the bill a second time. If it passed, the act would authorize the removal of the seat of government to another city and tie the return to the city of Washington only after the war had ended and peace was in place.

Mr. Rhea of Tennessee objected to the second reading of the bill because he believed the House ought to concern itself with matters that were more pressing to the nation as a whole, including recent dispatches from Europe that updated the Congress on the status of the peace negotiations.

Congressman Grosvenor of New York regretted the timing of the bill. Too many members of Congress were still absent, he felt, so they should wait until all had returned. Still another congressman believed that they should be focusing on funding the war. This bill delayed them from providing supplies to the army. A waste of time, it was.

Though expecting the measure to pass, Mr. Fisk, the bill's author, argued: "The increase of expense thus incurred amounted to a greater sum than would the cost of removal of the public officers to Philadelphia or New York."

Fisk had no sympathy for John Van Ness or other Washington residents. "To brave all these inconveniences merely in consideration of the interests of the people of this district, would be to pervert the constitutional provision which gives Congress exclusive legislation over the district and, instead of that would be giving to the district control over Congress."

Considering the interests of Washington residents to be the same as those of other Americans, Fisk believed that other citizens had "too much good sense and patriotism to ask Congress merely out of regard to their personal views to compromise the national interests."

Then he mocked those who had said that the enemy wouldn't come to Washington. He failed to mention that the man who most doubted the British would come to Washington was Armstrong—a New Yorker, not a local Washingtonian.

Knowing that those who supported removal were from the North and East and those who opposed it were from the South, Fisk put forward perhaps the real reason he had authored the bill: money. He favored monied men, as some described the banking class. He believed that the bankers of the North who'd loaned the government money deserved to know that their investment was safe. In Washington it wasn't, in his view. "Should not the creditors of the government be satisfied of the safety of Congress?" Yes, they should. Philadelphia and New York City offered better protection for Congress.

Such talk infuriated Mr. Wright of Maryland. Rising and speaking with vigor, he demanded that they vote and put the matter to rest. "Even the savages destroy their victim the same day they begin to inflict the deadly tortures on him." He hoped the "decision would then put eternally to rest the question of removal, and that this city, established by Washington, would never be broken up on the pretence that monied men would not lend their money here."

But the final vote didn't come that day. Not yet. By exercising his freedom to publish the proceedings, Gales knew the record might influence public opinion and the final vote.

━━━━━━

Dolley and James Madison sent a strong signal to the people of Washington in October of that year. While Congress debated whether to relocate the capital city, the president and his wife showed their intentions of staying. They moved into the Octagon, the finest private mansion in Washington City, only a short block west of the south grounds of the White House. By moving into this three-story red-brick residence with an oval or bow-shaped front, the Madisons demonstrated that they had no intention of going anywhere.

They also sent Congress another strong signal by entertaining again. The *Boston Commercial Gazette* took notice, too, reporting that "Mrs. Madison's levees have recommenced at Washington, not with the splendor of the former ones but apparently with unabated good cheer and hilarity."

Though a far cry from the stage they had created at the White House, the Octagon, owned by Colonel John Tayloe and designed by William Thornton, gave them a pleasant environment to entertain guests nonetheless.

By resuming entertaining the autumn of 1814, the Madisons showed that they'd been down, but they were not out. They wouldn't let the loss of the White House keep them from living life. Grief would not defeat them. They would make the most of the two years James had left in his term.

The Madisons put the past behind them by resuming their normal activities. Dolley invited Ruth Barlow for a more intimate dinner. She inscribed a kind note to the Russian diplomat's wife. She offered to help

Elizabeth Bonaparte, the American sister-in-law of the deposed Napoleon, to obtain discreet passage to Europe.

Deciding to honor the brave in the Battle of Fort McHenry and Baltimore, she sent a very special gift to Minerva Rodgers, the wife of Commodore Rodgers, who lived in Havre de Grace.

"I beg you and my estimable friend, your husband, to accept a dimijohn of pure wine saved from the President's House the morning of its destruction."

Together James and Dolley were leading Washington back to normal.

CHAPTER THIRTY-TWO

Presidents' Club

A s Madison emerged with determination in the autumn of 1814, he received direct and indirect strength from the three presidents who had preceded him. He also unknowingly directed the destiny of the three presidents to follow him.

"It is very long since I troubled you with a letter," Jefferson began, "but in the late events at Washington, I have felt so much for you that I cannot withhold the expression of my sympathies."

When he read Jefferson's letter a month after the destruction of the capital, Madison immediately detected the spirit of friendship and camaraderie that he'd long enjoyed with the bookish Jefferson. Years earlier the pair had selected books that should be part of a Library of Congress. Though initially rejecting Jefferson's books, Congress had established a library, which was lost to the fire.

Through Jefferson's letter that fall of 1814, Madison also experienced the unique fraternity found among presidents. Regardless of their differences, Madison, Jefferson, and Adams were members of the unofficial presidents' club. Jefferson knew what Adams also knew, and now Madison. Leadership was a lonely place. Much is beyond a president's control.

Jefferson put it this way in his letter, "For although every reasonable man must be sensible that all you can do is to order, that execution must depend on others, and failures be immutable to them alone, yet I know that when such failures happen, they afflict even those who have done everything they could to prevent them."

Then he invoked the most comforting words he could have mustered. "Had General Washington himself been now at the head of our affairs the same event would probably have happened." With such a statement, Jefferson humanized George Washington and tried to make Madison feel better.

Then Jefferson offered Madison solace by referring to recent victories, such as Fort McHenry. "While our enemies cannot but feel shame for their barbarous achievements at Washington, they will be shamed to the soul by these repeated victories over them on that element on which they wish the world to think them invincible."

Just as Jefferson gave Madison the gift of encouragement from someone who had walked in his buckled shoes, so he also gave him another gift, something more tangible and politically beneficial to keeping the capital in Washington, which may have been part of his motivation. "Learning by the papers the loss of the Library of Congress, I have sent my catalogue...to make their library committee the offer of my collection, now of about 9 or 10,000 volumes which may be delivered to them instantly, on a valuation by persons of their own naming, and be paid for in any way, and at any term they please."

Because they were personal friends and neighbors whose estates were located fairly close to one another, Jefferson knew that Madison could vouch for his collection. "I believe you are acquainted with the condition of these books should they wish to be ascertained of this."

Replacing the library was a gift to Congress and the public. "I have long been sensible that my library would be an interesting possession for the public, and the loss Congress has recently sustained, and the difficulty of replacing it, while our intercourse with Europe is so obstructed, renders this the proper moment for placing it at their service."

Jefferson's offer was also a political gift to Madison. It signaled that life should go on. The government could continue as it was before and rebuild. While not explicitly addressing the issue of relocating the capital city, the gesture underscored Madison's determination that the British invasion should be only a temporary interruption, not a permanent one.

"I learn that the library committee will report favorably on your proposition to supply the loss of books by Congress," Madison responded in a letter that signaled he was following up on his friend's offer. "It will prove a gain to them, if they have the wisdom to replace it by such a collection as yours."

He also discussed the war with his predecessor. The outcome would depend on two things: the ability of the peace commissioners to negotiate with the British and how well General Andrew Jackson would lead the southern army to defend Louisiana.

Madison also wrote Jefferson the latest information on peace: "We have just received dispatches from Ghent which I shall lay before Congress today.... Our ministers were all present and in perfect harmony and of opinion on the arrogance of such demands."

Jefferson understood the challenge that Madison faced when it came to peace. The war over impressment and trade rights appeared to have shifted. The enemy had changed the end game, as he'd written to Madison.

"The war," Jefferson explained, "now that these [impressment and trade rights] are done away by events, is declared by Great Britain to have changed its object, and to have become a war of conquest, to be waged until she conquers from us our fisheries, the province of Maine, the [Great] lakes, states and territories North of the Ohio, and the navigation of the Mississippi, in other words till she reduces us to unconditional submission."

Madison agreed. As he responded to Jefferson, he longed for the British government to change its demands but feared it would not. He thought a "rupture of the negotiation" was possible. He hoped that new events, such as the outcome of a likely battle in New Orleans, would pressure the Brits to reduce their demands. Because leaders in Europe were meeting to divide Napoleon's territories, this might change the dynamics in America's favor.

———

A want-to-be member of the presidents' club, Senator King, found himself receiving disapproval from a friend. His phoenix-like rise to support congressional action met with disapproval from his Federalist friend Gouverneur Morris. More extreme in his views than King, Morris was in a fit over the Federalists' fall of 1814 plan.

"I feel myself bound in duty and honor to declare that anything like a pledge by Federalists to carry on this wicked war, strikes a dagger to my heart. Whoever shall utter a word of that sort will repent it," Morris wrote to King.

He accused King of being cheated by contrivers. "What are you to gain by giving Mr. Madison men and money?"

Morris's objection was about finances. "If you go on at this present rate…you wage war at an expense which no nation can bear. Patriotism is one thing, but food is another, and tho' patriotism may turn out soldiers it cannot buy bread."

Morris didn't believe the enemy ever intended to attack New York. He knew his criticism of King was hurtful, "Hard words if you please, but they break no bones."

King and Morris agreed on one thing. Both believed the British's main objective now was to capture Louisiana, specifically New Orleans, and control the Mississippi River. In this way they could live to fight another war and thwart western expansion by the United States in the future, as King wrote: "If N.O. [New Orleans] passes under the dominion of the enemy, the war will be continued for many years."

How King longed for an end to the war. How he hoped that New Orleans would end it. Now more than ever he hoped that Madison would obtain a victory, one that would lead to a lasting peace for the United States of America.

━━━━━━━━

Still highly focused on the war, Madison directed the resources of the War Department toward New Orleans. By ordering James Monroe, now war secretary, to send a letter to General Andrew Jackson, he unknowingly directed the next steps of two future presidents, both Monroe and Jackson. During the third week of October, Monroe communicated the president's wishes, noting that Madison had approved of how Jackson had conducted himself on behalf of his country. This move was to fix the insult Armstrong had thrown at Jackson for promotion.

Monroe concluded his letter to Jackson, "Very important interests are committed to you, and great confidence is entertained that you will meet the expectation of the government in the discharge of your duties."

Madison, Monroe, and Jackson knew that the British had changed their focus. They were now heading south. Cockburn had headed toward Georgia while another squadron was preparing to attack New Orleans.

"It is thought very probably that the British forces, expected from Europe, under Lord Hill, will be directed against Louisiana," Monroe conveyed on Madison's behalf to Jackson. "To enable to meet this prospect, 7,500 men have been ordered from Tennessee, 2,500 from Kentucky, and alike number from Georgia, and it is expected that warriors of all the friendly tribes of Indians will be received by you, on our side."

The government was also sending money and blankets and other articles to ready Jackson's men for service.

━━━━━━━━

Once again, a member of the presidents' club gave Madison an opportunity to express his confidence in peace. Former President John Adams had forwarded him a letter from his son, John Quincy Adams, who was one of the peace commissioners. John Quincy had written his father asking for a history of the fishing rights on bodies of water used by both Americans and Canadians. He wanted to know how those rights had been determined in the negotiation to end the Revolutionary War. Though John Adams had participated in those negotiations, he had sent his son's letter and request to President Madison.

"I have caused the archives of the Department of State to be searched with an eye to what passed during the negotiation for peace on the subject of the fisheries. The search has not furnished a precise answer to the enquiry of Mr. Adams," Madison thoughtfully responded to Adams.

All they could find was that Congress had supported the common right to fish three leagues beyond the shores of Canada in instructions for a commerce treaty with Britain years earlier. The information was not specific enough to resolve the problem in the current negotiations.

Madison then shared the latest information that he had about Adams's son. "The view of the discussions at Ghent presented by the private letters of all our ministers there, as well as by their official dispatches, leaves no doubt of the policy of the British Cabinet."

Outlining the challenge the peace commissioners faced, he continued, "The point to be decided by our ministers is, whether during the uncertainty of events, a categorical alternative of immediate peace, or a rupture of the negotiation, would not be preferable to a longer acquiescence in the gambling procrastinations of the other party."

He knew that it was possible a rupture had happened. Even if this had taken place, he assured Adams of his confidence in his son's skills. "It is very agreeable to find that the superior ability which distinguishes the notes of our envoys, extorts commendation from the most obdurate of their political enemies."

Recognizing John Quincy's abilities, Madison also caught a glimpse of the diplomatic skills that would launch John Quincy Adams as the nation's sixth president, in ten years.

As the nation's fourth president, Madison had been directly touched and influenced by the first three. He had also been a touchstone for the next three by directing the destinies of Monroe, John Quincy Adams, and Jackson.

In the autumn of 1814, though Madison remained worried that peace had not yet come, he had three reasons to hope it was still achievable. He had used his presidential power to give the peace commissioners instructions that would lead to peace. He'd also directed resources to Andrew Jackson in New Orleans, and he'd sent an important signal to members of Congress.

While not directly communicating his intentions to Mr. Gales at the *National Intelligencer*, he coyly reminded an intermediary that when it came to the removal of the capital by Congress, he held the power of the veto. And more than that, he would use it.

CHAPTER THIRTY-THREE

Uplifting News

"The decision of the House of Representatives has, as we anticipated, put to sleep for now, and we trust forever, the project of a removal of the seat of government from Washington."

Nine votes. That's all. The final vote was that close. Seventy-four members voted for moving the capital city, while eighty-three voted against it. As relieved as he was optimistic, Gales printed the happenings in the *National Intelligencer* on October 18, 1814.

The cause of justice had triumphed. Knowing the president all too well, Gales had decided that Madison would've vetoed the measure if it had passed. This newspaperman had changed a bit, however, since the burning of the White House and Capitol. Concluding that it was time to show a little distance and independence from the president, Gales made it clear that he had not spoken to Mr. Madison directly on the matter: "We take this opportunity to disclaim any direct knowledge of the sentiments of the chief magistrate in respect to the seat of government."

Yet, he knew that the president's recent actions of convening Congress in Washington and moving with his wife into the Octagon House, among other decisions, signaled his intention not to go anywhere anytime soon. Gales didn't run a state or official government paper, but he understood the criticism that he had been too chummy with the administration. He also knew Madison's character and sensed his views on the issue, and printed his thoughts. "Entertaining that opinion which we do of his patriotic spirit and zeal for the integrity of the union, with the light afforded us by the part which he took in the proceedings of Congress in 1791 in regard to this subject, we would not doubt but he [the president] would reject any bill for the removal of the seat of government which should've passed Congress by bare majorities only."

Party lines and region played a role in the outcome. Forty-four of fifty-three Federalists voted for removal while only thirty of 104 Republicans voted for removal. Most northern members voted for removal, while most southern members voted against it.

The vote was most divided in Pennsylvania, the state most likely to benefit from moving the capital. Nine members from Pennsylvania voted for removal while seven opposed it. Party allegiance and a desire to spite the enemy by keeping Washington as the capital city prevailed.

The vote didn't stop the enthusiasm of Washingtonians to continue to court Congress. Launching an effort from local residents to contribute money and supplies to rebuild, the city council created gravel sidewalks around local boardinghouses to ease the discomfort of members of Congress as they endured the city's muddy streets. This gave lawmakers more reasons to stay.

Gales had come to America because his father had sought freedom of speech and of the press. Despite Cockburn's efforts to destroy Gales's business, this man with a nose for news rose from the ashes with a strong determination to not let the enemy win. He used freedom of the press to persuade others to keep Washington as the permanent capital city of the United States of America.

Less than two weeks after the vote, John Van Ness had even more reason to smile. Thomas Munroe, superintendent of public buildings, gave Congress a report on the feasibility of rebuilding the U.S. Capitol and White House. Because Munroe had been a clerk and bookkeeper under the original three-member board of commissioners for the District of Columbia mandated by the 1790 residence act, his credibility and experience were respected by residents and lawmakers alike.

Munroe reported on October 29, 1814, that the remains of the buildings had been surveyed carefully by "architects and master builders, all of whom report it as their opinions that the walls of the President's House, and both wings of the Capitol, with some inconsiderable repairs, will be safe and sufficient to rebuild on."

The big question was cost, as Van Ness knew intimately. Munroe estimated $460,000 for rebuilding the government buildings. Local bankers like Van Ness offered to loan the government $500,000 "exclusively to the purpose of rebuilding or repairing the President's House, Capitol, and public offices."

In the House of Representatives, Joseph Lewis of Virginia reported a bill authorizing the president "to cause to be forthwith rebuilt or repaired the public buildings on their present sites; and for this purpose exclusively to borrow such sum as necessary for the purpose from the banks or individuals within the district."

Van Ness was now as personally invested as possible. Madison appointed him along with a few others to be part of the commission to oversee repairing the buildings. Within a few months, the president would provide strict guidance for the commissioners to return the buildings to their original appearance. "In carrying into execution the law for rebuilding the public offices, it will best comport with its object and provisions, not to deviate from the models destroyed," he wrote.

General Van Ness understood Madison's meaning. Not only were the U.S. Capitol and White House to be rebuilt, but they were also to look the same as they had before. That gave him a big reason to smile.

———

The time was now right for Van Ness to put his opinions into writing on the failures leading to the Battle of Bladensburg and the destruction of Washington City. He was one of many that members of Congress had called upon. Each witness was to submit a statement on paper. Van Ness dated his letter November 23, 1814. His testimony was one of the most damaging, especially toward General Armstrong.

Van Ness's revelation that Armstrong continued to deny Washington as the British target was highly persuasive. His assessment of the military failures at Bladensburg was also important. Why did America fail to repel the British there? Raw troops. Unsupplied troops. Fatigued troops. No battle plan. Failing to harass the British as they arrived in Benedict and as they departed. Focusing too much on Baltimore. In the end, Van Ness once again placed the blame squarely on Armstrong.

"Although I cannot think the means we had on the spot were used to the best advantage, still I think General Winder was by no means furnished with sufficient or timely means; which I always considered it the special duty of the war department to have attended to."

Relieved that Congress had decided to keep Washington as the nation's capital and thrilled to serve on the commission for rebuilding its monuments, Van Ness believed it was his duty to tell the truth. In his statement's conclusion, he wrote, "Considering your call as imperative, and having always been of opinion that it was due to the American people that the facts and circumstances connected with the fall of the capital should be fully developed, I transmit it to you."

In this way Van Ness, like the many others who testified, showed that the militia system wasn't working. In order to have a secure country in the future, America would need to improve and expand its military. The country would need to shift from depending on militia to relying on regular troops for its independence. In the years to come, it did just that.

On December 3, 1814, Congress received a report of "all the many contradictory statements" leading to the fall of Washington. The committee leader "declared that the committee, with great labor, had collected all the facts in relation to the military movement, but expressed no opinion on it, leaving it to all to judge for themselves, what ought to have been done."

Many members were unhappy. Who could blame them? Though Congressman Ingersoll later used the report as a starting point for writing his *Historical Sketch of the Second War between the United States of America, and Great Britain,* he chafed at the failure of heads to roll, except for Armstrong's. "So far from clearing up the causes of our failure, it covered up a most disgraceful transaction, in a mass of prolixity and detail. Although the enemy landed within fifty miles of Washington, and 1200 of their army overcame all the force collected there, after two months' notice no opinion was expressed of these circumstances."

Ingersoll also held distinct opinions about Ross and Cockburn. He saw them as very different personalities. "General Ross was less rapacious, more clement, and stricter in punishing military excesses, than, secondly, Admiral Cockburn, who was the evil genius, delighting in pillage and destruction."

He reflected on how different the outcome would have been if Ross had been killed in Washington and not Baltimore. "If the murderous shot fired at Ross, as he rode into Washington, and killed his mare, had killed the rider, it seems to be universally believed, that, instead of the public buildings burned, Cockburn would not have left a house standing, public or private."

Ingersoll calculated the cost and determined that "the public property destroyed at Washington exceeded two millions of dollars worth."

While a high amount, thanks to Ross, the British didn't burn everyone's house in Washington City. If they had, Ingersoll believed that Congress would have relocated the nation's capital to another city.

Ingersoll blamed Washington's destruction on the lack of a stern, unyielding chief. "Seldom, says Voltaire, is anything great done in the world, except by the genius and firmness of some one man, contending with the prejudices of the multitude and overcoming them."

What Ingersoll failed to see is that while a lack of leadership and eagle eyes led to the city's fall, the rise of Washington as the nation's permanent capital was through the firmness and genius of many phoenixes: Madison, Gales, Van Ness, Rodgers, Key, and Dolley.

———

"The fate of New Orleans will be known today—on which so much depends," Dolley wrote to Hannah Gallatin.

It seemed that everyone in Washington was waiting to know the outcome of a battle in New Orleans and peace negotiations in Europe. Longing for news of a treaty, she added, "We hear nothing from Mr. Gallatin, but expect every day, some arrival. Our anxieties cannot be expressed."

———

Dolley and the rest of Washington soon learned of the fate of New Orleans. Thomas Johnson, the postmaster for New Orleans and brother-in-law of peace commissioner John Quincy Adams, wrote Dolley on January 19, 1815, to tell her the news.

"Madam, the American army in Louisiana has gained immortal glory. It has made a defense against the most valiant and fortunate troops of Europe," he wrote with relief. Louisiana had repelled its invaders and prevented conquest.

"The eighth of January will form an epoch in the calendars of the republic," he proclaimed, noting that General Jackson had recently reported the evacuation of the British from Louisiana. "The country is saved, the enemy vanquished and hardly a widow or an orphan whose tears damp the general joy. All is exultation and jubilee. What do we not owe a protecting Providence for this manifestation of his favor?"

Johnson offered his congratulations to Dolley "on this auspicious termination of our trials and dangers."

Why did he write Dolley? He knew that his sister, Louisa Adams, the wife of John Quincy Adams, had previously asked Dolley to secure a position for him. Johnson repaid her patronage by giving her news of the victory.

Illuminations galore lit Washington City to celebrate New Orleans. People fired rockets. Cheering throngs filled the streets of Washington, which were decorated by thousands of candles and torches to celebrate the most important triumph since Yorktown served as the last major battle of the Revolutionary War in 1780.

Also thrilled to hear the news, Senator King wrote his son Charles in England a detailed account of the Battle of New Orleans. As always, his eagle eye looked to peace: "We hope that this failure [by the British] will hasten the conclusion of peace."

What he didn't know, nor did anyone else in America, was that the peace commissioners had concluded their work two weeks earlier. They had signed the Treaty of Ghent on December 24, 1814.

The news arrived in Washington City in mid-February. Paul Jennings, one of Madison's most reliable servants, described the moment that the president's household learned of the treaty: "When the news of peace arrived, we were crazy with joy. Miss Sally Coles, a cousin of Mrs. Madison, and afterwards wife of Andrew Stevenson, since minister to England, came to the head of the stairs, crying out, 'Peace! peace!' and told John Freeman (the butler) to serve out wine liberally to the servants and others."

Paul joined in the celebration. "I played the President's March on the violin, John Sioussat and some others were drunk for two days, and such another joyful time was never seen in Washington. Mr. Madison and all his Cabinet were as pleased as any, but did not show their joy in this manner."

Senator King also kept his reserve in check. He wrote simply and happily: "We have received the treaty of peace: it will be considered by the Senate tomorrow...no one is authorized to expect more than the status ante bellum."

Yet, this is what King had wanted more than anything else. The man who had opposed the war and made mischief for James Madison at every turn had changed. In the aftermath of the burning of the White House, he rose to defend his country. Madison and King now had something in common. Both could smile at peace. Both could take comfort in knowing that their country's future was as bright as it was secure. Both knew that America had risen from the ashes as a phoenix, and the White House would soon follow.

The normally withered apple-john appearance of James Madison smiled in February 1815 as he sent copies of the peace treaty to Congress. While John Quincy Adams had written that the day they had issued the treaty, December 24, 1814, was the happiest in his life, Madison could say the same about the day he signed it, on February 17, 1815.

No longer able to sit at his desk in the green room of the White House, Madison signed the treaty in the beautiful drawing room of the Octagon. With joy flowing from his pen, he wrote a message to the American people.

"The late war," he explained, "although reluctantly declared by Congress, had become a necessary resort to assert the rights and independence of the nation."

Giving credit to many, Madison honored those who had contributed so much to the nation. "It has been waged with a success which is the natural result of the wisdom of the legislative councils, of the patriotism of the people, of the public spirit of the militia, and of the valor of the military and naval forces of the country."

Recognizing the timing of peace, the man who had once seemed too deferential wrote decidedly and glowingly. "Peace, at all times a blessing, is peculiarly welcome, therefore, at a period when the causes for the war have ceased to operate, when the government has demonstrated the efficiency of its powers of defense, and when the nation can review its conduct without regret and without reproach."

Peace hadn't come by acquiring Canada. Peace hadn't come through a Russian mediation. Peace had come from Madison's determination to find it any way he could. It had come from a president who was too trusting of his aides and nearly lost the nation's capital city. It had come from a man who had trouble getting approval for his commissioners but who took the beating and re-nominated them with renewed vigor.

But this scholarly man who had authorized a war emerged as a phoenix. He was more decisive, more in charge, more of what he needed to be. He had sent the right signals and given the right instructions. He wasn't just one of a multitude of phoenixes that arose from the ashes of the White House. He was their leader, the pilot guiding their flight.

━━━━━━━

Madison had told Benjamin Latrobe before the fires that he had become so unpopular that the military wouldn't hire him for engineering projects during the war. But Latrobe listened to his wife. Mary strongly encouraged him to write the president and Thomas Munroe to offer his services to rebuild.

To the president he wrote a letter on Feb. 25, 1815.

"I beg leave respectfully to offer you my services in the restoration of the public buildings in the city of Washington," Latrobe had written to President Madison, noting that he'd devoted the best part of his life to public service and possessed the professional qualifications and experience to do the job.

The last thing Latrobe must have expected when he left Washington City in 1813 was to return, much less to ask Madison for the job of rebuilding the U.S. Capitol. He admitted as much, writing, "I am conscious that I do not deserve it—still more so, that if I do, my error has produced no advantage to myself."

What changed in Latrobe? What motivated him to ask the president who had told him he was too unpopular to rebuild the Capitol? Perhaps he feared that Dr. Thornton would receive the job, which would have been an "implied censure," as he called it. With his fortunes failing and his debt rising in Pittsburgh, his wife Mary had to sell a piece of furniture each month to pay the rent. Without telling him, she had written President and Mrs. Madison requesting that they consider her husband for rebuilding. Then she encouraged him to reach out to men he knew in the government and then to write the president directly.

The heartbreak over the loss of the buildings had led him to the "excusable ambition which prompts me to wish that I may restore the works which I erected." He wanted a second chance to build. He also asked out of love. "Consideration for my family would render the situation I solicit highly desirable to me."

When "a large packet with the President's seal, containing a recall" arrived at the Latrobes' Pittsburgh house, Latrobe cried as if he were a child. Madison had appointed him to rebuild the U.S. Capitol and James Hoban, the original architect and master builder, to rebuild the White House.

Mary Latrobe wrote that there was "no man in the country to name but Mr. Latrobe as filling the situation he had hitherto held."

———

Where was Admiral Cockburn when news of peace arrived in America? He was in Georgia planning an attack. Though this Goliath had not been slain by an American slingshot, he had failed in his mission to defeat his enemy.

"We remained in Cumberland Island in the expectation of a reinforcement of troops, on the arrival of which it was the Rear Admiral's intention to attack Savannah; but ere they made their appearance, peace had been concluded between Great Britain and the United States," Scott explained.

The only thing for Cockburn to do now that peace had come was to go home and wait for his next assignment. Because he had not been in New Orleans and suffered defeat there, his prospects for his own professional future remained bright. After all, he was the admiral who had burned the seat of the U.S. government, as a portrait of him later showed. Though not immediate, admiral of the fleet was within his reach.

Dolley perhaps best expressed her joy about peace in a letter to Hannah: "I have rejoiced with you and for you—our glorious peace."

President Madison had rewarded the peace commissioners with new appointments. He'd named John Quincy Adams to the top diplomatic post in England and Albert Gallatin to France. Dolley was thrilled for Hannah's future. "I trust you are pleased with Mr. G——s appointment to France.... How I should like to go with you!!"

Peace had been a busy time. "Congress adjourned last night, still our house is crowded with company—in truth ever since the peace my brain has been turned with noise and bustle. Such over flowing rooms I never saw before."

Though peace was glorious, Dolley's best triumph and most eternal contribution as the wife of the president was yet to come.

CHAPTER THIRTY-FOUR

Rise of the First Lady

Mrs. Crowninshield, the wife of the new navy secretary, was so excited to pay a call on Mrs. Madison in November 1815 that she impulsively knocked on the president's door without giving advance notice or wearing what she considered proper attire.

"Our girls went with me. She [Dolley] lives in the same block with us. I did not alter my dress. Well, we rung at the door, the servant showed us to the room—no one there," Mrs. Crowninshield explained, noting that the windows in the large parlor were as patriotic as could be: blue curtains with red silk fringe.

They didn't have to wait long for Dolley. "In about two minutes the lady appeared, received us very agreeably, noticed the children much, inquired their names, because she told them she meant to be much acquainted with them."

With her charisma shining brightly, Dolley greeted them as warmly as if she'd been expecting them for a week. As usual, Mrs. Madison's attire caught her guest's attention. Mrs. Crowninshield described her "white cambric gown, buttoned all the way up in front, a little strip of work along the button-holes, but ruffled around the bottom. A peach-bloom colored silk scarf with a rich border over her shoulders by her sleeves. She had a spencer of satin of the same color, and likewise a turban of gauze, all of peach bloom."

Dolley's hospitality also stood out: "You could not but feel at your ease in her company."

The Crowninshields experienced in 1815 what people had encountered for years when meeting Dolley Madison. Her charisma was magnetic. Cousin Sally Coles described the phenomenon this way in a letter to Dolley: "For no heart has been able to resist you, and every tongue is eloquent in yours, and our dear Mr. Madison's praises."

Dolley's love of clothing was no secret. While people noticed her fashion sense, they also admired her internal beauty. One observer said of Dolley: "'Tis here the woman who adorns the dress, and not the dress that beautifies the woman."

This same person recognized Dolley's unofficial queenly stature, a position of influence that Mrs. Madison couldn't see. "I cannot conceive a female better calculated to dignify the station which she occupies in society than Mrs. Madison—amiable in private life and affable in public, she is admired and esteemed by the rich and beloved by the poor."

For years, everything she had done in the White House was for James, not for herself, except for indulgence in fashion. Early on, William Lee, a U.S. commercial agent in Bordeaux, had sent Mrs. Madison fineries from France after his wife had gone shopping for her. Recognizing Dolley's character, Lee invoked a blessing on her: "That you may long live the queen of the people's hearts."

Lee also had prophetically praised President Madison: "His administration will tend more to the formation of a national character and to the consolidating our independence than any that have preceded it and posterity will do him justice."

After the fire, Madison had done just that. With the war complete and peace sealed, the president could go on with life and conclude his term in harmony.

Dolley spent her remaining time as the president's wife doing something no other president's wife had yet done. In doing so, the queen of hearts became a first lady.

About a month later, during Christmas week, the entire Crowninshield family visited the Madisons. This time Dolley introduced Mrs. Crowninshield's daughters to their special pet. According to Mrs. Crowninshield, "She had the parrot brought in for the girls, and he ran after Mary to catch her feet. She screamed and jumped into a chair and pulled hold of Mrs. Madison. We had quite a frolic there."

Just prior to the British invasion the previous year, French John had rescued the bird by taking it from the White House to Octagon. Dolley kept this macaw in the corner window of their new residence at the Seven Buildings, where they had moved after concluding the Octagon's entertaining space was awkward.

The species' brightly colored feathers appropriately make it a symbol of vitality and health. No wonder it attracted the attention of local children, who would gather in front of the window to watch the bird's feedings.

Perhaps seeing children squeezing in front of the window had given Dolley an idea. Or maybe she came to the decision by riding the streets of Washington and seeing poverty in the faces of children and orphans on the cobblestones.

Perhaps the words of previous letters she'd received had affected on her. In July 1813, Mason Lock Weems, famous for perpetrating the myth that George Washington cut down a cherry tree as a child and refused to lie about it, sought a favor from Dolley.

"As I know of no lady who has so large an interest at stake in this country as Mrs. Madison has, nor any who holds so distinguished a place in it," Weems flattered in an attempt to seek her patronage for reprinting a book about women in the Bible.

Weems understood her unofficial power. He continued, saying, "It is certainly no adulation, Honor'd Madam to say that you are one of the 'favor'd few' who to do good need but to will it."

He also knew the source of her power stemmed from her charisma and social skills, which gave her an unparalleled ability to influence others. "The elevation of your rank, together with the charm of your benevolent spirit and polish'd manners diffused so widely as they are by the members of the national legislature and the brilliant crowds that attend your levees give you an influence which no other lady can pretend to especially among the fair sex of our country."

Also that same month, Dolley had received a letter from Lucy Rumney, a wife and mother of four from Georgetown. She was troubled by her husband's impulsive choices: "My husband is a soldier. He enlisted while under the influence of liquor, and not aware of the evil that he was going to bring upon his family. We are poor and dependant on our daily labor, and principally on him, for subsistence."

Mrs. Rumney then explained that her husband had deserted on more than one occasion and was facing court-martial that would affect his life. She told Dolley, "You, Madam can feel—I cannot express—the grief and misery in which the danger of my husband plunges me, and those of my children who are capable of estimating their loss!"

Her words were as touching as they were desperate. "Think of the wretchedness of a wife and a mother from a husband and the father of her children is just about to be torn forever."

Dolley very well understood what it was like when life took a husband from a wife and a father from his children.

Maybe now in 1815 she worried about the children of men who had died in the war, knowing especially that a woman couldn't easily make a living after her husband died.

However she came to the decision, starting an orphanage showed that Dolley viewed her role as more than just an opportunity to entertain and host parties for her husband, even if those opportunities had changed the culture in Washington. She could do much more with her role. This Quaker could do something long lasting, eternal. The newspaper first printed notification of it in a call to action led by Mrs. Madison in October 1815: "The ladies of the county of Washington are requested to meet at the hall of the House of Representatives this day at 11 o'clock for the purpose of joining an association to provide an asylum for destitute orphans."

The writer of the article, likely Dolley or one of the other ladies involved, explained that these orphans were placed by Providence under the protection of society. "It is hoped that the ladies, will show their interest that they take in the fate of these destitute and forsaken children, by their great zeal and humanity, in endeavoring to supply them, as far as in their power, the place of deceased parents."

The newspaper described the importance of caring for these children. "A nobler object cannot engage the sympathy of our females—when we reflect, too, on how uncertain are all human possessions, we know not, but that we may be providing a respectable and comfortable asylum to our descendents."

The orphanage was also born of faith. Ministers in the area had often preached charity sermons in the previous years that called on women to spin, weave, and provide clothing for the local poor. Sometimes these sermons were advertised in advance, such as a charity sermon delivered at a Methodist Church. The notification for this 1815 meeting about the orphanage used a passage from Ecclesiastes to explain the eternal value of conducting charitable work: "'Cast your bread upon the waters and after many days it shall return to you.' It is therefore hoped that there will be a full and punctual attendance; particularly by, those ladies who have already subscribed to that institution."

The women who attended that first meeting for the orphanage adopted an organization plan. They elected Dolley as the first directress and Maria Van Ness, the wife of John Van Ness, as the second directress. They also named a treasurer, secretary, and nine trustees.

As first directress, Dolley presided over all of the meetings of the society and trustees. She also gave money, a cow, and handiwork for seamstresses to make clothing for the girls.

Soon the orphanage was open. Finding a house at 10th Street and Pennsylvania Avenue Northwest, the board of women hired a governess. The plan was to educate the girls and prepare them for life. When these little ladies became of age, they were to move into the home of a respectable family to help them enter society.

The orphanage opened its doors to girls without both parents. They also agreed to consider exceptionally needy girls with one parent and would also consider extending benefits to male orphans as the organization became more established.

The orphanage would serve the children in the following ways: "The children shall be educated fed and clothed at the expense of the society and at the asylum—They must have religious instruction, moral example and habits of industry inculcated on their minds."

Faith in God was central to the project and motivation for the ladies. "But trusting in Him who is the orphan's help and pleading with the benevolent of Washington they cannot plead in vain."

At least one board member visited the orphanage each week to oversee its management and interact with the girls. Perhaps Dolley brought her pet macaw with her to entertain the children. The ladies also helped to raise money for the orphanage through theatrical benefit productions at local theaters and other ventures with proceeds going to the orphanage.

The orphanage was a success. Dolley, the Quaker who was taught to see the potential for God's grace inside every human heart, became the first president's wife to establish a charity during her husband's tenure. In this way, she led by doing. Average Americans, particularly the ladies of Washington, devoted themselves to others and community service. She set the model for future first ladies to use their time, treasure, and talents in service of others.

———

On December 6, 1815, while the orphanage was being organized, Commodore John Rodgers sent Dolley a very special gift. Because he had commanded the *President* during the war and captured twenty-three other vessels, he sent her a mat "composed of pieces taken from the flags of all the vessels, to the number of 23 captured by the *President* while under his command, and consequently belongs to the lady to whom it is now presented."

He asked Mrs. Madison "to accept it, not only as a proof of his respectful esteem, but also that it may sometimes remind her of a glorious aerie of the country over which her husband presided with so much honor."

From the burning of his house at Havre de Grace in May 1813 to the battlefield of Baltimore in September 1814, the war had affected Rodgers in many ways. By giving Mrs. Madison the mat, he presented her with tangible evidence of America's renewed sovereignty. He knew that she represented what it meant to be a queen of hearts.

━━━━━━━

In February 1816, Dolley hosted a special event. One visitor described it as "the most splendid Presidential reception ever given to that date." Once again her dress stood out: "She also wore a gold girdle and gold necklace and bracelets. This costume was completed by a turban of white velvet, trimmed with white ostrich tips, and a gold embroidered crown."

But the reason for the occasion was more significant than any dress or turban. The new minister or top diplomat from Great Britain, Sir Charles Bagot, was the guest of honor. His presence in Washington was a symbol of many things, of the rising phoenix of Washington City and the start of America's new relationship with Great Britain. That the Madisons could welcome him showed their strength of character and ability to let go of the past and move America forward.

Bagot's aristocratic background was both cultured and courteous. He was "fit to conciliate the countries at the conclusion of the war." That night he made an observation about Dolley: "She looked every inch a queen."

She had transformed the wife of the president into a new role, now known as first lady.

Epilogue

few years ago, I toured one of the most popular exhibits at the National Museum of American History in Washington, D.C., the exhibit on first ladies. Featuring their many contributions to public service, political campaigns, family life, and fashion sensibilities, this exhibit has expanded over the years. Though I'd been to this Smithsonian museum several times, I saw something that Saturday afternoon that I'd never before noticed.

While walking past the gowns of first ladies, I stopped and gazed at an ivory satin gown embroidered with butterflies and dragonflies that belonged to Dolley Madison. As I read the dress's description, my pulse quickened with excitement. Not only does the dress boast butterflies, but it also features phoenixes, the eagle-like bird symbolizing life after fire.

Obviously, this gown was not destroyed during the burning of the White House in 1814. Did Dolley purposefully add phoenixes to it as a symbol of their rise after the fire? I could only stare with wonder that day as I beheld her sly fashion statement.

At the New Year's public reception in 1816, Mrs. Crowninshield described Dolley's gown this way: "Mrs. Madison was dressed in a yellow satin embroidered all over with sprigs of butterflies, not two alike in her dress; a narrow border in all colors, made high in the neck; a little cape, long sleeves, and a white bonnet with feathers."

Though Mrs. Crowningshield doesn't mention phoenixes or dragonflies, her description does match the gown owned by the National Museum of American History.

Dolley wore that dress in 1816, the last year of her husband's presidency. She knew the James would soon take his final bow, bid adieu, and exit the stage of public life for retirement. Though they'd seen the ashes of the White House and U.S. Capitol, they, along with a phoenix multitude, had saved Washington nonetheless.

JAMES AND DOLLEY MADISON

After his presidency, James Madison retired with Dolley to Montpelier, their Virginia home. With Dolley's assistance, James organized his private papers from the U.S. Constitution and others with a plan to release them publicly. James died June 28, 1836, at age eighty-five. Impoverished and lonely, Dolley moved to Washington, D.C. There she lived in a row house on Lafayette Square across from the north side of the White House and became one of the most sought-after guests in Washington. In one month alone she paid sixty-five social calls. Congress also helped to alleviate her poverty by purchasing three volumes of Madison's papers for $30,000 in 1837 and another set in 1848 for $25,000, with most of the money placed in a trust. They also gave her an honorary seat in Congress, which allowed her to watch debates from the floor of the House of Representatives.

Fulfilling her husband's desire for a method for instant communication, she became the first private citizen to transmit a message through Samuel Morse's new invention, the telegraph. She had her photograph taken with President James Polk and watched the laying of the cornerstone of the Washington Monument from the White House in July 1848.

Dolley Madison died on July 12, 1849. Newspapers praised her as an excellent and venerable lady who spent her life well. Sitting President Zachary Taylor led the procession at her funeral, which took place at St. John's Episcopal Church, across the street from her row house and the White House. In his eulogy, he allegedly called her *first lady*. Though no written record exists of his speech, this may have been the first use of the term. Less than a decade later, the phrase *first lady* was used for the first time in print in a magazine to describe Harriet Lane, who fulfilled the hostess role for her uncle, President James Buchanan.

In her lifetime, Dolley directly influenced the women who later served as first lady. Wives of sitting presidents, including Julia Tyler and Sarah Polk, sought her advice and often invited her to the White House.

Mrs. Madison's legacy and legend continues. In 2007, Laura Bush, wife of President George W. Bush, hosted an event for the U.S. Mint in the East Room for the first spouse gold coin program. In attendance was Lucinda Frailly of the National First Ladies' Library. Ms. Frailly gave a dramatic interpretation of Mrs. Madison.

During a 1993 White House Halloween party, First Lady Hillary Clinton dressed as Dolley Madison and President Bill Clinton dressed as James Madison. A few years later in a White House ceremony, Hillary Clinton announced the release of a silver dollar coin commemorating the 150th anniversary of the death of Dolley Madison.

HILLCREST CHILDREN AND FAMILY CENTER IN WASHINGTON, D.C.

The charity that Dolley founded in 1815 through a charter from Congress is known today the Hillcrest Children and Family Center in Washington, D.C. Hillcrest is a nonprofit behavioral healthcare and social services agency providing behavioral health treatment and prevention along with community and family support services. The center continues to promote the well-being and holistic development of children, youth, and families.

THE REBUILT WHITE HOUSE AND
PRESIDENT JAMES MONROE

James Monroe took the oath of office as the fifth president of the United States on March 4, 1817. He moved into the rebuilt White House with an incomplete interior in October 1817. Instead of painting with whitewash, architect James Hoban directed workers to use white lead paint with a linseed oil base to paint the exterior stone.

Three months later, Monroe held the first public reception in the new White House, on New Year's Day, 1818. Newspapers praised the event as a return to normalcy. With his presidency known as the era of good feelings, Monroe served two terms and was followed by War of 1812 heroes John Quincy Adams, who served one term, and Andrew Jackson, who served two.

THE WHITE HOUSE: GEORGE WASHINGTON
PORTRAIT BY GILBERT STUART

Thanks to Dolley Madison, George Washington's best painting by Gilbert Stuart still hangs in the White House. Americans have seen the portrait through photographs and television shots of the East Room, where the president hosts large events. Sometimes those moments are serious, such as when a tearful President Barack Obama announced his intent to use executive action for gun control in 2016. Other times the mood is celebratory, such as when President George W. Bush stood in front of this painting to pay tribute to Kennedy Center honorees Steven Spielberg, Andrew Lloyd Webber, Dolly Parton, Smokey Robinson, and Zubin Mehta in 2006.

THE NATIONAL PORTRAIT GALLERY:
GEORGE WASHINGTON PORTRAIT BY
GILBERT STUART

Known as the Lansdowne portrait, Gilbert Stuart's full-length painting of George Washington also hangs at the Smithsonian Institution's National Portrait Gallery in Washington, D.C. The painting is called the Lansdowne portrait because Senator and Mrs. William Bingham of

Pennsylvania gave it as a gift to the Marquis of Lansdowne, an English supporter of American independence. Gilbert Stuart copied his work, which is why visitors to the White House and the National Portrait Gallery can see the same painting.

ADMIRAL GEORGE COCKBURN

After leaving America's shores in 1815, Rear Admiral George Cockburn became the jailer of Napoleon, who came out of exile for one hundred days only to lose the Battle of Waterloo and submit to exile again. Cockburn transported Napoleon to one of the most remote islands in the world, St. Helena off the west coast of Africa, in August 1815. Promoted to vice admiral a few years later and eventually full admiral, Cockburn won several elections to Parliament and served on the Admiralty Board for seventeen years. He became Rear Admiral of the United Kingdom and earned the highest possible promotion as Admiral of the Fleet in 1851. He died on August 19, 1853.

SENATOR RUFUS KING

Senator Rufus King became the presidential nominee for the Federalist Party in 1816 and lost to Secretary of War James Monroe. The dissolving Federalist Party never elected another presidential candidate. King was reelected to the Senate in 1818 and died on April 29, 1827. Charles King, his grandson, published King's correspondence, and the New York Historical Society later acquired his library.

JOHN ARMSTRONG

After resigning his position as war secretary, John Armstrong retired to private life on his farm in Red Hook, New York, where he wrote several books. He was the last member of the Continental Congress to die and the only one to have his photograph taken. He passed away in 1843.

BENJAMIN LATROBE

Benjamin Latrobe was America's first professional architect. After working to rebuild the U.S. Capitol following the 1814 fire, Latrobe resigned his position as Capitol architect in November 1817. He continued work on a design he had started years earlier in Baltimore for the first Catholic cathedral, called the Basilica of the National Shrine of the Assumption of the Blessed Virgin Mary. He also worked on the Baltimore Exchange and other buildings before traveling to New Orleans, where he'd designed a waterworks project similar to his Philadelphia waterworks plan. Latrobe died in Louisiana from yellow fever on September 3, 1820.

JOSHUA BARNEY

The city of Washington presented Joshua Barney with a sword of honor for his valor at the Battle of Bladensburg. Four years later, Barney died in Pittsburgh on December 1, 1818, from complications of the wounds he received at Bladensburg.

FRANCIS SCOTT KEY

After the War of 1812, Francis Scott Key continued his career as an attorney while writing other poems. Becoming district attorney for Washington in his later years, Key died in Baltimore on January 11, 1843. A collection of his poems was later published in 1857. Although "The Star-Spangled Banner" was popular in his lifetime, Key didn't know that the song would forever seal him as a patriotic legend. By 1917 the U.S. Army and U.S. Navy had declared it as the military's national anthem for ceremonial occasions. After a series of campaigns from patriotic groups, Congress designated "The Star-Spangled Banner" as the nation's official anthem and President Herbert Hoover signed it into law on March 3, 1931.

WASHINGTON IRVING

Accomplished in both fiction and biography, Washington Irving gave America its literary identity. His short stories about Rip Van Winkle and Ichabod Crane in *The Legend of Sleepy Hollow* became classics in America and in Europe, which made Irving the first beloved American author recognized worldwide. Irving eventually served in diplomatic posts, first as a secretary to America's top diplomat to England in 1830 and then in 1842 as America's lead diplomat to Spain. Not long after completing a multivolume biography of George Washington, Irving died in 1859.

JOSEPH GALES

After the War of 1812, Joseph Gales continued his career as a newspaperman, editor, and printer. He expanded his publications in 1816 by using his press to print the *Annals of Congress* and the *Register of Debates in Congress*. He operated the *National Intelligencer* until his death in 1860.

JOHN RODGERS

After the War of 1812, John Rodgers became the first president of the Board of Naval Commissioners, a new organization dedicated to aiding the secretary of the navy. Except for a two-year stint leading a squadron in the Mediterranean, he held the position for most of the rest of his career and retired in 1837 and died in 1838. Three ships were named after him, and five generations of his descendants served in the U.S. military.

Acknowledgments

"**A**llow me again, to thank you, with all my heart, for the trouble you have taken, in many instances, to oblige and accommodate me," Dolley Madison wrote in September 1809 to architect Benjamin Latrobe for his work on her behalf.

I feel the same way about several people who have made this book possible.

I'm grateful to Jonathan Clements, my longtime agent, for representing my books and screenplays. You're a master at building and keeping relationships in the ever-changing worlds of publishing, media, film, and entertainment. Thanks for sticking with me, this true story, and steering me aright.

A big thanks to Alex Novak and all of the unsung heroes at Regnery Publishing and Salem Communications for publishing this book. I appreciate your commitment to keeping our nation's history alive and for passing it along to generations of readers. Thanks as well to Daniel Allott for your editorial eye, journalistic savvy, and ability to work quickly and smoothly.

I'd also like to thank the White House Historical Association, which gave me an educational research fellowship in 2003 that started my book-writing career after I left my webmaster position at the White House.

Thank you also to Monica Lee Bellais for selecting *Saving Washington*, my screenplay adaptation of this book, for 2015's Spotlight on Screenwriters, a limited-edition catalog produced by Women in Film and Video of Washington, D.C. (WIFV).

Most of all, many thanks and much love to my husband, John Kim Cook, for your love and patience. You've driven our family to Fort McHenry in Baltimore and Montpelier, the home of James and Dolley Madison, in Orange, Virginia. There on Constitution Day, September 17, we met reenactors for James and Dolley Madison, who gave me a few tips for this book and the screenplay adaptation. On the 200th anniversary of the burning of the White House, you helped our older sons make a spyglass at the Decatur House in Washington, D.C. Later that day you helped them make Dolley Madison's recipe for ice cream and chased our toddler on the lawn of Dumbarton (Belle Vue), the historic house in Georgetown where Dolley took refuge after she fled the White House in 1814. Today the house is a museum and headquarters of the National Society of the Colonial Dames of America. This event allowed me to talk with other historians and reenactors of Albert Gallatin and Dolley Madison. Most of all, you were a good sport to don a Napoleon costume for a reenactment ball at Gadsby's Tavern and Restaurant in Alexandria in 2015 to celebrate the 200th anniversary of Madison's signing the Treaty of Ghent, which ended the War of 1812.

So, allow me again to borrow a line from Mrs. Madison, to thank you all, with all my heart, for the trouble you have taken to oblige and accommodate me.

—Jane Hampton Cook

Bibliography

"About Scimitars (Swords)." Middle Eastern Dance. http://middleeast-erndance.homestead.com/Movements/Props/Scimitars/Scimitar-About.html.

"An Act for the Gradual Abolition of Slavery, March 1, 1780." http://www.portal.state.pa.us/portal/server.pt/community/empower-ment/18325/gradual_abolition_of_slavery_act/623285.

Adams, Henry, ed. *The Writings of Albert Gallatin.* Vol. 1. Indianapolis: Liberty Fund Inc., 1879. http://files.libertyfund.org/files/1953/Gall-atin_1358-01_EBk_v6.0.pdf.

Adams, John Quincy. *Letter to Louisa Adams, October 4, 1814.* Letter. From Library of Congress, *Adams Family Papers.*

"Admiral Cochrane's Letter." *Columbian Register* 2, no. 97 October 1814): 2.

"Admiral Cockburn, Annapolis." *Franklin Herald* 23, no. 124 (June 1813): 4.

"Admiral; Cockburn; Annapolis; Warren; Cockburn." *Salem Gazette* 27, no. 49 (June 1813): 1.

"After the Fire: White House History." *Journal of the White House Historical Association* 35 (Summer 2014).

Alexandria Gazette. June 29, 1813.

Allgor, Catherine. *A Perfect Union: Dolley Madison and the Creation of the American Nation.* New York: Henry Holt and Company, 2006.

Annals of Congress, 13th Congress, 1st–3rd sess. http://memory.loc.gov/ammem/amlaw/lwac.html.

Annals of Congress, 13th Congress, 1st sess., 14, 84–85, 88–89, 244–5. http://memory.loc.gov/ammem/amlaw/lwac.html.

Anthony, Katherine. *Dolly Madison: Her Life and Times.* New York: Doubleday & Company, 1949.

—. *Dolley Madison: Her Life and Times.* In "Saving History: Dolley Madison, the White House and the War of 1812." White House Historical Association. http://www.whitehousehistory.org/whha_classroom/classroom_documents-1812.html.

Arnett, Ethel Stephens. *Mrs. James Madison: The Incomparable Dolley.* Greensboro: Piedmont Press, 1972.

"Author of the Star-Spangled Banner." *The Denver Post.* August 14, 1898.

Baltimore Patriot. June 30, 1813; July 23, 1813.

Baltimore Whig. April 25, 1810.

Benjamin Latrobe to Dolley Madison, March 17, 1809. Letter. National Archives, National Historical Publications and Records Commission. http://founders.archives.gov/documents/Madison/03-01-02-0066.

"Bill of Rights Transcript." National Archives. http://www.archives.gov/exhibits/charters/bill_of_rights_transcript.html.

"Bladensburg and New Scotland." Prince George's County, MD 1810 Federal Census. http://us-census.org/pub/usgenweb/census/md/princegeorges/1810/pgs-502-to-582.txt.

Boston Commercial Gazette. October 4, 1814; November 10, 1814.

Boston Daily Advertiser. June 30, 1813.

Brant, Irving. *The Fourth President: A Life of James Madison.* Indianapolis: The Bobbs-Merrill Company, 1970.

"The British Burn the White House." U.S. Capitol Visitor's Center. http://www.visitthecapitol.gov/british-burn-capitol-august-24-1814#.VHYVTtLF-Jo.

Bryan, Wilhelmus Bogart. *A History of the National Capital From its Foundation Through the Period of the Adoption of the Organic Act: 1790–1814.* New York: The MacMillan Company, 1914.

"Burning of the White House and the War of 1812." *Journal of the White House Historical Association* 4 (Fall 1998).

Butler, Stuart L. *Defending the Old Dominion: Virginia and Its Militia in the War of 1812.* Lanham: University Press of America, 2012.

"Capture of the City of Washington." *Annals of Congress.* 13th Congress, 3rd sess., 524–95. http://memory.loc.gov/ammem/amlaw/lwac.html.

Chamier, Captain Frederick. *The Life of a Sailor.* London: Richard Bentley, 1850.

Clark, Allen Culling. *Life and Letters of Dolly Madison.* Washington, D.C.: W.F. Roberts Company, 1914.

"Conflagration of Havre de Grace." *The North-American Review and Miscellaneous Journal* 5, no. 14 (July 1817): 157–163. http://www.jstor.org/stable/25121304.

"Constellation—A Stellar History." U.S.S. Constellation CVA/CV 64 Association. http://www.ussconstellation.org/constellation_history.html.

"Constitutional Convention." James Madison's Montpelier. http://www.montpelier.org/.

Cornman, Jr., A. "A Series of Tables of American Manufactures Exhibiting them in Every County in the United States." In *Book 2 of the Third Census.* Philadelphia, 1814.

"The Costs for a Bath, Lately Added for 50 Cents Per Bath or Three for a Dollar at John Macleod at Any Temperature from 6 am to 9 PM." *Washington City Gazette.* August 17, 1814.

"Destruction of Havre de Grace." *Independent American* 5, no. 35 (May 1813): 2–3.

Democratic Press. June 29, 1813; August 16, 1813; October 7, 1814; October 14, 1814. From GenealogyBank.com. http://www.genealogybank.com/gbnk/newspapers/.

De Zutter, Joris. *The Bicentennial of the Treaty of Ghent: 1814–2014.* Ghent: Department of Culture and Sports, 2014.

Downing, Sarah Jane. *Fashion in the Time of Jane Austen.* London: Shire Publications, 2013.

Dudley, William S. *The Naval War of 1812: A Documentary History.* Washington, D.C.: Naval Historical Center Department of the Navy, 1992.

"Dutch Colonies." National Park Service. http://www.nps.gov/nr/travel/kingston/colonization.htm.

"Evolution of the Capitol." http://www.visitthecapitol.gov/aboutthe-capitol/evolution_of_the_capitol/index.html

"Explanation of the Clerk of the House of Representatives Relative to the Loss of Books and Papers of His Office, the Library of Congress, and Vouchers for His Expenditures from the Contingent Fund." *Annals of Congress.* 13th Congress, 3rd sess., 253–62. http://memory.loc.gov/ammem/amlaw/lwac.html.

"Extract of a Letter Dated Norfolk, March 22." *Gazette* 14, no. 52 (April 1813): 2.

Freeman's Friend. May 19, 1810.

"General Eaton Is Reported." *Republican Watch-Tower.* January 30, 1807.

George, Christopher T. *Terror on the Chesapeake.* Shippensburg: White Mane Books, 2000.

George Cockburn to Admiral Warren, April 29, 1813. Letter. From Library of Congress.

"Georgetown: Monday, May 3." *Federal Republican* 7, no. 963 (May 1813): 3.

"George Washington: Houses and Palaces." *Journal of the White House Historical Association* (1999).

Green, Constance McLaughlin. *Washington: A History of the Capital: 1800-1950*. Princeton: Princeton University Press, 1962.

"Guide to Robert Troup Papers." New York Public Library.

Hamlin, Talbot. *Benjamin Henry Latrobe*. New York: Oxford University Press, 1955.

Hammond, Andrew. *Pop Culture Arab World!* Santa Barbara: ABC-CLIO, 2005.

"Havre de Grace." *Franklin Herald* 23, no. 119 (May 1813): 2.

"Havre de Grace Destroyed." *Daily National Intelligencer* 1, no. 107 (May 1813): 3.

Heidler, David S. and Jeanne T. Heidler, eds. *Encyclopedia of the War of 1812*. Annapolis: Naval Institute Press, 1997.

"History of the Washington Navy Yard." Naval History and Heritage Command. June 10, 2016. http://www.history.navy.mil/browse-by-topic/organization-and-administration/commands-and-installations/washington-navy-yard/history-of-the-washington-navy-yard.html.

Hunt-Jones, Conover. *Dolley and the "Great Little Madison."* Washington, D.C.: American Institute of Architects Foundation, 1977.

"If the dispatches." *The Federal Republican*. February 10, 1813.

"Inauguration Ball." *Monitor* 1, no. 23 (March 1809): 2.

Ingersoll, Charles J. *Historical Sketch of the Second War Between the United States and Great Britain*. Philadelphia: Lea & Blanchard, 1849.

Irving, Washington. "James Lawrence, Esq. New Brunswick." *Analectic Magazine*. Washington's Head: L. Deare, 1813.

—. "Biography of Oliver Perry." *Analectic Magazine*.

—. *Life and Letters of Washington Irving*. Edited by Pierre M. Irving. Memorial ed., Vol. 1. New York: G.P. Putnam's Sons. 1883.

"James Madison." Miller Center, University of Virginia. http://miller-center.org/president/madison/essays/biography/3.

"To James Madison." *Baltimore Whig*. April 25, 1810.

"To James Madison." *Freeman's Friend*. May 19, 1810.

To James Madison from Benjamin Henry Latrobe, May 29, 1809. Letter. National Archives, National Historical Publications and Records

Commission. http://founders.archives.gov/?q=latrobe%20expenditures%201809&s=1111311111&sa=&r=5&sr=.

Jennings, Paul. *A Colored Man's Reminiscences of James Madison: Electronic Edition*. Chapel Hill: University of North Carolina at Chapel Hill, 2001. http://docSouth.unc.edu/neh/jennings/jennings.html.

"John Pierre Sioussat." Ancestry.com. http://records.ancestry.com/jean_pierre_sioussat_records.ashx?pid=45885573.

—. *Journal of the House of Representatives of the United States*. 1st Congress, July 9, 1790.

—. *Journal of the Senate of the United States*. 1st Congress, September 24, 1789.

Kaplan, Edward S. *The Bank of the United States and the American Economy*. Westport: Greenwood Publishing Group, 1999.

Ketcham, Ralph. *James Madison: A Biography*. Charlottesville: University of Virginia Press, 1990.

Key, Francis Scott. *Correspondence to James Madison, January 26, 1807*. Letter. Library of Congress.

—. *Correspondence to Mrs. Ann Phoebe Key, January 2, 1814*. Letter. University of Virginia, Special Collections.

Key-Smith, F.S. "How Francis Scott Key Wrote 'The Star-Spangled Banner.'" 1814. The Legacy Preservation Library. www.usgennet.org/usa/topic/preservation/epochs/vol5/pg90.htm.

King, Rufus. *The Life and Correspondence of Rufus King: Comprising His Letters, Private and Official, His Public Documents, and His Speeches*. Edited by Charles King. Vol. 5. New York : G.P. Putnam's Sons, 1898.

Benjamin Latrobe to James Madison, May 29, 1809. With Account. Letter. Library of Congress, *The James Madison Papers*. http://hdl.loc.gov/loc.mss/mjm.11_0313_0315.

Lord, Walter. *The Dawn's Early Light*. New York: W.W. Norton & Company, 1972.

Madison, Dolley. *Selected Letters of Dolley Payne Madison*. Edited by David B. Mattern and Holly Cowan Shulman. Charlottesville: University of Virginia Press, 2003.

Madison, James. "To George Washington, Apr. 17, 1787." In *The Papers of James Madison*. Edited by William T. Hutchinson et al. Chicago: University of Chicago Press, 1962–77. http://press-pubs.uchicago. edu/founders/documents/v1ch8s6.html.

—. *The Writings of James Madison: 1808-1819*. Vol. 3. New York: G.P. Putnam's Sons, 1908.

Marrin, Albert. *1812: The War Nobody Won*. New York: Atheneum, Macmillan Publishing Company, 1983.

Molotsky, Irvin. *The Flag, the Poet and the Song*. New York: Plume, 2001.

Morriss, Roger. *Cockburn and the British Navy in Transition: Admiral Sir George Cockburn, 1773–1853*. Columbia: University of South Carolina Press, 1997.

Mount Vernon Digital Encyclopedia. s.v. "Rustication." http://www. mountvernon.org/research-collections/digital-encyclopedia/article/ rustication/.

"Mrs. Suter Rents for $700 per anum." *Daily National Intelligencer* 1, no. 150 (June 1813).

National Intelligencer. July 22, 1813; May 13, 1814; August 23, 1814; August 24, 1814; August 30, 1814; October 3, 1814; October 18, 1814.

"New Amsterdam Becomes New York: 1664." History Channel. http:// www.history.com/this-day-in-history/new-amsterdam-becomes- new-york.

New York Evening Post. September 19, 1814.

"Norfolk Naval Shipyard History." U.S. Navy. http://www.navsea.navy. mil/shipyards/norfolk/History/Home.aspx.

"One Thousand Dollars Reward." *Democratic Press*. August 16, 1813. www.GenealogyBank.com.

Pack, James. *The Man Who Burned the White House: Admiral Sir George Cockburn 1772–1853*. Ensworth: Kenneth Mason, 1987.

PBS American Experience. "Dolley Madison: America's First Lady." 2010. http://www.pbs.org/wgbh/americanexperience/films/dolley/.

Pitch, Anthony S. *The Burning of Washington: The British Invasion of 1814*. Annapolis: Naval Institute Press, 1998.

"Poor Madison." *Evening Post, New York*. March 9, 1812.

"Population of the 46 Urban Places: 1810." U.S. Bureau of the Census. Internet release date June 15, 1998. http://www.census.gov/population/www/documentation/twps0027/tab04.txt.

"Population of Virginia—1810." Ann Arbor: Inter-university Consortium for Political and Social Research. http://www.virginiaplaces.org/population/pop1810numbers.html.

"Presidential Inauguration Ceremony's Firsts Over Time." http://www.dcmilitary.com/article/20130124/NEWS12/130129983/0/SEARCH.

"President's Message." *Annals of Congress*. 13th Congress, 3rd sess., 11–14. http://memory.loc.gov/ammem/amlaw/lwac.html.

Proclamation—Announcement of a State of War Between the United States and the United Kingdom. June 19, 1812. From the University of California, Santa Barbara, the American Presidency Project. http://www.presidency.ucsb.edu/ws/index.php?pid=65943.

"Rebuilding the Capitol, President's House, and Other Public Buildings in the City of Washington, Communicated to the House of Representatives." *Annals of Congress*. 13th Congress, 3rd sess., 524–95. http://memory.loc.gov/ammem/amlaw/lwac.html.

Republican Watch-Tower. January 30, 1807.

Rutland, Robert Allen. *The Presidency of James Madison*. Lawrence: University Press of Kansas, 1990.

Scott, Captain James. *Recollections of a Naval Life*. Vol. 3. London: Richard Bentley, 1834.

Seale, William. *The Night They Burned the White House: The Story of Tom Freeman's Painting*. Washington, D.C.: The White House Historical Association, 2014.

—. *The President's House: a History*. Vol. 1 and 2. Washington, D.C.: The White House Historical Association with the cooperation of the National Geographic Society, 1986.

"A Self-Guided Tour of Historic Havre de Grace: Havre de Grace." Havre de Grace Historic Preservation Commissions. 2010.

"Sewall-Belmont House and Museum." Sewall Belmont House and Museum. http://www.sewallbelmont.org/learn/144-constitution-ave-ne/.

Shulman, Holly C., ed. *Dolley Madison Digital Edition.* University of Virginia Press. http://rotunda.upress.virginia.edu/

Skeen, C. Edward. *John Armstrong, Jr. 1758–1843.* Syracuse: Syracuse University Press, 1981.

Smith, Margaret Baynard. "Mrs. James Madison." In *The National Portrait Gallery of Distinguished Americans* conducted by James B. Longacre and Jams Herring under the superintendence of the American Academy of the Fine Arts. Philadelphia: H. Perkins, 1834–39.

Sparks, Jared. "Conflagration of Havre de Grace." *North American Review 5,* no. 14 (July 1817): 157–163.

"Sword and Balancing Dances, Sword Dances of the Middle East." November 2014.

http://www.shemsdance.com/articles/sword-and-balancing-dances/ accessed.

The Federal Republican-Georgetown, February 10, 1813; September 1, 1814; September 5, 1814; September 10, 1814; September 22, 1814; October 1, 1814.

"The Green Room." White House Historical Association. http://www.whitehousehistory.org/history/white-house-facts-trivia/tour-green-room.html.

The James Madison Papers at the Library of Congress. Library of Congress, Manuscript Division. http://memory.loc.gov/ammem/collections/madison_papers/.

"The Seat of Government." *National Intelligencer.* October 3, 1814.

The Second Bank of the United States. Federal Reserve Bank of Philadelphia. http://www.philadelphiafed.org/publications/economic-education/second-bank.pdf.

"The Star-Spangled Banner." Fort McHenry. www.nps.gov/fomc/learn/historyculture/the-star-spangled-banner.htm.

"Tyro to the Editor, dateline Washington, December 20, 1813." *Democratic Press*. December 24, 1813.

U.S. Census, 1810. Harford, County, Maryland. http://us-census.org/pub/usgenweb/census/md/harford/1810/.

U.S. Congress. *Journal of the House of Representatives of the United States*. 1st Congress, September 7, 1789.

"USF Constellation." Historic Ships in Baltimore. http://historicships.org/.

"USS Hornet sinks HMS Peacock, 24 February 1813." Naval History and Heritage. U.S. Navy.

"Virginia Argus." June 22, 1813. http://www.genealogybank.com/gbnk/newspapers/.

"Washington—History and Heritage." Smithsonian.com. November 6, 2007. http://www.smithsonianmag.com/travel/destination-hunter/North-america/united-states/east/washington-dc/washingtondc-history-heritage.html.

"Washington Navy Yard: History of Latrobe Gate." http://www.history.navy.mil/browse-by-topic/organization-and-administration/commands-and-installations/washington-navy-yard/latrobe-gate.html.

"White House History." *Journal of the White House Historical Association*, 1998.

Willets, Gilson. *Inside History of the White House*. New York: The Christian Herald, 1908.

"The Yellow Fever Epidemic." Harvard University Open Collections Project. http://ocp.hul.harvard.edu/contagion/yellowfever.html.

Notes

AUTHOR'S NOTE

1.   Allow me again: Holly C. Shulman ed., *Dolley Madison Digital Edition* (Charlottesville: University of Virginia Press), http://rotunda. upress.virginia.edu/.

PART I—1813: A FIERY PRELUDE

1.   If our first struggle: James Madison, *The Writings of James Madison: 1808–1819* vol. 3, (New York: G.P. Putnam's Sons, 1908), 407.

CHAPTER 1—THE PIRATE

1.   One thousand dollars: *Democratic Press,* June 29, 1813; Aug. 16, 1813; Oct. 7, 1814; Oct. 14, 1814, http://www.genealogybank.com/ gbnk/newspapers/.
2.   for the head: Ibid.
3.   or five hundred dollars: Ibid.

4. a warm fire was: William S. Dudley, *The Naval War of 1812: A Documentary History*, vol. II (Washington, D.C., Naval Historical Center Department of the Navy, 1992), 342.

5. their fire rather: Ibid.

6. I observed guns: Ibid., 341.

7. This of course: Ibid.

8. C'est Le Havre: "A Self-Guided Tour of Historic Havre de Grace: Havre de Grace," Havre de Grace Historic Preservation Commissions, 2010.

9. Resolved that the: U.S. Congress, *Journal of the House of Representatives of the United States*, 1st Congress, Sept. 7, 1789, http://memory.loc.gov/cgibin/query/D?hlaw:3:./temp/~ammem_GcbO.

10. Between the rivers: Ibid.

11. It having been judged: Dudley, *The Naval War of 1812*, 325.

12. very judiciously: Ibid., 342.

13. they commenced a: Ibid.

14. with which he: Ibid.

15. every opportunity of: Roger Morriss, *Cockburn and the British Navy in Transition: Admiral Sir George Cockburn, 1773–1853* (Columbia: University of South Carolina Press), 92.

16. had the satisfaction: Dudley, *The Naval War of 1812*, 342.

CHAPTER 2—MIGHTY LITTLE MADISON

1. The high character: *Annals of Congress*, 13th Congress, 1st Session, Library of Congress, May 3, 1813, http://memory.loc.gov/ammem/amlaw/lwac.html, 14.

2. Mr. Madison is a small man: Ralph Ketcham, *James Madison: A Biography* (Charlottesville: University of Virginia Press, 1990), 476.

3. We regard Erskine's: Rufus King, *The Life and Correspondence of Rufus King: Comprising His Letters, Private and Official, His public documents, and His Speeches*, vol. 5, ed. Charles King (New York: G.P. Putnam's Sons, July 1898), 187.

4. Hence the adjustment: Ibid., 190.

5. The high character: *Annals of Congress*, 13th Congress, 1st Session, Library of Congress, 14.

6. it was immediately: Ibid.

7. Three of our: Ibid.
8. further proof: Ibid., 14.
9. The issue of this: Ibid.
10. it of such: Jared Sparks, "Conflagration of Havre de Grace," *North American Review* 5, no. 14 (July 1817): 161.
11. This was not: Ibid.
12. should resistance: George Cockburn, *George Cockburn to Admiral Warren, April 29, 1813*, Library of Congress, 25.
13. found that the: Dudley, *The Naval War of 1812*, 342.
14. two or three: Sparks, "Conflagration of Havre de Grace," 161.
15. endeavored by: Ibid.
16. but when they: Ibid.
17. perforated with balls: Ibid., 162.
18. to cause the proprietors: Dudley, *The Naval War of 1812*, 342.
19. I embarked in: Ibid.
20. The most valuable works: Ibid.
21. and I have much: Ibid., 343.
22. But the most: Sparks, "Conflagration of Havre de Grace," 163.
23. They returned wretched: Ibid.
24. No reasons of: Ibid., 162.
25. assign any cause: Ibid.

CHAPTER 3—HELLO, DOLLEY

1. We cannot be: Shulman, *Dolley Madison Digital Edition*.
2. her complexion: Dolley Madison, *Selected Letters of Dolley Payne Madison*, David B. Mattern and Holly C. Shulman eds. (Charlottesville: University of Virginia Press, April 2003), 13.
3. stately step: Ibid.
4. She came upon: Ibid.
5. He thinks too much: Ibid., 27.
6. he hopes that: Ibid.
7. She could raise: "Dolley Madison: America's First Lady," PBS: American Experience, 2010.
8. I give my hand: Madison, *Selected Letters of Dolley Payne Madison*, 31.
9. In this union: Ibid.

10. Dolley Madison, Alas!: Ibid.
11. We cannot be: Shulman, *Dolley Madison Digital Edition*.
12. I trust in Heaven: Ibid.
13. situated up the: Dudley, *The Naval War of 1812*, 344.
14. only river or: Ibid.
15. sent forward the: Ibid.
16. assuring them if: Ibid.
17. that vessels and public: Ibid.
18. I am sorry to say: Ibid.
19. towns, which: Ibid., 345.
20. here I had the: Ibid.
21. well pleased with: Ibid.
22. I am assured that: Ibid.
23. I have little doubt: Talbot Hamlin, *Benjamin Henry Latrobe* (New York: Oxford University Press, 1955), 388.
24. An express arrived: Ibid.
25. which surrounds us: Ibid.
26. Our honest, patriotic, firm: Ibid., 385–86.
27. So I am going to: Ibid.
28. This war has among: Hamlin, *Benjamin Henry Latrobe*, 378.
29. But this unfortunate war: Ibid.
30. Before your receive: Shulman, *Dolley Madison Digital Edition*.
31. But tell him: Ibid.
32. every person condemns: Ibid.
33. I have shown: Ibid.
34. dignified representative: Madison, *Selected Letters of Dolley Payne Madison*, 120.
35. resemblance of your: Ibid.

CHAPTER 4—DUELING STRATEGIES

1. And now, if: Shulman, *Dolley Madison Digital Edition*.
2. It is to land as: Ibid.
3. For the last week: Ibid.
4. Madison and General Armstrong: Hamlin, *Benjamin Henry Latrobe*, 388.

5. Rules and Regulations: Edward C. Skeen, *John Armstrong, Jr. 1758–1843* (Syracuse: Syracuse University Press, 1981), 128.
6. So many false alarming: Ibid., 130.
7. We are making: Shulman, *Dolley Madison Digital Edition.*
8. I do not tremble: Ibid.
9. Mr. Madison, whom your mother: Hamlin, *Benjamin Henry Latrobe*, 386.
10. Tomorrow you will: Shulman, *Dolley Madison Digital Edition.*
11. But if you have: Ibid.
12. I am sorry: Ibid.
13. The dining room is: Ibid.
14. I therefore intended: Ibid.
15. But if you have: Ibid.
16. Your letter caused: Shulman, *Dolley Madison Digital Edition.*
17. We indulge this: Ibid.
18. and that of: Ibid.
19. Mr. M. can do: Ibid.
20. The winter is: Ibid.
21. in my eyes: Ibid.
22. A Mr. Elijah Mix: Dudley, *The Naval War of 1812*, 355.
23. You will furnish him: Ibid.
24. his plan is: Ibid.
25. He is an intrepid: Ibid.
26. If I were unmarried: Hamlin, *Benjamin Henry Latrobe*, 389.
27. mathematical instruments: Ibid., 391.
28. Mix should be: Ibid.
29. the spirit and manner: Madison, *The Writings of James Madison*, 246.
30. savage fury: Ibid.
31. a system of plunder: Ibid.
32. equally forbidden: Ibid.
33. In continuation of: Ibid.
34. highest praise: Ibid.
35. On the Lakes: Ibid.
36. I am a great favorite: Skeen, *John Armstrong, Jr.*
37. This cannot from: Ibid.
38. Nothing can exceed: Ibid., 117.

39. She plays her part: Ibid.
40. Armstrong may take: Ibid., 119.
41. Rules and Regulations: Ibid., 117.
42. To the astonishment: King, *The Life and Correspondence of Rufus King*, 227.

CHAPTER 5—KNICKERBOCKERS

1. You will have: King, *The Life and Correspondence of Rufus King*, 294.
2. Of one thing: Ibid.
3. I shall probably: Ibid.
4. communication from: *Annals of Congress*, 13th Congress, 1st Session, Library of Congress, 84.
5. dates at which: Ibid.
6. respectively received: Ibid.
7. that the President: Ibid.
8. to inform the Senate: Ibid.
9. I arrived at the: Allen Culling Clark, *Life and Letters of Dolly Madison* (Washington, D.C.: W.F. Roberts Company, 1914), 113.
10. our sides have been: Ibid., 116.
11. there are passages: Ibid.
12. So I mounted with: Ibid.
13. In a few minutes: Ibid.,128.
14. Mrs. Madison is a fine: Ibid., 113.
15. Her sisters, Mrs. Cutts and Mrs. Washington: Ibid.
16. The President, on its: Washington Irving, *Life and Letters of Washington Irving*, vol. 1, Memorial ed., Pierre M. Irving ed. (New York: G.P. Putnam's Sons, 1883), 132.
17. I should only look: Ibid., 131.
18. Should I not: Ibid., 129.
19. of studying: Ibid.
20. Which, if I have any: Ibid.
21. Of this, however: Ibid.
22. But whatever I may: Ibid.
23. tied by the leg: Ibid., 139.
24. wickedly made the: Ibid.

25. stagger under the trash: Ibid.
26. It was the most splendid: Ibid., 141.
27. The room was decorated: Ibid.
28. We are a nation: Skeen, *John Armstrong, Jr.*, 120.
29. they behave: Ibid., 122.
30. The effect will be to: Ibid., 119.
31. pedestal waiting: Seale, *The President's House: a History*, 14.
32. ought to be: "Evolution of the Capitol," U.S. Capitol Visitor Center, www.visitthecapitol.gov.
33. Why should you: Skeen, *John Armstrong, Jr.*, 158.
34. I speak to you: Ibid.
35. my constitution will not: Ibid.
36. sultry, fatiguing, dilatory: Ibid.

CHAPTER 6—TORPEDO

1. the boats of the: Dudley, *The Naval War of 1812*, 355.
2. This was no doubt: Ibid.
3. laudable: Ibid.
4. I think it extremely: Ibid.
5. unvaried examples: Ibid.
6. I have now closed: Ibid.
7. if the enterprise: Hamlin, *Benjamin Henry Latrobe*, 391.
8. I watch the decline: Ibid., 392.
9. the Senate are informed: *Annals of Congress*, 13th Congress, 1st Session, June 7, 1813, Library of Congress, 85.
10. We are at present: Madison, *The Writings of James Madison*, 243.
11. whether England: Ketcham, *James Madison: A Biography*, 550.
12. Mr. Madison reminded me: Clark, *Life and Letters of Dolly Madison*, 136.
13. Here's to they absent broadbrim: Ibid., 143.
14. And here's to: Ibid.
15. She wears a crimson: Ibid., 141.
16. Some splendid trimmings: Shulman, *Dolley Madison Digital Edition*.
17. Oh! I wish: Madison, *Selected Letters of Dolley Payne Madison*, 151.
18. There were many: "Tyro to the Editor, dateline Washington, December 20, 1813," *Democratic Press*, December 24, 1813.

19. Everybody loves Mrs. Madison: Catherine Allgor, *A Perfect Union: Dolley Madison and the Creation of the American Nation* (New York: Henry Holt and Company, 2006), 232.
20. That's because Mrs. Madison: Ibid.
21. I would describe: Clark, *Life and Letters of Dolly Madison*, 141.
22. but her demeanor is: Ibid.
23. I am by no means: Ibid.
24. the city is more: Shulman, *Dolley Madison Digital Edition*.
25. but this sad summer: Ibid.
26. The mornings are: Ibid.
27. Mr. M has received: Ibid.
28. I received one: Ibid.
29. there was now only: Dudley, *The Naval War of 1812*, 328.
30. he also added: Ibid.
31. and he assured me: Ibid.

CHAPTER 7—CHESAPEAKE FEVER

1. Before this: Madison, *Selected Letters of Dolley Payne Madison*, 163.
2. I believe there: Ibid., 154.
3. The brave Lawrence: Washington Irving, "James Lawrence, Esq. New Brunswick," *Analectic Magazine*, 1813, 41.
4. He passed from: Ibid., 10.
5. not merely to render Irving, *Life and Letters of Washington Irving*, 145.
6. Except in the: King, *The Life and Correspondence of Rufus King*, 314.
7. We think not: Ibid.
8. increasing disposition: Ibid.
9. In the instance: Ibid.
10. The cases described: Ibid.
11. But is his appointment: Ibid.
12. his estate and private: Ibid., 315.
13. not an absence: Ibid.
14. If such be the: Ibid.
15. the kind and affections: Shulman, *Dolley Madison Digital Edition*.
16. I hope however: Ibid.
17. She was certain: Ibid.

18. she had written: Ibid.
19. When I attempted: Ibid.
20. I have been: Ibid.
21. Of all the situations: "Constitutional Convention," James Madison's Montpelier, http://www.montpelier.org/.
22. Having been lately: James Madison, "To George Washington, Apr. 17, 1787," *The Papers of James Madison*, ed. William T. Hutchinson et al. (Chicago and London: University of Chicago Press, 1962–77), http://presspubs.uchicago.edu/founders/documents/v1ch8s6.html.
23. irreconcilable: Ibid.
24. I have sought for: Ibid.
25. disinterested: Ibid.
26. I would propose: Ibid.
27. You give me a: "Constitutional Convention."
28. the powers and duties: *Annals of Congress*, 13th Congress, 1st Session, June 14, 1813, Library of Congress, 85.
29. are so incompatible: Ibid.
30. at such time: Ibid., 87–88.

CHAPTER 8—SNUBBED BY DOLLEY

1. a bilious fever: Ketcham, *James Madison: A Biography*, 511.
2. think of thy: Madison, *Selected Letters of Dolley Payne Madison*, 66.
3. Mr. Madison has: Ibid., 560.
4. I went to the palace: Ibid., 561.
5. I think he will: Ibid.
6. perhaps never left: Ibid.
7. no pressure whatever: Ibid.
8. The thought of: Ibid.
9. I write to you: Shulman, *Dolley Madison Digital Edition*.
10. The anxiety of your mind: Ibid.
11. The dangerous sickness: Ibid.
12. Several times I: Hamlin, *Benjamin Henry Latrobe*, 395.
13. fixing a day: Ketcham, *James Madison: A Biography*, 561.
14. our minds have: *The James Madison Papers at the Library of Congress*, Library of Congress, Manuscript Division, Washington, D.C. http://memory.loc.gov/ammem/collections/madison_papers/.

15.   it is well known: Ibid.

16.   If men were angels: Ketcham, *James Madison: A Biography*, 297.

17.   Congress shall make: "Bill of Rights Transcript," National Archives, http://www.archives.gov/exhibits/charters/bill_of_rights_transcript. html.

18.   no person religiously scrupulous: Ketcham, *James Madison: A Biography*, 292.

19.   the introduction of: *The James Madison Papers at the Library of Congress*, June 17, 1813.

20.   And by our gracious Redeemer: Ibid.

21.   and most respectfully solicit: Ibid.

22.   They are now angels: Madison, *Selected Letters of Dolley Payne Madison*, 7.

23.   from what I have: Christopher T. George, *Terror on the Chesapeake* (Shippensburg: White Mane Books, 2000), 42.

24.   You will readily: King, *The Life and Correspondence of Rufus King*, 296–97.

25.   These politicians: Ibid.

26.   Before we part: Ibid.

27.   The only opposition: Ibid., 272.

28.   I regard the war: Ibid.

29.   The war cannot be: Ibid.

30.   A regular army will be: Ibid.

31.   I infer that the: Ibid.

32.   and if England: Ibid.

33.   Notwithstanding the: Ibid., 211.

34.   The imbecility of: Ibid., 275.

35.   I know that our political: Ibid., 278.

36.   I am convinced that: Ibid.

37.   Mr. Madison: Jane Hampton Cook, *Battlefields and Blessings Iraq/Afghanistan* (Chattanooga: God & Country Press, 2009), 476.

38.   The other to consist of: Ibid.

39.   The more lax: Ketcham, *James Madison: A Biography*, 210.

40.   There are foreign: Ibid.

41.   I am concerned: Ibid.

42.   Whatever may be: Ibid.

CHAPTER 9—WASHED UP AT CRANEY

1. On the issue of: Madison, *The Writings of James Madison*, 236.
2. They have retained: Ibid., 236–37.
3. compelling them to: Ibid.
4. The British cabinet: Ibid., 245.
5. And now we: Ibid., 236–37.
6. what is meant when: King, *The Life and Correspondence of Rufus King*, 187.
7. I have never allowed: Madison, *The Writings of James Madison*, 241.
8. be the greatest loser: Ibid.
9. The great road: Ibid.
10. If there be links: Ibid.
11. The sword was: Ibid., 238.
12. should the enemy: George, *Terror on the Chesapeake*, 42.
13. About daybreak the: *Boston Daily Advertiser*, June 30, 1813.
14. The batteries were: Ibid.
15. fired their 18-pounders: David S. Heidler, and Jeanne T. Heidler, eds., *Encyclopedia of the War of 1812* (Annapolis: Naval Institute Press, 1997), 130.
16. Our officers, soldiers: *Boston Daily Advertiser*, June 30, 1813.
17. I was so unwell: Madison, *Selected Letters of Dolley Payne Madison*, 74.
18. I have received: Ibid., 75.
19. The letters of my: Ibid., 77.
20. Your charming letter: Ibid., 71.
21. It is not probable: Shulman, *Dolley Madison Digital Edition*.
22. For the waste of: Ibid.
23. I beg you my: Ibid.
24. The error committed: Ibid.
25. poor me—I am: Ibid.

CHAPTER 10—ATROCIOUS HAMPTON

1. unfortunate females: Heidler, *Encyclopedia of the War of 1812*, 225.
2. Congreve rockets led: *Alexandria Gazette*, June 29, 1813.
3. The gallantry: Dudley, *The Naval War of 1812*, 362.
4. as well steading: Ibid.

5.   Our sod must be: *Baltimore Patriot*, June 30, 1813.
6.   We copy from the: *National Intelligencer*, July 22, 1813.
7.   It may be soon: Ibid.
8.   Having just returned: *Baltimore Patriot*, July 23, 1813.
9.   That the town and country: Ibid.
10.   Several gentlemen informed: Ibid.
11.   Why did you quit: Ibid.
12.   revenge for the refusal: Ibid.
13.   Her story was: *National Intelligencer*, July 22, 1813.
14.   to do justice: Ibid.
15.   electrify my countrymen: Ibid.
16.   This woman was: Ibid., 3.
17.   Her cries and: Ibid.
18.   whence she was dragged: Ibid.
19.   They had previously: Ibid.
20.   They followed her: *Baltimore Patriot*, July 23, 1813.
21.   Mr. Hope made off: *National Intelligencer*, July 22, 1813.
22.   But the enemy are: Ibid.
23.   Men of Virginia!: Ibid.
24.   wherever he dares: Ibid.
25.   and devote yourself: Ibid.
26.   every horror was: Heidler, *Encyclopedia of the War of 1812*, 225.
27.   Armstrong said Daschkoff: King, *The Life and Correspondence of Rufus King*, 320.
28.   that he knew: Ibid.
29.   Would to Heaven: Shulman, *Dolley Madison Digital Edition*.
30.   You can form: Ibid.
31.   They will find it: Ibid.
32.   But I forget how: Ibid.

CHAPTER 11—DEAR DOLLEY

1.   I have the happiness: Shulman, *Dolley Madison Digital Edition*.
2.   It has been three weeks: Ibid.
3.   Rumor with her hundred: Ibid.
4.   and most fervently: Ibid.

5.   was about to execute it: "Capture of the City of Washington," *Annals of Congress*, 13th Congress, 3rd Session, November 1814, 524–95, http://memory.loc.gov/ammem/amlaw/lwac.html.
6.   was only balancing: Ibid.
7.   The committee sincerely: *Annals of Congress*, 13th Congress, 1st Session, Library of Congress, 88.
8.   restored health: Ibid.
9.   That the Senate: Ibid., 89–90.
10. that they do not: Ibid.
11. That the granting: Ibid.
12. rights of the Senate: Ibid.
13. You have heard: Shulman, *Dolley Madison Digital Edition.*
14. Nothing however: Ibid.
15. Mr. A will tell: Ibid.
16. We console ourselves: Ibid.
17. Had you been: Hamlin, *Benjamin Henry Latrobe*, 392.
18. if I reproached you: Shulman, *Dolley Madison Digital Edition.*
19. every hour of your: Ibid.
20. and that the public: Ibid.
21. We are in: Ibid.
22. Poor Mr. Gaston: Ibid.
23. Oh my friend what: Ibid.
24. Kingston, therefore: Skeen, *John Armstrong, Jr.,* 158.
25. a pleasant work: Ibid.
26. You will learn: Madison, *The Writings of James Madison*, 252.
27. It is not easy: Ibid., 253.
28. It was calculated: Ibid., 254.
29. Should the mediation: Ibid.
30. a temper in the: Ibid., 255.
31. I have just recovered: Ibid., 255–56.
32. The physicians prescribe: Ibid.
33. be intercepted: Ibid.
34. I feel it right: Dudley, *The Naval War of 1812*, 365.
35. furnish with promptitude: Skeen, *John Armstrong Jr.,* 158.
36. under a wise organization: Madison, *The Writings of James Madison*, 246.

37. Bidding adieu:, Hamlin, *Benjamin Henry Latrobe*, 396.
38. starving doctors: Ibid.
39. The more your stir it: Ibid.
40. So you really think: Ibid.
41. As general, honest: Ibid.
42. All who have: *Maryland Gazette*, July 16, 1813; King, *The Life and Correspondence of Rufus King*, 321.
43. His talents are: Ibid.
44. and we do not think: Ibid.
45. With such a man: Ibid.
46. If ever there is: Ibid.
47. One thousand dollars: "One Thousand Dollars Reward," *Democratic Press*, August 16, 1813, www.genealogybank.com.

PART II—1814: WHITE HOUSE ABLAZE

1. There is a secret in life: "Dolley Madison: America's First Lady."

CHAPTER 12—THE WHITE HOUSE

1. I will turn Jefferson: "General Eaton Is Reported," *Republican Watch-Tower*, January 30, 1807, 3.
2. If the dispatches: Ibid.
3. the American people: "To James Madison," *Baltimore Whig*, April 25, 1810.
4. duty to steer: Ibid.
5. you hear no language: Ibid.
6. the next presidential: "To James Madison," *Freeman's Friend*, May 19, 1810.
7. dazzled with the blaze: Ibid.
8. enveloped in the smoke: Ibid.
9. we have ladies: Shulman, *Dolley Madison Digital Edition*.
10. the White House: "Tyro to the Editor, dateline Washington, December 20, 1813."
11. You can little: Ibid.
12. There is an utter: Ibid.
13. splendor: Ibid.
14. There are no museums: Ibid.

15. I must not forget: Ibid.
16. It was a novelty: Ibid.
17. It was with: Ibid.
18. Refreshments were very: Ibid.
19. The president: Ibid.
20. But for the drawing room: Ibid.
21. and the men: Ibid.
22. By appropriating two: Ibid.
23. General. Harrison was there: Ibid.
24. If you have not: Ibid.
25. My observations at: Ibid.
26. The little president: Ketcham, *James Madison: A Biography*, 565.
27. In fine, the war: Madison, *The Writings of James Madison*, 265.
28. We have met the: Ketcham, *James Madison: A Biography*, 565.
29. that the union of these States: Madison, *The Writings of James Madison*, 265.
30. to the decisions of: Ibid.
31. At 10 AM: Washington Irving, "Biography of Oliver Perry," *Analectic Magazine*, 501.
32. the dying words: Ibid.
33. don't surrender the ship: Irving, "James Lawrence, Esq. New Brunswick," 41.
34. don't give up: Irving, "Biography of Oliver Perry," 501.
35. In future times: Ibid, 508.
36. The fisherman: Ibid.,167
37. Whatever we may: Irving, *Life and Letters of Washington Irving*, 150.
38. He who fancies: Ibid.
39. Whenever our arms: Ibid.
40. Other nations will: Ibid.
41. but will extend to: Ibid.

CHAPTER 13—HOSPITALITY AND HOSTILITY

1. Messrs. King and Gore: Shulman, *Dolley Madison Digital Edition*.
2. we may conclude: King, *The Life and Correspondence of Rufus King*, 356.
3. With sixty thousand: Ibid.

4. The report of the: Ibid.
5. We shall expect: Dudley, *The Naval War of 1812*, 33.
6. The enemy has a: Ibid.
7. her hair bound tight: Madison, *Selected Letters of Dolley Payne Madison*, 93.
8. more like a harvest-home: Ibid., 46.
9. she thought abundance: Ibid.
10. arouse from the happy: Ibid.
11. The other evening: Madison, *Selected Letters of Dolley Payne Madison*, 61.
12. mentioned that the: Ibid.
13. Mrs. M. instantly: Ibid.
14. I fear he: Dudley, *The Naval War of 1812*, 17.
15. Have you quite: Shulman, *Dolley Madison Digital Edition*.
16. I wrote a few: Ibid.
17. Your winter campaign: Ibid.
18. My husband desires: Ibid.
19. having met with: Ibid.
20. to know that is: Ibid.

CHAPTER 14—NOSES FOR NEWS

1. Armstrong was decided: King, *The Life and Correspondence of Rufus King*, 370.
2. That an understanding: Ibid.
3. What a golden: "Wilkinson to Armstrong," *Annals of Congress*, 13th Congress, 1st Session, Library of Congress, 244–45.
4. That Mr. Armstrong: King, *The Life and Correspondence of Rufus King*, 370.
5. speaks respectfully: Ibid., 371.
6. Wilkinson and Hampton: Ibid.
7. if you could possibly: Shulman, *Dolley Madison Digital Edition*.
8. everybody, affected or disaffected: Allen Culling Clark, *Life and Letters of Dolly Madison* (Washington, D.C.: W. F. Roberts Company, 1914), 157.
9. Her majesty's appearance: Ibid.
10. The members of Congress: Shulman, *Dolley Madison Digital Edition*.

11. They have a report: Ibid.
12. Should Mr. G: Ibid.
13. The policy which: Ketcham, *James Madison: A Biography*, 568.
14. A bad cold which: Shulman, *Dolley Madison Digital Edition*.
15. While I was nursing: Ibid.
16. You are at perfect: Dudley, *The Naval War of 1812*, 51.
17. Their government authorizes: Ibid.
18. they must be made: Ibid.
19. This is now: Ibid.
20. system of retaliation: Ibid., 28.
21. Their seaport towns: Ibid., 52.
22. It is therefore: Ibid.
23. Allow me: Ibid., 41.
24. all your views: Ibid., 46.
25. but the conduct of: Ibid.
26. and induces me: Ibid.
27. I have just: Ibid., 54.
28. each wishing: Ibid.
29. We were doing: Ibid.
30. I supposed whatever: Ibid., 15.
31. everything that can: Ibid., 54.
32. It would appear: Ibid.
33. I enclose you the: Ibid.
34. I do not know: Ibid.

CHAPTER 15—NOT YOUR AVERAGE NEWS DAY

1. There will be: King, *The Life and Correspondence of Rufus King*, 390.
2. Your have then: Ibid.
3. I have altered: Ibid.
4. a war pulse: Ibid.
5. In this case: Ibid
6. Are you not mistaken: Ibid.
7. What reason have: Ibid.
8. It cannot: Ibid., 391.
9. Do you believe: Ibid.

10. I do not: Ibid.
11. It is to be sought: Ibid.
12. was at no loss: Ibid.
13. If there be a: King, Ibid., 392.
14. If Congress remain: Ibid.
15. If ministers be: Ibid.
16. moreover dispatches: Ibid.
17. I hope that if: Ibid.
18. The turn of recent: *The James Madison Papers at the Library of Congress.*
19. I am just possessed: Ibid.
20. The admonish us: Ibid.
21. to indicate the: Ibid.
22. Would it not be: Ketcham, *James Madison: A Biography*, 148.
23. to depend as: Ibid., 149.
24. among those the: *The James Madison Papers at the Library of Congress.*
25. What, though the enemy: Charles Ingersoll, *Historical Sketch of the Second War Between the United States and Great Britain* (Philadelphia: Lea & Blanchard, 1849), 157.
26. the neighboring militia: Ibid.
27. We have powder and ball: Ibid., 158.
28. As to his near approach to the capital: Ibid., 157.
29. Yesterday a gentleman: Dudley, *The Naval War of 1812*, 99.
30. that if they: Ibid.
31. I had him arrested: Ibid.
32. The militia have: Ibid.
33. The enemy has come: Ibid., 101.
34. The American Papers: Ibid., 65.
35. I am sure: Ibid.
36. and the government: Ibid., 66.
37. I am rather surprised: Ibid.

CHAPTER 16—SUPERABUNDANT FORCE

1. the convenience and: "Capture of the City of Washington," 580.
2. Shall a treaty of: Madison, *The Writings of James Madison*, 280–81.

3. received intelligence that: Dudley, *The Naval War of 1812*, 76–77.
4. will be their: Ibid., 80.
5. It is manifest: King, *The Life and Correspondence of Rufus King*, 397.
6. I am of a: Ibid.
7. I think England: Ibid.
8. The continent is: Ibid.
9. Spain, Portugal: Ibid.
10. I mean peace consistent: Ibid.
11. We must not: Ibid.
12. a long time cannot: Ibid.
13. The president must: Ibid.
14. Not only can: Ibid.
15. I pushed on towards: Dudley, *The Naval War of 1812*, 113.
16. and as Marlborough: Ibid.
17. and we were allowed: Ibid.
18. I am decidedly: Ibid., 116.
19. but the country: Ibid.
20. they have induced: Ibid., 65.
21. and I can truly: Ibid., 117.
22. but should you: Ibid., 122.
23. This kind of warfare: Ibid., 204
24. Deserters, of whom: Ibid.
25. The force of the enemy: Ibid.
26. Such as force will: Ibid., 106.
27. Hence I believe: Ibid.
28. A well-organized and: Henry Adams ed., *The Writings of Albert Gallatin*, vol. 1 (Indianapolis: Liberty Fund Inc., 1879), 602–7.
29. and they will: Ibid., 620.
30. How ill-prepared we: Ibid., 602–7.
31. The hope: Ibid.
32. In the intoxication: Ibid.
33. To use their own: Ibid., 617.
34. You are sufficiently: Ibid., 602–7.
35. The numerous English: Ibid., 616.
36. and agreed to by: Madison, *The Writings of James Madison*, 280–81.
37. This morning at 4 AM: Dudley, *The Naval War of 1812*, 123.

38. after two hours: Ibid.
39. I am moving up: Ibid.

CHAPTER 17—TWENTY THOUSAND REINFORCEMENTS

1. Lord Hill and 15,000: Dudley, *The Naval War of 1812*, 129.
2. by the account I have: Ibid.
3. with them [slave soldiers]: Ibid.
4. Barney had got: Ibid., 151.
5. Mr. Madison: Ibid.
6. 10,000 militia: Madison, *The Writings of James Madison*, 282.
7. the Secretary of War: Ibid.
8. the other more: Ibid.
9. a circular communication: Ibid.
10. adequate portions: Ibid.
11. them in the best: Ibid.
12. the intention: "Capture of the City of Washington."
13. if it were: Ibid.
14. if it were: Ibid.
15. It was decided: Ibid.
16. Annapolis is tolerably: Ibid.
17. Together with: Ibid.
18. a small work: Skeen, *John Armstrong, Jr.*, 188.
19. Baltimore is likewise: Ibid.
20. and a fort: Ibid.
21. to put Washington: Ibid.
22. bayonets are known: Ibid.
23. But both Annapolis: Ibid.
24. and from the moment: Ibid, 139.
25. and popular clamor: Ibid.
26. Boston, and New York: Dudley, *The Naval War of 1812*, 133.
27. that the most advantageous: Ibid.
28. After leaving Baltimore: Ibid., 134.
29. Should Washington: Ibid.
30. could not be warned: Ibid.
31. If troops arrive: Ibid., 131.

32. in case of actual: Ibid., 189.
33. You are hereby: Ibid., 140.
34. her proportion: Ibid.
35. my belief is: Skeen, *John Armstrong, Jr.*, 188.
36. in short it is: Dudley, *The Naval War of 1812*, 135.
37. Thus, I foresee: Ibid.
38. and popular clamor: Ibid.
39. I can only say: Ibid.
40. He consoled the: Ibid., 167.
41. I have no hesitation: Ibid.
42. advantages might: Ibid., 138.
43. by an assurance: Ibid.
44. I therefore most: Ibid.
45. always so great: Ibid.
46. as the other places: Ibid.
47. One day a lady: "Dolley Madison; America's First Lady."
48. I wish you would: Madison, *Selected Letters of Dolley Payne Madison*, 70.
49. You know I am: Ibid.
50. nor will there be: Ibid.
51. Yours of the first: Ibid., 72.
52. Your question as: Ibid.
53. If a general war: Ibid.
54. The power: Ibid.
55. We have been in: Shulman, *Dolley Madison Digital Edition*.
56. and the disaffected: Ibid.
57. such a place: Ibid.
58. I wish (for my own part): Ibid.
59. among other exclamations: Ibid.
60. I am not the least alarmed: Ibid.
61. our preparations for: Ibid.
62. I desired Mr. Astor: Ibid.
63. It had a distressing effect: Ibid.
64. I find that I owe: Madison, *The Writings of James Madison*, 287.
65. without the knowledge: Ibid.
66. subsequently made: Ibid.

CHAPTER 18—HANGING MADISON

1.   All letters giving: Madison, *The Writings of James Madison*, 287.
2.   The charge that opposition: King, *The Life and Correspondence of Rufus King*, 405.
3.   That such opinions: Ibid.
4.   To produce such: Ibid.
5.   If war suppresses opposition: Ibid.
6.   Neither the administration: Ibid.
7.   have no confidence: Ibid.
8.   have not brought: Adams, *The Writings of Albert Gallatin*, 616.
9.   If you prosecute: King, *The Life and Correspondence of Rufus King*, 406.
10. a belief is said: Adams, *The Writings of Albert Gallatin*, 617.
11. We are still: Shulman, *Dolley Madison Digital Edition*.
12. If you have not: Ibid.
13. I write you: Ibid.
14. Not a line from: Ibid.
15. Nothing has occurred: Ibid.
16. The British on our: Ibid.
17. If the war: Ibid.
18. farewell, may Heaven: Ibid.

CHAPTER 19—INVASION

1.   Their Lordships entrust: Dudley, *The Naval War of 1812*, 72.
2.   as it will rarely if: Ibid.
3.   You will also: Ibid., 73.
4.   Rear Admiral Cockburn: Captain James Scott, *Recollections of a Naval Life*, vol. 3 (London: Richard Bentley, 1834), 272–73.
5.   They were as wild: Ibid.
6.   It is a singular fact: Ibid.
7.   Oh yes!: "Capture of the City of Washington," 580.
8.   but they certainly: Ibid.
9.   No, no! Baltimore: Ibid.
10. If the force of the: Madison, *The Writings of James Madison*, 291.
11. want of precaution: Ibid.
12. He may be bound: Ibid.

13. to accompany him: "Capture of the City of Washington," 580.
14. I acknowledge the justness: Dudley, *The Naval War 1812*, 108.
15. Appearances indicate: Ibid.
16. If however their force: Ibid.
17. I determined not: "Capture of the City of Washington," 581.
18. I plainly discovered: Dudley, *The Naval War of 1812*, 196.
19. Here, then, was: Scott, *Recollections of a Naval Life*, 277.
20. The admiral, dashing: Ibid.
21. we observed the sloop: Dudley, *The Naval War of 1812*, 196.
22. And in a few minutes: Scott, *Recollections of a Naval Life*, 277.
23. almost cracked the drums: Ibid.
24. The enemy are: Madison, James. *The Writings of James Madison*, 293.
25. The papers of all: Ibid., 292.
26. fear not much: Ibid.
27. But the crisis I: Ibid.
28. No complete organization: "Capture of the City of Washington," 526.
29. no part of it: Ibid., 524.

CHAPTER 20—THE BRITISH ARE COMING

1. All my affection: Madison, *Selected Letters of Dolley Payne Madison*, 71.
2. Give Miss P.: Ibid.
3. to find that you love: Ibid., 67.
4. My husband left me: Shulman, *Dolley Madison Digital Edition*.
5. Dear Sister: Ibid.
6. He inquired anxiously: Ibid.
7. beseeching me to: Ibid.
8. A number of valuable: *National Intelligencer*, May 13, 1814.
9. has been anxious: Shulman, *Dolley Madison Digital Edition*.
10. I have therefore: Ibid.
11. Nearly all the rumors: Joseph Gales, *National Intelligencer*, August 23, 1814.
12. Each man brings the: Ibid.
13. I have since: Shulman, *Dolley Madison Digital Edition*.
14. The reports as to: Madison, *The Writings of James Madison*, 293.

15. unless it be from: Ibid., 293–94.
16. they may have a: Ibid.
17. the last is alarming: Shulman, *Dolley Madison Digital Edition*.
18. that the enemy: Ibid.
19. I am accordingly ready: Ibid.
20. The captain of the: Scott, *Recollections of a Naval Life*, 280.
21. A long discussion ensued: Ibid.
22. and finally an order: Ibid., 280–81.
23. The orders contained: Ibid.
24. But, upon the receipt, Ibid., 281–82.
25. I am determined: Shulman, *Dolley Madison Digital Edition*.
26. My friends and acquaintances: Ibid.
27. Dear Sister—tell me: Ibid.
28. in a wagon if: Ibid.
29. French John: Ibid.
30. To the last proposition: Ibid.
31. Have they artillery?: Ingersoll, *Historical Sketch of the Second War Between the United States and Great Britain*, 168.
32. We are more frightened?: Ibid.
33. If they want to?: Ibid.
34. Having perused it: Scott, *Recollections of a Naval Life*, 283.
35. If we proceed: Ibid.
36. I know their force: Ibid.
37. Well, be it so: Ibid., 284.
38. a low murmuring burst: Ibid.
39. and we were not: Dudley, *The Naval War of 1812*, 220.
40. In conformity therefore: Ibid.
41. I also most: Ibid.
42. and bivouacked before: Ibid.

CHAPTER 21—SPYGLASSES

1. We feel assured that: Gales, *National Intelligencer*, August 24, 1814.
2. The Baltimore troops: Ibid.
3. In a few hours we: Ibid.
4. monument to bad: "Washington Navy Yard: History of Latrobe Gate," http://www.history.navy.mil/browse-by-topic/

organization-and-administration/commands-and-installations/
washington-navy-yard/latrobe-gate.html.

5. more like a fat goose: Ibid.
6. fitter for a: Ibid.
7. not until the extinction: Ibid.
8. the latter had been: Madison, *The Writings of James Madison*, 295.
9. he was asked: Ibid.
10. was grieved to: Ibid.
11. I could scarcely conceive: Ibid.
12. I hoped he had: Ibid., 296.
13. at such a juncture: Ibid.
14. The sun beat: Ingersoll, *Historical Sketch of the Second War Between the United States and Great Britain*, 172.
15. on reaching which place: Dudley, *The Naval War of 1812*, 221.
16. several troops coming: "Capture of the City of Washington," 557.
17. Mr. Madison! The enemy: George, *Terror on the Chesapeake*, 95.
18. The British are now: Ibid.
19. He said that he: Madison, *The Writings of James Madison*, 297.
20. I have no news: Madison, *Selected Letters of Dolley Payne Madison*, 75.
21. I can give you: Ibid.
22. We are to have: Ibid., 78.
23. Wednesday morning: Shulman, *Dolley Madison Digital Edition*.
24. but, alas: Ibid.
25. On the opposite: Ingersoll, *Historical Sketch of the Second War Between the United States and Great Britain*, 175.
26. What will be said: Ibid.
27. If it rain militia: Ibid.
28. In the present state: Shulman, *Dolley Madison Digital Edition*.
29. Mr. Jones is deeply: Ibid.
30. busy packing up: Ibid.

CHAPTER 22—BLADENSBURG RACES

1. roars of musketry: Scott, *Recollections of a Naval Life*, 286.
2. conspicuous gold laced: Ibid., 288.
3. I trust, Sir: Ibid.

4. Poh! Poh! Nonesense: Ibid., 288–89.
5. Capital! Excellent: Ibid., 289.
6. a musket shot passed: Ibid.
7. dismissed my assistant: Ibid.
8. When it became manifest: Madison, *The Writings of James Madison*, 297.
9. Three o'clock: Shulman, *Dolley Madison Digital Edition*.
10. Mr. Madison comes not: Ibid.
11. At this late hour: Ibid.
12. Our kind friend, Mr. Carroll: Ibid.
13. This process was found: Ibid.
14. I have ordered the: Ibid.
15. and the precious: Ibid.
16. And now, dear sister: Ibid.
17. When I arrived: "Capture of the City of Washington," 579.
18. I sent an officer: Ibid.
19. During this period: Ibid.
20. At length the: Ibid.
21. In a few minutes: Ibid.
22. By this time: Ibid.
23. one of which shot: Ibid., 580.
24. to my great mortification: Ibid.
25. At this time: Ibid.
26. Three of my officers: Ibid.
27. In that part: Ibid., 582.
28. Several of the officers: Ibid.
29. inglorious circumstances: Ibid.
30. in a few minutes: Ibid., 580.
31. that is not Admiral: Ingersoll, *Historical Sketch of the Second War Between the United States and Great Britain*, 179.
32. It is Admiral Cockburn: Ibid.
33. Oh, Cockburn is: Ibid.
34. Do not let us speak: Ibid.
35. Well, Admiral: Scott, *Recollections of a Naval Life*, 291.
36. Quite enough to: Ibid.
37. Those officers behaved: "Capture of the City of Washington," 580.

38. Barney was a brave: Ingersoll, *Historical Sketch of the Second War Between the United States and Great Britain*, 179.
39. If I had had: Scott, *Recollections of a Naval Life*, 291.
40. that the enemy: Dudley, *The Naval War of 1812*, 221.
41. and a victory gained: Ibid.
42. the contest being completely: Ibid.

CHAPTER 23—CAPITOL CONFLAGRATION

1. In the land of liberty: Scott, *Recollections of a Naval Life*, 297.
2. and on the general: Dudley, *The Naval War of 1812*, 221–22.
3. these were: Ibid., 222.
4. All of this is even: Ingersoll, *Historical Sketch of the Second War Between the United States and Great Britain*, 182.
5. Common sense should: Scott, *Recollections of a Naval Life*, 301.
6. every possible precaution: Dudley, *The Naval War of 1812*, 215.
7. A deputation also: Ibid., 217.
8. I would delay the: Ibid.
9. he could protect: Ibid., 215.
10. the matches were applied: Ibid., 217.
11. sent me to a stable: Paul Jennings, *A Colored Man's Reminiscences of James Madison: Electronic Edition*, http://docSouth.unc.edu/neh/jennings/jennings.html.
12. in the mean time: Ibid.
13. It was an unfinished: Scott, *Recollections of a Naval Life*, 297.
14. The interior accommodations: Ibid.
15. infected with an unseemly: Ibid., 300.
16. Taken in the President's: James Pack, *The Man Who Burned the White House: Admiral Sir George Cockburn 1772–1853* (Ensworth: Kenneth Mason, 1987), 17–18.
17. surmounted by a gilt eagle: Scott, *Recollections of a Naval Life*, 301.
18. Shall this harbor: Ingersoll, *Historical Sketch of the Second War Between the United States and Great Britain*, 185.
19. All for it will: Ibid.
20. Its funeral pile: Scott, *Recollections of a Naval Life*, 301.
21. The position of the: Ibid.

22.   Silence! If any man: *Georgetown Federal Republican*, September 10, 1814.

23.   Gentlemen, I presume: Ibid.

24.   I hope, Sir: Ibid.

25.   Yes, Sir, we pledge: Ibid.

26.   Be under no: Ibid.

27.   Where is your President: Ibid.

CHAPTER 24—WHITE HOUSE INFERNO

1.   Come, Madam: Ingersoll, *Historical Sketch of the Second War Between the United States and Great Britain*, 186.

2.   preferred her house: Ibid.

3.   a poor British soldier: Ibid.

4.   he should return: Ibid.

5.   A large store of: Scott, *Recollections of a Naval Life*, 303.

6.   We found the cloth: Ibid.

7.   Never was nectar: Ibid.

8.   to peace with: "Burning of the White House and the War of 1812," *Journal of the White House Historical Association* no. 4 (Fall 1998): 16.

9.   must give it to the flames: Margaret Bayard Smith, *The First Forty Years of Washington Society* (New York: C. Scribner's Sons, 1906), 16.

10.   This will remind me: Ibid.

11.   the little president America: Ibid.

12.   The beautiful apartments: Scott, *Recollections of a Naval Life*, 303.

13.   I accordingly doffed: Ibid.

14.   On the walls hung: Ibid.

15.   Our sailors were artists: "Burning of the White House and the War of 1812," 562.

16.   Washington was: Scott, *Recollections of a Naval Life*, 301.

17.   preferred the light: Ingersoll, *Historical Sketch of the Second War Between the United States and Great Britain*, 186.

18.   It was near midnight: Scott, *Recollections of a Naval Life*, 305–6.

19.   It had ever taken: Ibid., 306.

20.   Its fate was decreed: Ibid.

21. Well, good people, America: Smith, *The First Forty Years*, 112.
22. Never fear: Ingersoll, *Historical Sketch of the Second War Between the United States and Great Britain*, 189.
23. The success of the fair: Scott, *Recollections of a Naval Life*, 308.
24. Why, that is the vile: Ibid.
25. A half-uttered shriek: Ibid.
26. My plighted word: Ibid.
27. the Americans always: Ibid.
28. harlequin of havoc: Ingersoll, *Historical Sketch of the Second War Between the United States and Great Britain*, 189.
29. I make no war: George, *Terror on the Chesapeake*, 107.
30. I cannot think: Ingersoll, *Historical Sketch of the Second War Between the United States and Great Britain*, 189.
31. I am a married man: Ibid.
32. I have heard so: George, *Terror on the Chesapeake*, 107.

CHAPTER 25—DISPLACED OR CONQUERED?

1. Make sure all the C's: George, *Terror on the Chesapeake*, 109.
2. I'll punish Madison's man: Ingersoll, *Historical Sketch of the Second War Between the United States and Great Britain*, 189.
3. The reams of paper: Scott, *Recollections of a Naval Life*, 306.
4. the instruments of: Ibid.
5. in short: Dudley, *The Naval War of 1812*, 222.
6. About noon: Scott, *Recollections of a Naval Life*, 313.
7. many of the latter: Ibid.
8. The object of the: Dudley, *The Naval War of 1812*, 224.
9. The lady of the house: Jennings, *A Colored Man's Reminiscences of James Madison.*
10. Hearing the tramp: *Records of the Columbia Historical Society* (Charlottesville: University Press of Virginia, 1984), 104, https://archive.org/stream/recordscolumbia00unkngoog#page/n15/mode/2up.
11. Great God, Madam!: Ibid.
12. No, Sir. This is: Ibid.
13. All the villagers: Madison, *The Writings of James Madison*, 298.
14. My Dearest: Ibid., 300.

15. I have just received: Ibid.
16. you will all of: Ibid.
17. I know not where: Ibid.
18. I may fall in with: Ibid.

PART III—PHOENIX BY THE DAWN'S EARLY LIGHT

1. The smoldering fires: Ingersoll, *Historical Sketch of the Second War Between the United States and Great Britain*, 197.

CHAPTER 26—PHOENIX SPICES

1. War America would: Walter Lord, *The Dawn's Early Light* (New York: W.W. Norton & Company), 302.
2. the reign of Madison: Ibid.
3. It was an attack: Ingersoll, *Historical Sketch of the Second War Between the United States and Great Britain*, 197.
4. After twenty-five years: Ibid., 190.
5. The object of the expedition: Ibid., 182.
6. There is scarcely: John Quincy Adams, *Letter to Louisa Adams, Oct. 4, 1814, Adams Family Papers,* Library of Congress.
7. The army of Napoleon: Ibid.
8. John Armstrong is a traitor: Lord, *The Dawn's Early Light*, 216.
9. Fruits of war: Ibid.
10. This is the city of: Ibid.
11. George Washington founded: Ibid.
12. The immediate and: Ingersoll, *Historical Sketch of the Second War Between the United States and Great Britain*, 197.
13. Sir, do you seize: Irving, *Life and Letters of Washington Irving*, 151.
14. Let me tell you: Ibid.
15. The country is insulted: Ibid.
16. Believe us fellow: Ibid.
17. You're here?: Ibid., 155.
18. During which time: Ibid.
19. The smoldering fires: Ibid.

20. And glory, like the: Lord Byron, "Phoenix," *Oxford English Dictionary*, 1809.
21. O golden bird: Thomas Watson, "Phoenix," *Oxford English Dictionary*, 1582.
22. He seems to think: John Wesley, "Phoenix," *Oxford English Dictionary*, 1775.
23. I stopped at General: Madison, *The Writings of James Madison*, 300.
24. I observed to him: Ibid., 301.
25. that violent prejudices: Ibid.
26. received a message: Ibid.
27. what was best to: Ibid.
28. aware of the excitement: Ibid.
29. that a temporary: Ibid., 302.
30. in relation to the: Ibid.
31. he had not taken: Ibid.
32. I could not in: Ibid.
33. that he had omitted: Ibid.
34. that it was the: Ibid., 303.
35. had never appeared: Ibid.
36. a single precaution: Ibid.
37. I had selected: Ibid.
38. leaving my country: Ibid., 303–4.
39. I have received: Dudley, *The Naval War of 1812*, 244.
40. The people now begin: Ibid.
41. with a view: Ibid.
42. It is believed here: Ibid.
43. consequently I could: Ibid.
44. I shall be ready: Ibid.
45. I repeat again, that: Ibid.

CHAPTER 27—PHOENIX MULTITUDE

1. After an intermission: Gales, *National Intelligencer*, Aug. 30, 1814.
2. The country must be: *Georgetown Federal Republican*, September 1, 1814.

3. The expenses of living: Francis Scott Key, *Correspondence to Mrs. Ann Phoebe Key, January 2, 1814*, University of Virginia, Special Collections.

4. I really think: Ibid.

5. I have not determined: Ibid.

6. It is absolutely necessary: *Georgetown Federal Republican*, September 1, 1814.

7. The admiral has said: Ibid.

8. omit no sacrifice: Ibid.

9. No man who is mindful: Ibid.

10. Whereas the enemy: Madison, *The Writings of James Madison*, 304.

11. they wantonly destroyed: Ibid.

12. Whereas it now appears: Ibid., 305.

13. principles of humanity: Ibid.

14. at the very moment: Ibid.

15. to chastise: Ibid.

16. exhorting all the good: Ibid.

17. be vigilant and alert: Ibid.

18. none will forget: Ibid.

19. the glory acquired: Ibid., 306.

20. We are constrained: Francis Scott Key, *Correspondence to James Madison, January 26, 1807*, Library of Congress.

21. The disgraceful loss: King, *The Life and Correspondence of Rufus King*, 410.

22. My object was to: Ibid.

23. the time had arrived: Ibid.

24. he should be obliged: Ibid.

25. ruin yourself if it: Ibid.

26. We are in a critical: Ibid., 413.

27. The enemy is at: Ibid., 411.

28. Sir, do you seize: Irving, *Life and Letters of Washington Irving*, 151.

29. Let me tell you: Ibid.

30. The country is insulted: Ibid.

31. Believe us fellow: Ibid.

32. You're here?: Ibid., 155.

33. During which time: Ibid.

34. I have before: Dudley, *The Naval War of 1812*, 228.
35. To Rear-Admiral Cockburn: Ingersoll, *Historical Sketch of the Second War Between the United States and Great Britain*, 166.
36. Whether Madison will: King, *The Life and Correspondence of Rufus King*, 411.
37. So far as regards: Ibid., 414.
38. I shall not be: Ibid., 411.
39. Where Congress will meet: Ibid., 414.
40. Philadelphia should be: Ibid.
41. In the present alarm: Ibid., 411.
42. We have no tidings: Ibid., 415.
43. nothing favorable to peace: *Georgetown Federal Republican*, September 5, 1814.
44. Your letter of this: Dudley, *The Naval War of 1812*, 261–62.
45. I can assure you: Ibid.

CHAPTER 28—WHITE HOUSE PHOENIX

1. The spirit of the: Lord, *The Dawn's Early Light*, 216–17.
2. As soon as the: Dudley, *The Naval War of 1812*, 269.
3. the most democratic town: Ibid.
4. this town ought: Ibid.
5. when he is better: Ibid.
6. He looks shaken: Lord, *The Dawn's Early Light*, 216.
7. Mrs. M. seem'd much: Smith, *The First Forty Years*, 110.
8. in short, it would: Ethel Stephens Arnett, *Mrs. James Madison: The Incomparable Dolley* (Greensboro: Piedmont Press, 1972), 249.
9. We stepped in to see: Ibid., 248.
10. She had better: Ibid.
11. Never was a man: Lord, *The Dawn's Early Light*, 216.
12. Dr. Beanes shall be released: George, *Terror on the Chesapeake*, 132.
13. Dr. Beanes having: Ibid.
14. The friendly treatment: Ibid.
15. I shall accordingly: Ibid.
16. Ah, Mr. Skinner: Lord, *The Dawn's Early Light*, 256.

17. Sometimes when I: F.S. Key-Smith, "How Francis Scott Key Wrote 'The Star-Spangled Banner,'" *The Literary Digest*, April 29, 1911, www.usgennet.org/usa/topic/preservation/epochs/vol5/pg90.htm.
18. To make my feelings: Ibid.
19. I reached here the: Dudley, *The Naval War of 1812*, 263.
20. Forts, redoubts and: Ibid.
21. It is understood: Ibid.
22. I hope to leave: Ibid.

CHAPTER 29—DAWN'S EARLY LIGHT

1.   I'll eat in Baltimore: Lord, *The Dawn's Early Light*, 262.
2.   They are mainly militia: Ibid., 261.
3.   I don't care if it: George, *Terror on the Chesapeake*, 137.
4.   I'll bring up the column: Scott, *Recollections of a Naval Life*, 334.
5.   it is with the most: Dudley, *The Naval War of 1812*, 279.
6.   that whilst his wounds: Ibid.
7.   It is impossible for: Ibid., 277.
8.   It is for Colonel Brook: Ibid.
9.   without this can be: Ibid.
10. At any rate a very: Ibid.
11. have a flag so large: "The Star-Spangled Banner," Fort McHenry, www.nps.gov/fomc/learn/historyculture/the-star-spangled-banner.htm.
12. Whose broad stripes: Ibid.
13. O'er the ramparts: Ibid.
14. Gave proof through: Ibid.
15. O say does that: Ibid.
16. O thus be it ever: Ibid.
17. Then conquer we must: Ibid.
18. And the star-spangled: Ibid.
19. The enemy has been: Dudley, *The Naval War of 1812*, 293.
20. I shall give you: Ibid.

CHAPTER 30—RELOCATING THE CAPITAL CITY

1.   The destruction of the: *New York Evening Post*, September 19, 1814.
2.   unfortunately the lapse: Scott, *Recollections of a Naval Life*, 317.

3. arraign the conduct: Ibid.

4. It is easy to pronounce: Ibid.

5. our acts are not: Wilhelmus Bogart Bryan, *A History of the National Capital From its Foundation Through the Period of the Adoption of the Organic Act: 1790–1814* (New York: The MacMillan Company, 1914), 8.

6. the puzzling question: Ibid., 14.

7. If it were possible: Ibid., 30–31.

8. an act for establishing: Ibid., 31.

9. We hear some indistinct: Gales, *National Intelligencer*, October 3, 1814.

10. on old shell of: Jennings, *A Colored Man's Reminiscences of James Madison.*

11. both houses of Congress: Ibid.

12. Mr. Gales is not an: *Boston Commercial Gazette*, October 4, 1814.

13. a return of peace: Madison, *The Writings of James Madison*, 306.

14. infer that a spirit: Ibid., 307.

15. This is as it should be: *Georgetown Federal Republican*, September 5, 1814.

16. we trust that no representative: Ibid.

17. The character of the nation: Ibid.

18. however deeply to: Madison, *The Writings of James Madison*, 306–8.

19. I would take the liberty: *The James Madison Papers at the Library of Congress.*

20. without a precaution: Ibid.

21. A gentleman had left: *The Federal Republican-Georgetown*, September 22, 1814.

22. He watched the flag: Ibid.

23. Resolved that a committee: *The Federal Republican-Georgetown*, October 1, 1814.

24. If proper preparations: Ibid.

25. Let us not gratify: Ibid.

26. The following communication: *National Intelligencer*, October 3, 1814.

27. want of room: Ibid.

28. The corporation of Georgetown: Ibid.

29. It is said that the: Ibid.
30. Can it be that any: Ibid.
31. They cannot be so: Ibid.
32. Under a law of: Ibid.
33. contracts have been made: Ibid.
34. If then the government: Ibid.
35. Our disgrace would indeed: Ibid.
36. It would be considered: Ibid.
37. Our national character: Ibid.
38. It is laughable to see: *Massachusetts Spy*, October 5, 1814.
39. The editor of that: Ibid.
40. No drudgery is too low: Ibid.
41. I thank you: Hamlin, *Benjamin Henry Latrobe*, 432–33.
42. I know exactly: Ibid.
43. President Washington: *The Federal Republican-Georgetown*, October 1, 1814.
44. and thus the city: Ibid.
45. but these inconveniences: Ibid.
46. The President's House: Ibid.
47. Because we have suffered: Ibid.
48. No, from you we: Ibid.

CHAPTER 31—POOR MRS. MADISON

1. Poor Mrs. Madison: Shulman, *Dolley Madison Digital Edition*.
2. The disgraceful and distressing: Ibid.
3. The derangement occasioned: Ibid.
4. The expectation of a: Ibid.
5. The discussion has created: Ibid.
6. How it has been permitted: *Democratic Press*, October 7, 1814.
7. There is a determination: Ibid.
8. The removal of the seat: Ibid.
9. If you were to see: Ibid.
10. There is said: Ibid.
11. Resolved, that we view: *National Intelligencer*, October 10, 1814.
12. repugnant to the Constitution: Ibid.

13. Enclosed I send: King, *The Life and Correspondence of Rufus King,* 417.
14. It would appear: Ibid.
15. The enemy now demand: Ibid., 418.
16. would in effect: Ibid.
17. Our rulers can neither: Ibid.
18. The country is invaded: Ibid., 419.
19. it has become: Ibid., 423.
20. Congress should therefore: Ibid.
21. The Federalists have: Ibid.
22. The subject of removal: Ibid., 422.
23. Whether an adjournment: Ibid.
24. Unless we go: Ibid.
25. The increase of expense: *National Intelligencer,* October 14, 1814.
26. To brave all these: Ibid.
27. too much good sense: Ibid.
28. Should not the creditors: Ibid.
29. Even the savages: Ibid.
30. decision would then: Ibid.
31. Mrs. Madison's levees: *Boston Commercial Gazette,* November 10, 1814; Shulman, *Dolley Madison Digital Edition.*
32. I beg you and: Shulman, *Dolley Madison Digital Edition.*

CHAPTER 32—PRESIDENTS' CLUB

1. It is very long since: *The James Madison Papers at the Library of Congress.*
2. but in the late events: Ibid.
3. for although every: Ibid.
4. Had General Washington: Ibid.
5. We all remember: Ibid.
6. while our enemies: Ibid.
7. Learning by the papers: Ibid.
8. I believe you are acquainted: Ibid.
9. I have long been sensible: Ibid.
10. I learn that the: Madison, *The Writings of James Madison,* 313.
11. We have just received: Ibid.

12. Our ministers were all: Ibid.
13. not that these are: *The James Madison Papers at the Library of Congress.*
14. rupture of the negotiation: Ibid.
15. I feel myself bound: King, *The Life and Correspondence of Rufus King*, 429.
16. What are you: Ibid.
17. If you go on: Ibid.
18. Hard words if: Ibid.
19. If N.O. passes: Ibid., 448.
20. Very important interests: *The James Madison Papers at the Library of Congress.*
21. It is thought very: Ibid.
22. To enable to meet: Ibid.
23. I have caused: Ibid.
24. The view of the discussions: Ibid.
25. The point to be decided: Ibid.
26. It is very agreeable: Ibid.

CHAPTER 33—UPLIFTING NEWS

1. The decision of the: *National Intelligencer*, October 18, 1814.
2. We take this opportunity: Ibid.
3. Entertaining that opinion: Ibid.
4. architects and master builders: "White House History," *Journal of the White House Historical Association* (1998): 26.
5. exclusively to the purpose: Ibid.
6. to cause to be forthwith: Ibid.
7. In carrying into execution the: Ibid.
8. Although I cannot: "Capture of the City of Washington," 583.
9. Considering your call: Ibid.
10. declared that the committee: Ingersoll, *Historical Sketch of the Second War Between the United States and Great Britain*, 170.
11. So far from clearing: Ibid.
12. General Ross was: Ibid., 171.
13. If the murderous shot: Ibid.
14. The public property destroyed: Ibid., 196.
15. Congress would have: Ibid., 171.

16. Seldom, says Voltaire: Ibid.
17. The fate of New Orleans: Shulman, *Dolley Madison Digital Edition*.
18. We hear nothing: Ibid.
19. Do you know of: Ibid.
20. I understand my: Ibid.
21. How often do I: Ibid.
22. I hope you may: Ibid.
23. Madam, the American army: Ibid.
24. The eighth of January: Ibid.
25. The country is saved: Ibid.
26. We hope that: King, *The Life and Correspondence of Rufus King*, 466.
27. When the news: Jennings, *A Colored Man's Reminiscences of James Madison*.
28. I played the: Ibid.
29. We have received: King, *The Life and Correspondence of Rufus King*, 470.
30. The late war: Madison, *The Writings of James Madison*, 324.
31. It has been waged: Ibid.
32. Peace, at all times: Ibid.
33. I beg leave respectfully: Hamlin, *Benjamin Henry Latrobe*, 434.
34. I am conscious: Ibid.
35. implied censure: Ibid.
36. excusable ambition: Ibid.
37. implied censure: Ibid.
38. a large packet: Ibid., 435.
39. No man in: Ibid.
40. We remained in Cumberland: Scott, *Recollections of a Naval Life*, 335.
41. I have rejoiced: Shulman, *Dolley Madison Digital Edition*.
42. I trust you are: Ibid.
43. Congress adjourned last: Ibid.

CHAPTER 34—RISE OF THE FIRST LADY

1. Our girls went: Clark, *Life and Letters of Dolly Madison*, 190.
2. In about two minutes: Ibid.
3. She was dressed: Ibid.

4.   You could not but: Ibid., 113.
5.   For no heart: Shulman, *Dolley Madison Digital Edition.*
6.   Tis here the woman: Seale, *The President's House: a History*, 128.
7.   I cannot conceive: Ibid.
8.   That you may: Shulman, *Dolley Madison Digital Edition.*
9.   His administration: Ibid.
10. She had the parrot: Clark, *Life and Letters of Dolly Madison*, 192.
11. As I know of: Shulman, *Dolley Madison Digital Edition.*
12. It is certainly: Ibid.
13. The elevation of: Ibid.
14. My husband is: Ibid.
15. You, Madam can feel: Ibid.
16. Think of the wretchedness: Ibid.
17. The ladies of the: *National Intelligencer*, October 10, 1815; Shulman, *Dolley Madison Digital Edition.*
18. it is hoped that: Schulman, *Dolley Madison Digital Edition.*
19. A nobler object: Ibid.
20. Cast your bread upon: Ibid.
21. The governess must: "Constitution, Washington Orphan Asylum, Dec. 18, 1815," quoted in Shulman, *Dolley Madison Digital Edition.*
22. The children shall: Ibid.
23. By trusting in Him: Ibid.
24. Such, find a friend: Ibid.
25. composed of pieces: Shulman, *Dolley Madison Digital Edition.*
26. to accept it: Ibid.
27. the most splendid: Clark, *Life and Letters of Dolly Madison*, 193.
28. She also wore: Ibid., 194.
29. fit to conciliate: Ibid., 195.
30. She looked every inch: Ibid., 19

EPILOGUE

1.   Mrs. Madison was dressed: Clark, *Life and Letters of Dolly Madison*, 192.

ACKNOWLEDGMENTS

1.   Allow me again: Shulman, *Dolley Madison Digital Edition.*

Index